PRAIS

UNCOMMON L

●●●●◡◡

"I have read lots of management books; however this book was different. I couldn't put it down! The case studies and examples really helped reinforce and bring alive the 5-S leadership model. It gave me an opportunity to revisit my own leadership approach. I recognized my own good practice against the 5-S model and looked for ways I could implement new ways of working. The examples helped me see how different ways of thinking can have a massive impact on results, whether that is with your people, your customers, performance or just the way you do things." **Sarah Parr, Director of SIA Service and Customer Access Service, Liverpool Direct Limited**

"A distinctive approach . . . (for) all those faced with the common challenge of leading businesses and organizations of any shape and size in the modern world. This is a practical book, grounded in sound scholarship which will help anyone to make sense of leadership." **Professor David Major, consultant in work-based and lifelong learning**

"Comprehensive, provides a fresh perspective and illustrates what the best leaders do well to develop competitive advantage . . . brings together the best thinking on this topic to provide leaders with a practical, insightful and informative toolkit." **David Robertson, Vice President and Executive Consultant, The Forum Corporation (EMEA)**

UNCOMMON LEADERSHIP

HOW TO BUILD COMPETITIVE ADVANTAGE BY THINKING DIFFERENTLY

PHIL
HIGSON

ANTHONY
STURGESS

KoganPage

LONDON PHILADELPHIA NEW DELHI

First published in Great Britain and the United States in 2014 by Kogan Page Limited

2nd Floor, 45 Gee Street	1518 Walnut Street, Suite 1100	4737/23 Ansari Road
London EC1V 3RS	Philadelphia PA 19102	Daryaganj
United Kingdom	USA	New Delhi 110002
		India

www.koganpage.com

ISBN 978 0 7494 7104 0
E-ISBN 978 0 7494 7105 7

British Library Cataloguing-in-Publication Data

A CIP record for this book is available from the British Library.

Library of Congress Cataloging-in-Publication Data

Higson, Phil.
  Uncommon leadership : how to build competitive advantage by thinking differently / Phil Higson, Anthony Sturgess. – 1st Edition.
    pages cm
    Includes index.
    ISBN 978-0-7494-7104-0 – ISBN 978-0-7494-7105-7   1. Leadership. 2. Competition (Psychology) I. Title.
  HD57.7.H5334 2014
  658.4'092—dc23

                                                                                    2014005699

Typeset by Amnet
Print production managed by Jellyfish
Printed and bound by CPI Group (UK) Ltd, Croydon, CR0 4YY

CONTENTS

●　●　●　●　●

LIST OF FIGURES

● ● ● ● ●

FOREWORD

I really liked this book. It addresses the elephant that has been in the room for some time. Everyone knows that effective leadership makes the difference and yet we continually see the same issues time and again, where leaders are under the spotlight. The book makes the case for, and illustrates, a more holistic view of leadership that encourages leaders to become more conscious of their role requirements and impact in five key areas:

- Creating and using a compelling vision to make sense of the business and distil meaning.

- Influencing appropriately to shape the organization in line with the vision.

- Modelling appropriate behaviours and skills and setting the standards.

- Building strong networks and effective relationships with internal and external customers.

- Fostering collaborative leadership.

Containing good, solid references throughout, this is a comprehensive book which provides a fresh perspective, and illustrates what the best do well to develop competitive advantage through their leadership approach. The learning suggestions are practical and insightful. The book brings together the best thinking on this topic to provide leaders with a practical, insightful and informative toolkit.

The book is certainly comprehensive in terms of leadership models and frameworks but I also really like the integration of examples and stories. I love the idea of sense-making conversations and wished leaders would find time to do this more, perhaps using advocacy and inquiry for skilful and balanced conversations. I also liked the detail on building a vision, the resource strategies, and the section on leading with service which links to the importance of building trust and encouraging engagement – currently one of the biggest issues in leadership.

I believe that climate is where leaders need to focus. Climate is something they directly impact and which drives performance (self, team and customer). While culture is so big, and difficult for a leader or even a community of leaders to change quickly, climate is local and is driven by what leaders do. This links to the section on leading with purpose, which relates to the leader's need to set a strong personal climate, in order to influence the team and customer climate. Interestingly, research has shown that customers can sense climate within two seconds of interacting with a team member; you cannot conceal it.

David Robertson,
Vice President and Executive Consultant,
The Forum Corporation (EMEA)

PREFACE

● ● ● ● ●

Our original inspiration for this book was an insight from renowned management thinker Charles Handy. We were both very taken by his distinction of what separated thought-leaders from the rest. Thought-leaders, according to Handy, are special because they find the sense before it becomes common sense. This posed some interesting questions for us. Firstly, is finding sense before it becomes common sense something all leaders should think about? And if so, how can they do this and perhaps more importantly, put it into action? We thought the answer to the first question was almost self-evident – of course they should. But responding to the others wasn't quite so easy.

So we began addressing these questions in our consultancy work with managers and leaders. We designed and delivered workshops which were based on uncommon ideas and insights, rather than just theories and models. These encouraged delegates to think differently about leadership, and challenged them to take action based on what they found. The workshops struck a real chord with those attending, and we found the whole idea of uncommon insights into leadership gathered momentum. We were pleased by the feedback we received from the delegates, who felt the content was 'of real substance which made you think and act!' Others thought our approach led them to 'think differently,' finding it 'thought-provoking ... very encouraging and motivating.' They particularly commented on our use of stories and 'loved all the analogies', finding them 'enlightening and helpful'. So this evidence convinced us that there was something significant about our approach. After all, how often do delegates at such workshops comment that they found them inspiring, thought-provoking, encouraging and motivating? We were discovering that using uncommon ideas about leadership both prompted 'radical thinking' and crucially, left delegates 'keen to put into practice' some of the insights they had found.

Receiving such an enthusiastic response made us keen to help more leaders and managers benefit from our approach. Which is why we decided to write *Uncommon Leadership*, a book based on our practical work, but which includes a much wider collection of ideas and insights about good leadership. The overall aim of this book is to explore the things that good leaders have in common, and to suggest ways to make these more common in organizations. The key to this is encouraging leaders to think differently, but this alone is not enough. Business leaders need to develop competitive advantage, by challenging conventional wisdom, by asking different questions, and by connecting the 'new' common sense to opportunities. We hope *Uncommon Leadership* can help you to do all of these things. It was written to stimulate your thinking, sharpen your practice, and act as a springboard for better leadership and better organizations. It is packed with anecdotes, quotes, stories and challenging research, all brought to life with an emphasis on the uncommon insights which can help leaders to think and act differently.

So we'd like to introduce the book, with a special thanks to all those managers and leaders who have shared their experiences, helped us hone our ideas, and spurred us on to write the book by their encouraging feedback. We wrote this with you in mind!

ACKNOWLEDGEMENTS

●●●●●

Books seldom come together without a good deal of support and encouragement and *Uncommon Leadership* is no exception. There are many people who have inspired us to write this book, and many more who have helped us to make it a reality. The latter includes the team at Kogan Page who have been both supportive and informative as we've worked through our first book together. So thanks to them and, in particular, to Liz Gooster for firstly giving us the opportunity to write the book, then for providing us with critical insights, positive feedback, and invaluable support.

We both owe a deep debt of gratitude to our families and friends. From Anthony, special thanks go to Val and their children, Dan, Heather and Alison. And from Phil, to his children Joanna, Mark, David and Laura, and to Maryellen. To each of these, and to the many other family members who have encouraged and supported us, we can't say a thank you that is big enough.

We'd like to thank Sarah and Jade, and their teams, for keeping us supplied with coffee through the long hours we spent developing our ideas in two of Chester's finest coffee shops. We'd also like to thank our many friends for their support, especially our mutual friends Andy, Anita, Lawrence, Julie, Ian and Judy. And finally, we'd like to dedicate *Uncommon Leadership* to Ian McDonald – an incomparable colleague who became an irreplaceable friend.

Phil Higson and Anthony Sturgess

INTRODUCTION
THE UNCOMMON SENSE OF LEADERSHIP

● ● ● ● ●

The only explanation is leadership

Leadership in the real world rarely fits exactly into neat theories. The messy reality of the workplace puts a stop to that. Being a leader is seldom easy and always challenging, but it can also be very rewarding. And there is no doubting the value of good leadership to an organization. One chief operating officer of a retail company makes the point very clearly:

> *You take the same company, the same system, and basically the same pay scale, and yet you get tremendously different attitudes among employees from different stores… The only logical explanation is leadership.[1]*

But US leadership expert Warren Bennis makes an even stronger point. He thinks good leadership is actually a matter of survival, calling for a 'new generation of leaders – leaders not managers.'[2] This begs a critical question. If leaders are so important, are we doing enough to help them succeed in such demanding and high-impact roles? Not according to recent reports that suggest a shortage of leadership skills and competence, which give considerable cause for concern. In the UK, although improved leadership is seen as being crucial to sustainable economic growth, 75 per cent of organizations reported a deficit of leadership skills.[3] And if that isn't bad enough, 42 per cent of managers rate their own line-manager as ineffective. Similar concerns have been expressed in the US. According to one report, nearly 70 per cent of Americans still believe they have a crisis of leadership. What's more, 70 per cent agree that unless leadership improves, the US will decline as a nation.[4]

Business leadership is also being challenged from another standpoint. Following the global financial crisis, questions of a more fundamental nature are being asked about leadership in our organizations. Some leaders who until recently were praised for their success, have found themselves under fire for their failures. This criticism has led to a focus on several key issues, including:

- the importance of integrity, to address a loss of confidence in the motivations and actions of some leaders;

- the desirability of more shared leadership throughout organizations, to reduce the damage caused by too much power being concentrated in the hands of too few people;

- the need for a more holistic view of leadership, to help cope with the complexity of the business environment, and the growing importance of relationships between organizations.

Time for a fresh look at leadership?

So there are compelling reasons to re-think leadership, and now is a timely opportunity to do so. There is a clear need for effective leadership, yet there is also credible evidence of a shortage of skilled leaders. And it therefore follows that there must also be a problem in the way we support and develop leaders. Add to that the more fundamental questions raised in the wake of the financial crisis, and the conclusion is obvious: it really is time to take a fresh look at leadership. Of course all leaders and managers need to update and renew their thinking, but to respond to the challenges we've outlined above, something more is needed: leaders need to think differently. We can all benefit from thought-provoking insights. But often it's only by looking at something differently that leaders can get the fresh perspectives and renewed energy they need to make a real impact in their organizations. That is precisely what this book is about.

Over the years, our work with leaders and managers has given us some fascinating insights into their work. This experience has also filled us with a great sense of respect and of privilege as, time and again we've witnessed the talent and commitment of junior, middle and senior leaders and managers. But in listening to how they cope, adapt and succeed, often in very difficult situations, one thing stands out. Leadership may be important and rewarding, but it's also hard work. So what helps?

As we deliver our workplace programmes and workshops, we find that leaders and managers need more than theories, regardless of how good these might be. What helps them most are ideas and insights, sparking fresh thinking and new perspectives. So this has prompted us to ask a different question about leadership: What might be common to good leadership, but is not commonly practised?

The answers are in *Uncommon Leadership*. The practice of leadership is always played out in a particular context. This presents leaders with a choice to make: whether they will be shaped *by* that context or *do* the shaping. It's leaders themselves who must determine how they will respond to the challenges ahead. And in doing so they must shape their own approach to leadership. *Uncommon Leadership* can help you to do this by:

- offering thought-provoking insights for a fresh perspective on leadership;

- developing the skills you need to succeed in demanding leadership roles;

- encouraging you to think differently about the meaning of leadership.

The 5-S leadership framework

To help bring all this together, *Uncommon Leadership* is structured around our '5-S leadership framework'. Whilst techniques, tools and theories can be useful in leadership development, if we're not careful they can also be limiting. If we allow our thinking to stay within the confines of theories or models, these can actually end up being counter-productive. What organizations really need are leaders who can help them gain advantage by thinking differently. So our framework is designed to encourage leaders to think differently about five key, leadership themes: *seeing; showing; shaping; serving*; and *sharing* (Figure 0.1).

But this book is not just about leadership, it's about *uncommon leadership*. So each of the next five chapters also relates one of these themes to an uncommon insight into leadership:

1 *Seeing* – finding the sense before it becomes common.

2 *Shaping* – making good sense into common sense.

3 *Showing* – doing the common things uncommonly well.

4 *Serving* – having the common touch.

5 *Sharing* – making uncommon leadership more common.

FIGURE 0.1 Introduction: the 5-S leadership framework

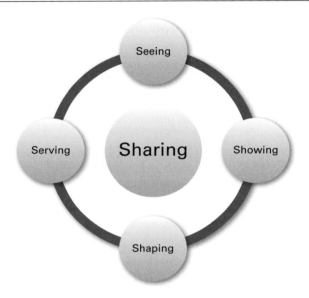

Inside *Uncommon Leadership*

We begin by exploring a counter-intuitive idea – that of seeing the things that others have missed. To do this requires not just the ability to see the 'uncommon sense', which is hard enough, but to see it *before* it becomes common sense. Chapter 1 is about challenging conventional wisdom and asking different questions. We'll do this by introducing some remarkable leaders and their surprising stories. For example, little-known Save the Children workers Jerry and Monique Sternin, and better-known Steve Jobs, on his successful return to an ailing Apple Corporation. All three overcame seemingly intractable situations by finding sense before it became common sense. And we'll introduce you to other practical ways to find the uncommon sense, such as tipping-point leadership like that displayed by Bill Bratton whilst head of the New York City Transit Police, succeeding by separating the trivial many from the vital few. But it's one thing seeing sense before it becomes common, it's quite another making that sense more common within your organizations. We explore this in the next chapter.

In Chapter 2 we examine some common-sense approaches to leadership that, as it turns out, aren't really that common. As leaders turn their attention from sense-making to sense-giving, we think about how they influence and shape their organizations. We'll see what a world-famous, classical musician, busking anonymously in a Washington subway station, can teach us about influencing. And we'll see how leaders turn sense into common sense, as when Richard Branson thought he could provide a better airline service and in so doing change an industry. Or through bricolage leadership, introduced in the story of the Apollo 13 near-disaster. The world of bricolage leadership – where resourceful leaders find ways through, even in the toughest times – is untidy and fraught. It's a world of scarce resources and of competing demands. So how do you cope with such a world? To answer that question we'll help you challenge some conventional views on how to get your organization into shape. For example, we'll suggest some practical ways to apply bricolage leadership. Then we'll consider the most powerful way for leaders to shape culture, according to leadership expert Edgar Schein.

Leaders get organizations into shape in order to improve performance. In Chapter 3 we'll see how leaders who show the way can help organizations to do the common things uncommonly well. This means ensuring that what leaders *do* resonates with what they *say*. And as you'll see, this is something that can be easily done, but very easily undone, sometimes with spectacular results. We'll also ask you some provocative questions, such as: Would people pay to see your work team perform? And if you were offered something that could have a significant impact on your business but which required neither capital investment nor a spending commitment, would you be interested? And what if this was wholly within your power and remit, and offered your organization a real competitive advantage? Would you do it? You might think this all sounds too good to be true but maybe it's just about doing the common things uncommonly well.

Chapter 4 explores the idea of leaders who serve, both employees and customers, and who demonstrate the common touch by being in touch. It's a chapter about upside-down thinking. To lead you need to serve. To build customer loyalty you need to *be* loyal. And sometimes, as we shall see, to make a big impact you need to focus on the small things. Like a small alteration to a sandwich barcode that saved one company half-a-million pounds. Or how small things can have an even bigger impact still, such as when one simple act of courtesy transformed a young boy and his entire nation. But important as the common touch may be, keeping it is sometimes not that easy. When the pressure is on, leaders may find the problems at hand can seem all-consuming, which is when it's easy to lose touch. So in this chapter we look for answers from a leader known for being in touch, and from the intriguing story of two 19th-century British prime ministers. Not to mention from another well-known leader, talking about: 'the best leadership I ever gave'.

The first 4Ss will certainly make a difference to leadership in our organizations. But if we are to make uncommon leadership a reality, it needs to become far more common. So Chapter 5 is about sharing – making uncommon leadership more common, both within your organization and beyond. We start this chapter with a story about a strange decision. Why did a US basketball team ignore conventional player statistics and buy what appeared to be an 'average' player, in an attempt to improve their results? The answer to this question sparks an interesting debate, which challenges some well-established assumptions about leadership. Assumptions challenged by organizations such as W L Gore & Associates, which succeed by making shared leadership fundamental to the way they work. We look at four specific ways in which leaders can build a shared approach to leadership, by sharing vision, enthusiasm, strengths and influence. And we consider the importance of collaborative leadership – sharing good practice and increasingly constrained resources *between* organizations.

To conclude, we show how each of these uncommon themes points to an advantage to be gained from thinking differently. But it's not enough to just think differently, gaining competitive advantage means taking action. So we finish the book by identifying five key leadership roles to help you turn our ideas into uncommon competitive advantages. Our first three uncommon leadership themes were about challenging conventional wisdom, asking different questions and connecting the new common sense to opportunities. These can give organizations:

- *An uncommon advantage* – through pathfinders, who find the sense before it becomes common.

- *A transforming advantage* – through game-changers, who make sense into common sense.

- *A value advantage* – through rain-makers who do the common things uncommonly well.

But the real secret of uncommon leadership is to build a strong sense of togetherness within the organization, helping people to fulfil their potential. That's what we concentrate on in our last two themes:

- *A customer advantage* – through bridge-builders, who apply the common touch.

- *A collaborative advantage* – through play-makers, who make leadership more common.

At the heart of *Uncommon Leadership* is the idea of realizing a very powerful advantage. That of finding the sense before it becomes common sense: an uncommon advantage.

Balancing optimism and realism

But it's not easy to gain advantage in an increasingly difficult business world. It requires leaders who are prepared to challenge conventional wisdom, and that can be a difficult balancing act. So to help you get that balance right, we introduce *Uncommon Leadership* with our first two insights. The first asks whether leaders should spend their time on the 'balcony' or on the 'dance floor'. The second considers the balance between optimism and realism.

The balcony and the dance floor

One fresh approach to leadership, developed by Harvard professor Ronald Heifetz, is called adaptive leadership. This is the kind of leadership needed when things are unpredictable and uncertain. One of the more colourful insights from Heifetz's work is the idea of the balcony and the dance floor. This analogy is useful both as a way to think about your own approach to leadership, and as a way to use this book. Heifetz, and his colleague Marty Linsky (2002) put it this way: 'The only way you can gain both a clearer view of reality and some perspective on the bigger picture is by distancing yourself from the fray… [but if] you want to affect what is happening, you must return to the dance floor.'[5]

Balcony and dance floor leaders interchange between the two. They balance the bigger picture, viewed from the balcony, with spending time on the dance floor. Because it's only there that you'll really be in touch with the people in your organization, and with your customers. And, of course, the dance floor is where the action is!

Warning: this costume does not enable flight or super-human powers!

In 2007, *Forbes* published an entertaining web article, which listed some bizarre product warnings.[6] These included a US costume company which warned that its Superman capes did not enable flight or super-human powers. So before you read any further, let's pause for a reality check, based on another balancing act: the need to balance optimism and realism.

Shawn Achor (2010) uses a similar Superman cape example in his highly readable book, *The Happiness Advantage*.[7] He does so to inject some words of caution into his advice on adopting a more positive approach to life: 'Whilst it's important to shift our fulcrum to a more positive mindset, we don't want to shift it too far – in other words, we have to be careful not to have unrealistic expectations about our potential.' And in much the same way, we feel it's important to be realistic about what we can achieve in our organizations. We think optimism should be balanced with realism, but that's not to say the balance needs to be equal. So what you'll find in this book is a clear focus on positive, thought-provoking approaches to leadership. And you'll also find some real insights into how thinking differently can help you build competitive advantage.

Perhaps it is time to shift the balance – to a focus on optimism tempered with realism. And time to balance seeing the bigger picture from the balcony, with getting down to where the action is on the dance floor. Perhaps it's time for some uncommon leadership.

Bibliography

1 Schwartz, T (2000) [accessed 19 April 2013] The greatest sources of satisfaction in the workplace are internal and emotional, *Life/Work – Issue 40* [Online] http://www.fastcompany.com/40847/life-work-issue-40

2 Bennis, W G (1989) Managing the dream: leadership in the 21st century, *Journal of Organizational Change Management*, **2** (1), pp 6–10

3　Department for Business Innovation and Skills (2012) *Leadership and Management in the UK – The key to sustainable growth*, London, Department for Business Innovation and Skills

4　National Leadership Index (2012) A national study of confidence in leadership, Harvard Kennedy School Center for Public Leadership

5　Heifetz, R and Linsky, M (2002) *Leadership on the Line: Staying alive through the dangers of leading*, Boston, MA, Harvard Business School Press

6　Nelson, B and Finneran, K (2011) [accessed 28 October 2013] In Pictures: 24 Stunningly Dumb Warning Labels, *Forbes* [Online] http://www.forbes.com/2011/02/23/dumbest-warning-labels-entrepreneurs-sales-marketing-warning-labels_slide_20.html

7　Achor, S (2010) *The Happiness Advantage: The seven principles of positive psychology that fuel success and performance at work*, London, Virgin Books

01

LEADING WITH VISION

SEEING THE SENSE BEFORE IT BECOMES COMMON

KEY TOPICS

- Seeing the sense before it becomes common.
- Sense-making.
- Lessons from a fire.
- Vision – a different view of the future.
- Vision – what's the problem?
- Finding the sense before it becomes common.
- Tipping point leadership.

FIGURE 1.1 Seeing

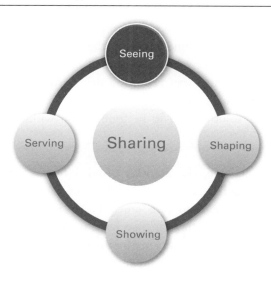

Short of time, short of money and faced with an intractable problem, Jerry and Monique Sternin achieved a remarkable turnaround in tackling malnourished children in Vietnam. They did it quickly, the improvements were remarkable, and the benefits were long lasting. How they did it has lessons for us all.

Jerry Sternin recounts a conversation with a high-ranking government official only a week after arriving in Vietnam in 1990. He and wife Monique were just starting a Save the Children project with local, malnourished children. 'Sternin, there are many officials who do not want you in this country,' he was warned. 'You have six months to demonstrate impact, or I'm afraid my ministry will be unable to extend your visa.'[1]

Six months to turn around a shocking level of child malnutrition? At that time, around two thirds of all Vietnamese children under the age of five suffered some degree of malnutrition. As if that wasn't enough, the Sternins knew there was no money for conventional approaches, using external experts, to deal with this intractable problem. A problem made worse by the fact that Vietnam was still suffering from a US-led economic embargo. Short of time, short of money and faced with these seemingly impossible problems, how did the Sternins respond? The answer lies at the very heart of leading with vision and of seeing the sense before it becomes common sense.

What do you do if there are insufficient funds to find and sustain a solution to child malnutrition? Do you try persuading an already over-stretched Vietnamese government of the project's value? Or do you try to find more external funding? Or do you pack up and go back to the US? That was the dilemma facing Jerry and Monique Sternin as the clock ticked towards their visa expiry date. Typically, conventional approaches to such issues involved external experts identifying the problem, then proposing appropriate nutritional and agricultural solutions. But on this occasion there was no money to do this. A solution had to be found from within the resources available.

With little money or time, the Sternins decided to ask some different questions. They noticed that not all children in the community were malnourished. Some seemed to fare much better than the majority of malnourished children, even though they lived in the same impoverished conditions. Why, amongst so many malnourished children, was there a relatively small number who were comparatively healthy?

Jerry Sternin had come across an obscure research construct called 'positive deviance', an idea originally developed by Professor Marian Zeitlin at Tufts University. [2] In short, the idea is that somewhere in a community or organization someone *already* has the answer to any problem you are facing. So the Sternins asked villagers in the communities they were working in to show them the children who were better nourished than the others. Initially they chose six of the poorest families who nonetheless had well-nourished children. What the Sternins found was that the mothers of these well-nourished children all had one thing in common. They ignored conventional wisdom. These mothers had found the sense before it was common sense.

The Sternins found the well-nourished children were fed more times a day than the norm. Most families fed their young children only twice a day but because of their small stomachs, the children were only able to eat a relatively small percentage of the rice available to them. In contrast, the well-nourished children were fed up to four or five times a day, which meant overall their food intake was higher. But not only did their mothers feed them more frequently, they also served them different food: food that was normally ignored by the communities. This group of mothers quite happily added sweet potato greens to the children's rice, and fed them other foods such as shrimps and crabs which, although abundant and freely available in the paddy fields, were generally considered to be inappropriate or dangerous for children. When added together, these seemingly small actions combined to make a significant difference. [3]

On seeing this, the Sternins encouraged the villagers to spread these ideas and practices to the other mothers in the village. The results were both rapid and remarkable. The first year of implementation saw such a significant improvement in child health that Save the Children was able to move on to other programme sites. [4] Within two years, malnutrition had dropped by about 74 per cent in every village in which the Sternins had worked. Moreover, these improvements were also long-lasting. A follow-up study found that the benefits were still evident up to four years after the programme began. [5] What's more, the benefits were found to be greatest amongst the very young, children who hadn't even been a part of the original project.

In some ways, our workplaces are not unlike those Vietnamese villages. Like them, we may be trying to deal with serious issues but without any extra resources. Or worse still, we may even be facing resource cuts. Yet, again like the Vietnamese villagers, there may be solutions to seemingly intractable issues on our doorsteps. It's quite possible that problems are already being solved by others in the organization, or at least that the seeds of progress are being sown.

So what were the Sternins able to do that has such a resonance with organizations? Firstly, they made sense of a difficult and confusing context. They did this by finding the uncommon sense that wasn't commonly practised. It is this striking ability to see what others don't that points towards a particular kind of vision. It's the kind that tries to make sense of unclear situations, and the kind that sees the sense before it becomes common.

How did the Sternins manage to see what others had missed? They began by applying an uncommon insight. They adapted the idea of positive deviance – that the solution to the problem might well be already apparent within the organization or community. This led them to ask different questions of the situation, concentrating on what was *working* rather than what was *wrong*. The approach required the villagers themselves to recognize the differences, then to spread their knowledge. The Sternins found the sense before it became common, then set about making it common sense.

So we'll begin this chapter by exploring a counter-intuitive idea – that of seeing things others have missed. To do this we'll need to think about a different kind of vision. Not just the ability to see the uncommon sense, which is hard enough, but to see it *before* it becomes common sense. The nature of uncommon sense is that, often, it doesn't initially make sense to others – that's why it's uncommon! So leaders not only need to find uncommon sense. First they need to make sense of it to themselves, then help others to see it. As we shall see, making sense when things aren't certain is different to conventional approaches to building a vision. It suggests seeing vision less as a rational process and more as the crafting of meaning in complex business environments. This is the concept known as 'sense-making', an idea that can provide some valuable tools to help us make sense. To illustrate this, we'll draw insights from two, very diverse examples. Firstly, from the late Steve Jobs on his return to save Apple, when the company was only two months from bankruptcy. Then, from a fire-related tragedy, where sense-making became crucial to a different kind of survival. Of course, a fire tragedy is not the same as an organizational issue, but there are still important lessons to be learned by any leader. Fires can create difficult situations where vision may become unclear or clouded – often with deadly consequences. So one notable academic and thought-leader used just such a story to illustrate principles for sense-making that have significant implications for all leaders trying to make sense of difficult environments. The main implication being: it's only as you make sense of the context that you can begin to build a vision.

Building a vision using uncommon sense is no easy thing. Whilst 'finding the sense before it becomes common' might be a catchy phrase, it does beg the question: just how might leaders do this? So at the end of the chapter we'll unpack some counter-intuitive ideas and insights on how to find the sense before it becomes common. Ways, as we shall see, that emerge from insights into the Sternins' experience in Vietnam.

How did the Sternins make sense of their context? Firstly they refused to compromise on their goal of improving nutrition for children, even when compromise seemed inevitable. They held the tension between competing and conflicting demands. Secondly, the Sternins sought ways to make change happen relatively quickly, yet within significant constraints of budget and time. They found a tipping point. Thirdly, the Sternins looked for and found the small things, those that can make both a big difference and a lasting difference. To reveal the sense, the Sternins looked for the examples that bucked the norm, the vital few that held the answer to the problem. Fourthly, it was also striking from their story that the answer was actually hidden in plain view. The reasons why a small number of children were thriving in the same conditions as so many who were malnourished were actually very obvious. Fifthly, they found the seeds of a future solution in the few who were doing something differently.

These five insights from the Sternins' experience: 'tensions'; 'tipping points'; 'trivial many and the vital few'; 'the obvious in plain view'; and 'the future', provide a springboard into our own guidelines on practical ways to find the business sense before it becomes common. The first two thought-provokers: 'tensions' and 'tipping points', suggest where to look for the uncommon sense. Can a commitment to holding the tension between competing and conflicting demands lead to some uncommon insight? Tipping points, on the other hand, look to the small things that can make a big impact.

Further sense-finding clues emerge in the contrast between what has become known as 'the trivial many and the vital few', and a rather more subtle thought-provoker: the 'obvious in plain view'. The first challenges leaders to find the few things that might matter amongst the many that don't. The second counsels against missing the obvious hidden in plain sight.

Finally, we return to the idea that vision is all about the future, and the future is notoriously difficult to predict. That's why our fifth and final suggestion about thinking differently explores the idea of three futures. These offer a challenge to help ensure leaders consider a range of different perspectives on the future.

Tensions, tipping points, the trivial many and the vital few, the obvious in plain view, and three futures all help us to see the sense before it becomes common. But before looking at those in more detail we'll introduce the idea of uncommon sense with another story – this time from the world of business.

CASE STUDY   Two months from bankruptcy: the obvious and the unexpected

What would you do if you only had two months to save an iconic business from bankruptcy? That's the position that Steve Jobs found himself in, when returning to Apple in 1997. What he did 'was both obvious and, at the same time unexpected' – he shrunk Apple to a more manageable scale and scope. But what is particularly interesting is how he did it, by successfully combining simplicity and focus.

At that time, the Apple product range included around 15 different, desktop computers. Here's how Jobs explained the significance of this fact to US academic and strategist, Richard Rumelt: 'A friend of the family asked me which Apple computer she should buy. She couldn't figure out the differences among them and I couldn't give her clear guidance, either.'[6] This is a salutary example of the obvious test, an idea we'll return to later in this chapter. Put simply, if your idea isn't simple enough to explain to others in a way that grabs their attention, then it's not obvious. This kind of focus, said Rumelt drawing on his own experience, is very rare in industry. As Steve Jobs was about to prove.

On his return to Apple, Jobs reviewed the company's product portfolio. Calling his teams together, he drew a two-by-two matrix on a whiteboard. On one axis he put the labels 'consumer' and 'pro'. On the other axis he put the labels 'desktop' and 'portable'. He then told his people that their job was to 'focus on four great products, one for each quadrant. All other products should be cancelled.' Simplifying what Apple did, and focusing on what they should do, saved the company. In applying this uncommon sense, Jobs proved that deciding what *not* to do is as important as deciding *what* to do. 'That's true for companies,' said Jobs, 'and it's true for products.'[7]

Jobs's actions saved Apple, but the story doesn't end there. Rumelt then asked Jobs a very perceptive question: 'What are you trying to do in the longer term?' Jobs had initially applied an unexpected but simple response that addressed Apple's immediate problems. But this was not going to take Apple forward. Jobs's answer to Rumelt's question was both simple and uncommonly insightful: 'I am going to wait for the next big thing.'[8] Rumelt went on to conclude: 'It would be two years before he would make that leap again with the iPod and then online e-music. And after that, with the iPhone.' Rumelt pointed out that whilst the response from Jobs is not an answer for every situation, for Apple it was a wise move at the time – given their 'situation at that moment, in that industry, with so many new technologies seemingly just around the corner.' You don't often hear CEOs say their plan is to wait for the next big thing, but that's exactly what Jobs did. In effect, he was saying he'd wait for the next tipping point – something which would revolutionize the market, but which he might see and exploit before others. And with the iPod (and later the iPhone and iPad) he did indeed see the sense before it became common. Which is exactly what this chapter is all about.

Seeing the sense before it becomes common

The first element of the 5-S leadership framework is *seeing* or leading with vision. Leading with vision means several things but here we want to think of a particular kind of vision, seeing things that others don't, can't or won't.

It's worth pausing to ask, where do you look to see the sense before it becomes common? Leadership knowledge is not static. It must be dynamic if it's to help us respond to the constantly changing environment in which our businesses operate. Some ideas may well have a timeless quality about them, others may have had their time and have a diminishing relevance for the future. Therefore, what we know about leadership, business, and customers should be under regular review.

Charles Handy is a world-renowned writer on organizations and organizational behaviour. His name ranks alongside the greats of management and leadership thinking. Indeed, one of the many endorsements of Handy's work comes from Warren Bennis. Regarded by many to be a pioneer of leadership studies, Bennis is often quoted as saying: 'If Peter Drucker is responsible for legitimizing the field of management and Tom Peters for popularizing it, then Charles Handy should be known as the person who gave it a philosophical elegance and eloquence that was missing from the field.'[9]

It's significant then, that Handy has placed a particular emphasis on the way in which thought-leaders use common sense. Handy was asked by the UK public broadcasting institution the BBC to write and record a series of talks entitled *The Handy Guide to the Gurus of Management*.

The idea of management gurus is often ridiculed, associated as it can be with the creation and exploitation of 'the next big thing' in management thinking. Nonetheless, serious thinkers support the role of serious management gurus. Charles Handy makes the case: 'Great ideas lie wasted unless someone turns them into a viable activity or a business, through management.'

Perhaps this is reason enough to explain why good leaders learn from the best! Handy goes further though, explaining that the role of a guru is: 'to interpret and spread around what seems to be working, helping managers to cope in a world that changes fast.'

Of course we need to exercise some caution when thinking about gurus. Some would argue that gurus only complicate or embellish things, and that we would be better without them. In his book *The Halo Effect... and the eight other business delusions that deceive managers*, Phil Rosenzweig makes some timely caveats. He points out that: 'for all the self-proclaimed thought leadership, success in business is as elusive as ever.'

He also persuasively argues that busy managers, who are under constant pressure, 'naturally search for ready-made answers, for tidy plug-in-and-play solutions that might give them a leg up on their rivals. And the people who write business books – consultants and business school professors and strategy gurus – are happy to oblige.'[10] Nonetheless, there is clearly much to learn from the work of some thought leaders and business gurus.

Learning from the best

So how do you ensure you learn from the best without being taken for a ride on the latest, soon-to-be-forgotten, 'next big thing'? Here are six suggestions to help:

1 *Learn from the best first.* Build on what has gone before, especially the wisdom of others. Many new ideas are not really new, often they come from the wisdom of others. Become a student of great thinkers on leadership. What ideas have shaped success in other organizations? What are the current ideas and insights that might shape how you think about leadership, management and business? Be informed by the best.

2 *Learn from the tried and tested.* Some ideas have a good evidence base; they have stood the test of time. Many mistakes can be avoided by learning from ideas that are tried and tested. Of course, whilst some ideas may have stood the test of time, they might need interpreting differently in new situations.

3 *Learn to distinguish between fad and fact.* In the haste to keep up with a fast-changing business world, it's all too easy to jump on bandwagons. Just because something seems to have worked elsewhere doesn't necessarily mean it will work in your situation. Pay careful attention to the evidence that supports any new idea. Then think carefully about how ideas might need to be adapted to your organizational context.

4 *Learn from those around you.* There are numerous opportunities to learn from the wisdom of those around you. Seek out the leaders and managers who best support and encourage learning. Learn from these people by asking questions and seeking to understand their methods, philosophies and the reasons for their success. What do your colleagues know that could have an impact? What do customers think?

5 *Learn to change the way you lead and manage.* The world of leadership and management is changing. Just as business is constantly changing; so too are the skills and knowledge needed to lead and manage effectively. Virtual teams, collaborations, new organizational structures and outsourcing capabilities all demand radically different ways of leading, managing and working. These evolving changes to the way we work will have a significant impact on how we lead and manage. Think about what you'll need to do to change the way you lead and manage.

6 *Learn to learn.* A key skill for any leader or manager is to develop an inquisitive and disciplined approach to learning. Knowledge often has a sell-by date and needs to be refreshed and renewed as the

business context changes. That's why it's important to build-in regular time to keep up to date, and to reflect on your practices as a leader. Take how you learn seriously. Learning is more about setting a course than taking a course!

As new ideas emerge it takes leadership to implement them

Learning from the best is one important lesson to adopt, but it's not the only one that can be drawn from Handy's discussion of thought leaders. Handy's definition of a management guru is both pithy and pragmatic: someone who interprets and spreads ideas and practices that seem to be working. But there is something even more significant. According to Handy, what differentiates gurus is that they, 'often use common sense, but they see the sense before it becomes common and that's what can give companies and their managers the competitive edge. The insights and methods of the gurus can make a big difference to the way we manage our organizations.'

The implication for organizational leaders is obvious. What is true of Handy's thought-leaders should be true for business leaders. One key attribute that sets successful leaders apart from the crowd is their ability to see things before others do. In other words, to find the sense before it becomes common. But regardless of how original or insightful, simply seeing the sense is not enough. Leaders must also make sense – of events, relationships, opportunities, threats, trends, and so on.

We'll return to consider how you might find the sense before it becomes common sense after discussing a fundamental point. If leaders are to *find the sense* before it becomes common sense, they need to be able to *make sense*. In other words, they need to be sense-makers. Why? Because, although it's nice to think of vision in clear-cut terms, the reality is often far less clear. More often than not, it's difficult to confidently pick a way forward. This is where the view of vision as sense-making can be helpful. For Professor Karl Weick, the world of sense-making is 'built out of vague questions, muddy answers, and negotiated agreements that attempt to reduce confusion.'[11] Weick's expert views on sense-making were informed from his studies of a range of situations, from difficult to fraught to disastrous. From these he drew some valuable advice for organizations, suggesting how they might cope with unpredictable and unclear circumstances.

Sense-making

Sense-making is an essential leadership role and an essential precursor to developing a vision. It's, '… the way managers understand, interpret, and create sense for themselves based on the information surrounding the strategic change.'[12]

Sense-making and sense-giving

In their early work on the subject, Dennis Gioia and Kumar Chittipeddi saw sense-making as inseparable from sense-giving. They argued that the two processes were reciprocal. Sense-making led to sense-giving, the need to influence and persuade others of the sense you have made of the situation. Feedback and other interactions would then often necessitate further reflection from sense-giver – a return to more sense-making. We'll consider sense-giving in more detail in the next chapter.

What is interesting about Gioia and Chittipeddi's study is that the situation they analysed, in contrast to Weick's example, was not a crisis. Although their study was more about conventional organizational change, they still found similar, unpredictable conditions. They found that ambiguity and uncertainty were both still evident from the start, and that leaders in the organization worked towards finding 'a sensible, workable interpretation of a revised organisational reality.'[13] When the future is inherently unpredictable, sense-making becomes a crucial leadership skill. It requires the ability to make sense of what is going on, both outside and within your organization, to inform your vision for change.

'Sense-making involves coming up with a plausible understanding – a map – of a shifting world; testing this map with others through data collection, action, and conversation; and then refining, or abandoning, the map depending on how credible it is.'[14]

Sense-making means:

- Scanning and information-seeking.
- Searching the internal and external environment for meaning, in order to develop a vision and plans for change.
- Mapping a plausible understanding of an uncertain context.

CASE STUDY   Lessons from a fire

If you want to study sense-making in a difficult context then few situations can be more unpredictable, and therefore more appropriate, than a forest fire. This is what Karl Weick explored in his article about the tragic loss of a fire-fighting team. Drawing insights and lessons from the incident, Weick explored one question of particular relevance here: how can organizations be made more resilient? The answer reveals some helpful advice about sense-making.

In his book, *Young Men and Fire*, Professor Norman Maclean recounted the gripping story of how 13 fire-fighters died tragically on 5 August, 1949.[15] Trained smoke-jumpers, these men were part of a crew parachuted into Mann Gulch, in the remote mountains of Montana. At first their crew leaders thought they were dealing with a small fire, taking early, preventative action to stop a much bigger conflagration. But conditions and circumstances soon changed dramatically. Turbulent winds and soaring temperatures whipped the fire into a raging inferno.

The crew foreman, Wagner Dodge, was new to this team — a fact that was to have tragic significance. Dodge realized that the speed and ferocity of the fire was overtaking the young fire-fighters, as they made for the safety of a rocky ridge. With great presence of mind, Dodge took quick action. To save his men from the onrushing blaze he lit an 'escape' fire. He signalled them to drop their equipment and shelter with him in the burned-out area he'd created. Dodge survived but tragically, his men ignored him and ran off to their deaths.

This tragedy happened for several reasons but primarily it was due to issues in teamwork and sense-making. Due to the confused situation, only Dodge had seen the bigger picture, which meant he alone made sense of the changing circumstances. Lacking time to communicate fully, his instruction was neither immediately understood, nor acted upon by the crew. In not being able to see the bigger picture, they had lost their own ability to make sense of what was happening. To further complicate things, they didn't know Dodge well enough to instinctively trust his leadership. When Dodge lit the escape fire, and in so doing fought fire with fire, the rest of the crew looked on in disbelief. This was the pivotal point where the crew lost both their ability to make sense of things, and their trust in their leader. It is also a crucial point from which Weick seeks answers to his question, and draws organizational lessons about resilience. He thought the Mann Gulch incident clearly illustrated a range of issues facing organizational leaders:

> *For those of us concerned about leadership in organizations, the episode illuminates problems facing corporate leaders… minimal organizations, exemplified by the crew at Mann Gulch and found at a growing number of businesses, are susceptible to sudden and dangerous losses of meaning… the level of disorganization at Mann Gulch is not all that different from what companies face today. People are often thrust into unfamiliar roles to fulfil difficult tasks, and small mistakes can combine into something monstrous.[16]*

Weick thought today's leaders need to develop resilient teams that are capable of four things:

1 *Improvisation* – the ability to remain creative under pressure. In the story, Dodge does the unusual, with what is to hand – asking his colleagues to drop the tools they would normally use to fight the fire.

2 *Wisdom* – avoiding extremes of over-confidence and excessive caution. The 'group wisdom' at Mann Gulch was based on an underlying assumption that the fire was smaller than it was. Countering the risk of relying too heavily on assumptions requires an attitude that balances being over-confident and being overly cautious.

3 *Respectful interaction* – with each other, other teams, the wider organization, customers, and with stakeholders related to their organization. Trust needs to be built, and the limited time Dodge had with his team meant they neither respected nor trusted his leadership when faced with the crisis situation.

4 *Communication* – which is effective, timely and appropriate to the audience, and the situation. The answer to the lack of communication as Mann Gulch is perhaps summed up by Weick himself when he said: 'Evidence is growing that nonstop talk is a crucial source of co-ordination in complex systems that are susceptible to disasters.'[17]

Weick's resilience factors combine to form a bedrock from which to make sense-making more effective. Sense-making would be both easier and more effective in organizations, when this foundation is in place.

Steps to sense-making

So how do you sense-make? Drawing on Weick's insights and the discussion so far, we think there are six key approaches that will help leaders with sense-making:

1   scanning and searching;

2   finding the sense before it becomes common;

3   crafting and adapting;

4   balancing knowing and doubting;

5   having sense-making conversations;

6   asking the right questions.

1   *Scanning and searching*. Sense-making suggests an on-going vigilance, continually scanning and searching the context you are in. It means noticing things but also trying to see things differently. This is what the Sternins did in Vietnam. They paid attention to what was working, then asked why. They also took note of the surprising. In the midst of so much malnutrition, what surprised was that some children were so well nourished. Keeping your eyes open means that you notice changes. Scanning and searching also means recognizing change, especially recognizing changing patterns. Pattern recognition asks questions about what seems to be emerging in your organizational context. For example, greater vigilance at Mann Gulch, by the whole team, might have picked up the dangerously changing conditions more quickly. Seeing what is different or emerging is important, but so too is the need for leaders to see what is missing. Scanning and searching means also looking for discontinuities and gaps. And don't be afraid of finding a big gap! David Lloyd George, the highly energetic UK prime minister who led Britain through the First World War, is quoted as saying: 'Don't be afraid to take a big step if one is indicated; you can't cross a chasm in two small jumps.' Which is just what Steve Jobs found on his return to Apple: when you are two months away from bankruptcy, big steps need to be taken.

Scanning and searching means continually seeking to understand. It helps to prompt a scan or search with some key questions, such as:

What can thought-leaders help you to see? How can customers give you a different perspective? What do your front-line staff know that could change your business? What can you learn from your competitors?

2 *Finding the sense before it becomes common.* A critical step in sense-making should be to look for the uncommon sense. The awareness, vigilance and perceptions gathered from continually scanning and searching can provide the spark to make sense of the context. Things began to make sense to the Sternins when they applied an uncommon insight – by adapting the idea of positive deviance. Weick's fire story contained some uncommon insights. At Mann Gulch it was fighting fire with fire, a technique relatively unknown at that time.

3 *Crafting and adapting.* Sense-making brings thought and action together. It's about trying to interpret a situation, then thinking about what is currently working, and what could work in the future. It is highly likely that any solutions will involve *improvisation*. This means adapting in order to respond flexibly to a changing context. It is about testing an idea to see if it works, then adapting as you gain more awareness of whether your actions are achieving the outcomes you want. As Karl Weick said: 'By improvisation, I mean bringing to the surface, testing, and restructuring one's intuitive understandings of phenomena on the spot, at a time when action can still make a difference.'[18]

Improvising is also about creatively using what you already have to hand, a concept referred to as 'bricolage'. We will explore this further in the next chapter by referring to the Apollo 13 mission, itself a great example of sense-making and improvisation.

4 *Balancing knowing and doubting.* Holding the tension between knowing and doubting is particularly important when facing an unpredictable future. In those circumstances there can be a strong temptation towards either over-confident knowing or overly-cautious doubting. A wise leader resists these temptations by maintaining a balance between knowing and doubt. This means testing underlying assumptions that might lead to over-confident or unfounded conviction.

Of course, there can be as much value in knowing what you *don't know* as there is in asserting your conviction about what you *do know*. According to Plato, Socrates once questioned a man with a reputation for being knowledgeable, who seemed to be wise both to himself and to others. Socrates is quoted as thinking: 'I went away thinking to myself that I was wiser than this man: the fact is that neither of us knows anything beautiful and good, but he thinks he does know when he doesn't, and I don't know and don't think that I do: so I am wiser than he is by only this trifle, that what I do not know I don't think I do.'[19]

Or as US academic J A Meacham is quoted as saying: 'The essence of wisdom is in knowing that one does not know, in the appreciation that knowledge is fallible, in the balance between knowing and doubting.'[20]

5 *Holding sense-making conversations.* To be really effective, sense-making needs to be done with others. Other people may well have insights that can shed light onto the situation. But even when we are looking for such input, it may not always be forthcoming. Others may be reluctant to engage for any number of reasons – lack of opportunity, lack of communication channels, lack or trust. Pro-actively seeking and holding sense-making conversations is an essential step to overcoming such matters. And it is far easier to extol or extract wisdom where people are respectful of the interactions that hold the group together. To do this, Weick suggests that there needs to be respect borne of trust and communication. According to Weick, this is built on three foundations:

- Trust: listening to, respecting and acting on input from others.
- Honesty: communicating in a way that enables others to make sense of your input.
- Self-respect: integrating the above without losing your own self-belief.[21]

The notion of sense-making conversations, is captured by leadership and management expert, Jay Conger. Professor of Leadership Studies at Claremont McKenna College, Conger states that:

> *The most effective leaders study the issues that matter to their colleagues... in... conversations... they collect essential information. They are good at listening. They test their ideas with trusted confidants, and they ask questions of the people they will later be persuading. These explorations help them to think through the arguments, the evidence, and the perspectives they will present.*[22]

Sense-making conversations help leaders to gain clarity and build a shared sense of what is happening.

6 *Asking the right questions.* There is more to sense-making than conversations. To be effective, leaders must also ask questions – preferably, the right questions. In fact, it could be argued that the best leadership tool of all is – a good question! Good questions are at the heart of any attempt to make sense of a situation. As no less an authority than Albert Einstein once said: 'If I had an hour to solve a problem and my life depended on the solution, I would spend the first 55 minutes determining the proper question to ask, for once I know the proper question, I could solve the problem in less than five minutes.'

Questions serve different purposes, there is a 'pecking order' implied by the question's words. The more powerful questions begin with why, how or what. These are followed by who, when, where. Finally, the least powerful questions are those beginning with which, or those that can be answered with a yes or no.

As we have seen with the Sternins in Vietnam, the kind of questions we ask can lead us in a certain direction. For example, limiting the scope of our questions means limiting the kind of solutions we may find to problems or issues. So, it matters how we frame questions, especially if we are seeking to find opportunities from problems. Framing questions positively changes the process. It elevates problem solving from simply trying to fix something that's wrong, to exploring the possibilities and potential to create improvement from the problem, and something of value. The Sternins could have continued asking questions about what was wrong. And they could have continued to focus on fixing the problem by studying the malnourished children. Instead they asked a different question: what is working?

The kind of question we ask will lead us in a certain direction. Returning to save Apple, Steve Jobs could have just focused on typical actions, such as cutting costs. And surely selling more of what you've got would seem a less risky option than reducing your product range, just when you need as much turnover as you can get. But Jobs asked a different question: how do we shape what we offer so that our customers understand it, and so that we focus on a few great products? As we'll find out in Chapter 5, how we frame things can make a big difference to the decisions we make.

Today's sense, tomorrow's vision

Sense-making is rooted in the real world – a world of confusion, limited clarity, change and uncertainty. Yet perhaps the real value in sense-making is that it helps to shape the future. It's about understanding the context from which leaders must try to craft a way forward. Seeing and understanding that current context is important but arguably the critical role of the leader is to see beyond what is happening now. It might not be possible to actually see into the future, but effective leaders must still have a vision of how that future might look. Making sense of things leads to the creation of a vision.

Vision: a different view of the future

 Where there is no vision, the people perish
(Proverbs 29 v18, King James Version)

So too for organizations! You don't need to look far in any book on leadership to realize the importance of vision. Indeed the central, recurring need for leaders is to have a vision. For some leaders, vision may arrive in a moment of inspiration. But more often, organizational vision is formed over a period of time. As we have just discussed, vision *emerges,* as leaders begin to make sense of a situation.

Ideally that vision will focus on achieving improvement. It should be an optimistic vision, albeit one rooted in realism. In setting a course of action, there is always a danger that changes proposed or made will not bring about improvement. It's a truism that all improvement is change, but not all change is improvement. Much better then, to set off with a focus on improvement, rather than just on change.

Of course, you don't need to create your vision entirely on your own. Others can help to shape the vision. In fact one of the most effective ways to visualize and realize a leadership vision is to build it with the people you are leading. This is a point well made by authors and academics, Jim Kouzes and Barry Posner (2009): 'The best way to lead people into the future is to connect with them deeply in the present. The only visions that take hold are shared visions – and you will create them only when you listen very, very closely to others, appreciate their hopes, and attend to their needs.'[23]

Where change is needed, a vision needs to hold a significantly different view of the future. This future should be about creating a better place than the present. At the same time a vision should develop a sense of necessity, a sense that this has to be done. Ideally, it should be a future which employees are inspired to create together.

A good vision is not easily put together. It needs to be a compelling picture of the future, a future that resonates with colleagues. It then acts as a strong motivator to maintain high standards where they exist, or to make changes for the better where needed.

Building a vision

Building a vision from sense-making won't come easily. It will take more than a few strategic planning sessions or away-days for senior managers. That's not to say that scheduling time away from day-to-day pressures won't help you gain a different perspective. But developing and crystallizing a meaningful vision, with real input from those you are leading, requires significant conversations and compelling insights.

Significant conversations

Many leaders listen to, or engage in, conversations in order to help them crystallize a vision. But the critical issue is ensuring that such conversations are more than superficial or token. They need to be significant. This requires meaningful conversations with people across the entire organization, and possibly even further afield. This makes it easier to build a shared vision, from widespread involvement in the organization, rather than just sharing an 'ordained' vision.

How are significant conversations different from the sense-making conversations we referred to earlier? Significant conversations could be thought of as the next 'stage' of conversation, one that moves things on from sense-making to vision-building. But in reality, the two kinds of conversations may well overlap.

Reg Revans,[24] founder of the Action Learning approach to management development, argued that building wider action means identifying three kinds of people: those who know; those who care; and those who can.

Or better still, in finding people who combine all three! Either way, significant conversations should engage with:

- People who know – about the problems to be tackled, about how things are currently done, and about how they might be done differently in the future.

- People who care – about the organization and the people in it, and genuinely want improvement.

- People who can – who have enough power to get something done.

Compelling insights

Building a vision that will inspire also requires compelling insights – ideas that make people think or see things differently. Often, these come from thinking about what we've learned from making sense of context. What sense have you discovered before it becomes common sense?

Insights can also come from what is happening outside the organization, combining with the best ideas and insights from those within it. One excellent source of insight can be from the organization's customers and from those colleagues who work most closely with them. This can be especially true of leaders who experience things as the customer does.

Of course, compelling insights alone are not enough. These must be weaved into a vision that is inspiring but also clearly-stated, concise, tangible and real. For a vision to have impact it needs to engage, connect and spread. To explore how leaders can do this it's helpful to borrow two concepts from sociologists: bridging and bonding.

Leading with vision: bridging and bonding

Another reason for the Sternins' remarkable success is that they were able to draw from an often-overlooked resource – the community. They made the important distinction of seeing the community as having assets and resources, rather than simply being in need of help. This is just as important in our business communities, where it's easy to undervalue the resource potential in employees, customers, and the wider community within which a business fits. The Sternins certainly saw the existing and potential resourcefulness of the community's social capital. Sociologists refer to social capital as the connectedness that builds a strong society. It has been defined as: 'the sum of the actual and potential resources embedded within, available through, and derived from the network of relationships possessed by an individual or social unit.'[25]

In his best-selling book, *Bowling Alone*, Robert Putnam talks about social capital in two ways: social capital which *bonds* and that which *bridges*. He explains the difference in lay terms: '... bonding social capital constitutes a kind of sociological superglue, whereas bridging provides a sociological WD-40.[26]

Bonding connections reinforce similarities amongst individuals, whereas bridging connections span differences. In practice, most societies combine both to one degree or another. Bonding is about building a sense of togetherness, and cohesiveness with teams and departments, engaging everybody with the vision. Bridging refers to looser ties we may have to distant contacts, rather than the stronger, bonding ties we have with closer relationships. Bridging connects parts of the organization that don't normally connect, or makes links and networks outside the organization perhaps with customers. This wider connecting may produce synergies and help to spread the vision.

Putnam quotes Xavier de Souza Briggs who suggests that bonding social capital is good for 'getting by', but bridging social capital is crucial for 'getting ahead'. Bridging generates broader identities and reciprocity, whereas bonding bolsters a narrower perspective. In this sense then, leading with vision promotes a sense of common purpose through internal bonding. It also builds external bridges, capitalizing on new opportunities outside of the organization.

It is the leader's role to *bridge* current reality and new vision, defining goals and showing how they are attainable. It's also the leader's job to help make that vision a reality, and this is more easily done when there is an adequate focus on *bonding*.

One powerful illustration of the importance of vision is expressed in the classic 'stonecutter' story.

Building a cathedral

There are several versions of the stonecutter story, and several ways to interpret its timeless lessons. Whether you think you're just earning a living, doing the best at your job, or you're leaving a legacy, this story demonstrates that there is great value in thinking positively and in seeing the bigger picture.

The three stonecutters

One day a traveller, walking along a lane, came across three stonecutters working in a quarry. Each was busy cutting a block of stone. Interested to find out what they were working on, the traveller asked the first stonecutter what he was doing.

'I am cutting a stone!'

Still no wiser the traveller turned to the second stonecutter and asked him what he was doing.

'I am cutting this block of stone to make sure that it's square, and its dimensions are uniform, so that it will fit exactly in its place in a wall.'

This gave the traveller slightly more information but he was still unclear about what the stonecutters were actually working on. So he turned to the third man. This stonecutter seemed to be the happiest of the three and when asked what he was doing he replied:

'I am building a cathedral.'

The stonecutter story beautifully illustrates the essence of leading with vision – seeing the bigger picture. All three stonecutters were *doing* the same thing but each gave a very different answer. Each knew *how* to do his job but what set the third stonecutter apart? It may simply have been that he was a naturally enthusiastic or positive person – one of life's optimists! But it's also possible that he was well led. Perhaps what motivated him in his work was:

- knowing not just *how* and what to do, but knowing *why* he was doing it;
- viewing the whole and not just its parts;
- seeing a vision, a sense of the bigger picture;
- having the ability to see significance in work, beyond the obvious;
- understanding that a legacy will live on, whether in the stone of a cathedral, or in the impact made on other people.

This story illustrates the importance of vision in affecting the way people work. It also illustrates that vision is not just what leaders have, it's what they create, impart and embed in the organizations or teams they lead.

Vision is undoubtedly critical to good leadership. But like most things worth having, it's not always easy to come by. We have seen how vision is often borne of difficult circumstances. Perhaps it comes from leaders trying to make sense of unpredictable or unclear contexts and situations. We've also seen how vision can come from engaging with people throughout the organization, especially those who know, who care or who 'do'. Whilst vision, when it is done well, engages and energizes colleagues, it can also be a tricky process to get right. For many people, there are some inherent problems with vision, and no small degree of scepticism.

Vision – what's the problem?

Has the notion of vision been sullied by trivial attempts to produce emotive slogans and to market a set of values around the organization? In some cases the idea of a vision seems to be more about a nice choice of words and images imposed on a workforce that might be ill-prepared, unwilling, uninformed or even resentful. Can visions cause more problems than they solve?

The problem with vision is that many employees see them as too distant or irrelevant. A vision is seen by many to be exactly that – just a vision. A vision that bears little or no resemblance to what people are experiencing here and now will need some selling! Perhaps worst of all is the feeling that senior managers and leaders aren't aware of the disconnect between vision and current reality. Without acknowledgment of this gap, or of steps needed to bridge them, even the best vision can actually be counter-productive. Instead of being an inspirational guide to change and growth, such a vision may actually result in de-motivation, apathy or even resentment.

Yet vision is exactly what is needed in any organization. Vision should lift aspirations above the mundane, create images of what could and should be, and articulate the route to making them a reality. Properly done, a vision should express the intent of the organization, and what it hopes to contribute to staff, customers, wider stakeholders and society in general.

A vision needs to be a compelling picture of the future. But achieving the vision is much more likely if it is grounded in reality. The vision must resonate with employees as a strong motivator to encourage change. The contrast to the current situation should inspire an achievable challenge, not offer an unfeasible disconnect between reality and aspiration. How can this be done? By creating visions that hold a significantly different view of the future, which are desirable, and which employees *want* to create together.

Or better still, a vision that develops a sense of necessity – creating a feeling that it simply *has* to be done.

There are always tensions with vision because a good vision describes something that is not yet in place. This tension, between what is and what is hoped for, can often result in frustration. However, if that frustration leads to renewed energy to realize the vision, then that can be a good thing. As St Augustine once famously said: 'If you would attain to what you are not yet, you must always be displeased by what you are. For where you are pleased with yourself there you have remained. Keep adding, keep walking, keep advancing.'

Not surprisingly though, encouraging people to move from current reality to new ground can cause tension. Peter Senge likens this tension to a rubber band which connects a current situation to a desired outcome. The tension can be relieved in one of two ways: either by 'lowering' the vision or by moving the current reality closer to that vision. Lowering the vision might seem the easier route to take, especially if the tension is causing problems. Sadly, this is what happens all too often. [27]

But rather than lowering vision, it's the leader's job to bridge current reality and new vision, defining goals and showing how they are attainable. That job becomes much easier if, as Senge advocates, the vision is shared. Creating a shared vision is much more preferable than simply sharing a vision and 'bridging' towards it. People will be more willing to bridge to a vision that they have helped to shape.

The idea of holding tensions can be an important consideration for anyone trying to lead with vision. It's also a good example of how to find the sense before it becomes common sense.

Finding the sense before it becomes common

It's easy to talk about finding the sense before it becomes common sense, but can you actually do that? How can you recognize sense before it becomes common? Perhaps the key is being able to think differently. To help you do that, we've brought together the five thought-provoking insights we mentioned earlier. Drawn from the Sternins' experience in tackling malnutrition in Vietnam, these insights are:

- tensions;
- tipping points;
- the trivial many and the vital few;
- the obvious in plain view;
- three futures.

The first two, tensions and tipping points, give some clues about where to look for the uncommon sense. Where are the tensions between competing demands in your organization? What small things can be done which, when brought together can have a big impact – can create tipping points?

Next we contrast two more thought-provokers. How do you find the significant few things that really matter, amongst the many that don't? Then how do you develop a more obvious skill – not missing the critical things that are in plain view – the obvious? The final technique for thinking differently takes us back to vision and the future. Whilst there is much we don't know about the future there are some clues that often are missed. So we finish by suggesting three ways for you to think about the future.

Holding tensions: why not find the glass?

We began this section by reflecting on the Sternins, as they faced some impossibly conflicting demands. Perceived wisdom was that to improve nutrition, they needed a team of experts to analyse the situation. The problem was, they had no money to pay for the project, the experts, or to ensure any improvements can be sustained. Faced with such a dilemma, what would you do?

Competing tensions in work and life often result in the need to make compromises. It's usually just too difficult, or even impossible, to ensure that competing demands and priorities can all be satisfied. In some circumstances finding the middle ground may be the right path to take. To achieve this something usually has to give, leading to compromise. Usually, but not always! Sometimes, especially over important issues, why not try thinking differently before settling for a compromise?

Why not?

As he took the last photograph and rewound the film in the camera, Edwin reminded his daughter that she'd have to wait until the roll of film was developed. The usual film-processing time was one week and for almost everybody this seemed acceptable. Everybody, that is, except the child.

'Why,' she asked, 'do I have to wait so long to see my pictures?'

A reasonable question as, after all, a week can be a long time for a young child. Edwin could have responded like countless parents faced with this most ubiquitous of childhood questions.

'Because that's just the way it is.'

Instead, Edwin Land chose to say, 'Why not?' His daughter's simple question ignited a challenge that he had never thought about before.

'Why can't you create instantaneous pictures from a camera?'

Land set to work seeking a solution. Within approximately four years, Edwin Land had commercialized a product. Revolutionary in its time, the Polaroid Land camera was the world's first camera capable of taking photographs that developed within minutes.[28]

When faced with a situation where compromise seems to be the only option, you could think like Edwin Land, and ask: 'Why not'? Edwin Land has been described as the Steve Jobs of his day. Interestingly Land was one of Jobs's heroes and the two men had actually met. What they shared in approach has some resonance with the Sternins' sense and belief that the solution was already out there. Here's how John Sculley, then CEO of Apple,[29] recollects the meeting between Land and Jobs. Land's perception of invention was different as he explained: 'I could see what the Polaroid camera should be. It was just as real to me as if it was sitting in front of me before I had ever built one.'

And Steve said: 'Yeah, that's exactly the way I saw the Macintosh.'

Land went on to make an interesting point: 'The world is like a fertile field that's waiting to be harvested... the seeds have been planted, and what I do is go out and help plant more seeds and harvest them.'[30]

Both Land and Jobs were describing an ability to see what they felt was already there. They saw something that already existed but which was either hidden from the view of others, or which needed to be harvested. Their view of vision, as being able to see what they had discovered before it had been made, is reminiscent of the great Michelangelo. In his famous words: 'Every block of stone has a statue inside it and it is the task of the sculptor to discover it.'

Find the glass

Land and Jobs typify an approach that refuses to compromise. This is our version of a great story, which we first came across in *The Three Tensions* by Dominic Dodd and Ken Favaro.[31] It's the story of a leader who, when confronted by colleagues with seemingly intractable problems, reminded them about glass. When people lived in mud huts they had the choice of light or warmth. They could make a hole to let daylight in, and face the consequences of the cold. Or they could block the hole, stay warm but dwell in the dark. Glass changed all that, making it possible to do both. The leader told his managers to stop thinking about 'either/or'. He told them to think 'and' – to 'find the glass'.

FIGURE 1.2   Find the glass

Work needn't always mean 'or'. Think about how and when it could mean 'and'? Thinking 'and' can make you think differently about two terms or ideas which are seemingly irreconcilable. For example, holding the tension between:

- Long term and short term – often the long term can be sacrificed to achieve short-term goals. How can you achieve both?

- Satisfied employees and satisfied customers – It's hard enough trying to keep customers happy without trying to pander to staff needs too.

If you pay too much attention to staff needs you'll take your eye off the customer, won't you?

- More choice and simplified operations – offering more choice will mean our operations will become more complex and costly, won't they?

- Better quality and lower price – providing better quality will cost more won't it?

Asking 'why not', or finding the 'and' may not be easy, but identifying the tensions is a good place to start. If you want to find the sense before it becomes common, try finding the tension first.

If a tension is an indicator of where uncommon sense might be found, we'll turn next to a very different kind of indicator. The world of tipping points is a world where small changes make a big impact.

Tipping point leadership

Imagine creating the conditions where you can accelerate the speed of change – even where this seems difficult or impossible. Think about the momentum that could be gained if a critical mass of people in your organization got behind the idea. Or think about the effect on your organization of generating a critical mass of customers in key areas. How can this be achieved even when the size and scale of the change agenda seems to weigh heavily on you? How do you overcome hurdles such as:

- struggling to make changes;

- being stuck in the status quo;

- limited and constrained budgets and resources;

- staff motivation and morale issues.

Returning once again to the experience of the Sternins, they faced almost all of these situations. They certainly had no extra money and very little time to achieve a turnaround in dealing with Vietnam's malnourished children. Nor did another successful leader, Bill Bratton of the New York City Transit Police, when trying to turn around a poor performing organization, with low staff morale and a restricted budget. What did they each do differently? They found a tipping point.

Tipping points

A tipping point is the point at which something begins to change substantially. At the tipping point, a number of small factors combine, resulting in significant change. In an organization, a tipping point is when: '… the energy and belief in an organization reaches a level that brings about change quickly.'[32]

The critical question for leaders is: can tipping points be created or managed? Given the potential benefits, as illustrated by the Sternins in Vietnam, it's well worth understanding and applying tipping-point principles. The idea of tipping points first came to prominence with the influential book of the same name by Malcolm Gladwell. But for our understanding of tipping point leadership we'll turn to two academics from the European INSEAD Business School. They tell the story of the dramatic turnaround at the New York City Transit Authority.

Tipping points in action

The changing fortunes of the New York subway in the late 1980s is one of the most famous examples of a tipping point in action. David Gunn and William Bratton led the significant few who totally changed the status quo in that failing organization. Not unlike the Sternins who found a different approach to a seemingly intractable problem, Bratton also applied an uncommon insight. Whereas the Sternins used the principle of positive deviants (a few who bucked the trend), Bratton used the idea of 'broken windows'. *Broken Windows* was the title of a 1982 article by George Kelling and James Wilson. They developed their idea based on the research of Philip Zimbardo, a Stanford psychologist whose work fostered the idea that a single broken window in a neighbourhood increased the likelihood of further destruction. As Wilson and Kelling put it: 'One unrepaired broken window is a signal that no one cares, and so breaking more windows costs nothing.'[33]

This idea was counter-intuitive. It suggested that a focus on what most police officers would consider small, insignificant things could have a big impact on overall crime, and build safer communities.

David Gunn was president of the New York Transit Authority from 1984 to 1990 and William Bratton was appointed its Chief of Police in 1990. On his arrival, Bratton was faced with crime figures that had risen 25 per cent per year in the past three years – twice the overall rate for the city. In the short space of just two years, he turned the situation around completely. By the end of that period, fare evasion was cut in half and serious crime reduced by 22 per cent. How did he do it? That's what Chan Kim and Professor Renée Mauborgne from INSEAD answered in their Harvard article.[34]

They found that Bratton adopted a zero-tolerance attitude to the rampant graffiti and crime on the subway. His persistent application of small principles – daily removal of graffiti and enforcement of fare rules and criminal laws – changed the subway's environment. Bratton's officers were initially sceptical. They felt they were being asked to focus on small crimes when so much more serious crime should demand their attention. But it turned out that most of the fare jumpers weren't ordinary citizens, simply committing minor misdemeanours. In reality, one out of every seven fare dodgers caught was wanted for more serious crimes. More significantly still, 1 in 21 was carrying a weapon.[35]

Gradually, Bratton's zero-tolerance to the small things began to influence offender behaviour until finally, a tipping point was reached. As a result, the New York subway was totally transformed in the space of just a few years. Some time later, when starting his new role as commissioner of NYPD, Bratton was to use the same approach. He promised that he would 'attack the largest crimes by focusing on the smallest.'[36]

Gunn and Bratton achieved these results regardless of seemingly insurmountable hurdles. The subway was transformed despite limited resources, chronic low staff morale, and an organization that was stuck in the status quo, struggling to change. Kim and Mauborgne synthesized the lessons learned from the New York subway example. They concluded that teaching a tipping point requires four steps:

1 Taking a cognitive step through which individuals become convinced of the change.

2 Overcoming resource hurdles, where change can be achieved within the resources available.

3 Motivating others by identifying and utilizing those people who carry influence.

4 Overcoming political barriers to change.

Can tipping points be created and managed? Bill Bratton demonstrated that the answer is yes, even without increased resources. Both Bratton and the Sternins found the few things amongst the many that made a big impact. To help you create and manage tipping points, we have adapted and extended these four points. We've incorporated the uncommon insight which was a key feature of their approach with another principle, that of the 'vital few':

- *Apply an uncommon insight* – search for the counter-intuitive ideas that can give insight into the context you are dealing with. For Bratton this was the 'broken window' principle. For the Sternins it was developing the idea of positive deviance.

- *Experience the problem/situation as the customer does* – none of Bratton's officers used the subways to commute. Bratton asked all his officers to commute to work by the subway (as he did himself). They quickly saw the issues for themselves. The Sternins went out to the villages and asked village representatives to show them the families where children were well-nourished. In both examples they saw things as their customers did.

- *Concentrate resources* – Bratton didn't have any more money to improve the organization. So he concentrated resources where they would have the most impact, at the few stations that saw the majority of crimes. With no money to bring in the professionals, the Sternins also concentrated resources, both financial and communal. They called upon the resources of the community to help them identify and solve the problem. The key message in both cases was to concentrate current resources on areas in most need of change.

- *Engage key influencers* – motivate key people in the organization. Find the few people who are opinion-formers, capable of spreading changes/ideas quickly and widely. This is what Malcolm Gladwell refers to as connectors – people who are not just important for how many people they know, but crucially for the 'kinds of people they know'. They aren't just connected, they are *well*-connected.[37] And for the Sternins, finding the mothers within the community who behaved differently allowed others to see that behaviour-changing ideas were both local and hidden in plain view.

- *Deal with the politics* – don't ignore the political context in your organization. Politics can kill a change. Ask yourself: who do you need on board? Who can influence the political agenda in the organization?

● *The vital few* – find the few things that can have a big impact. For the Sternins this meant finding the few children who were bucking the trend. For Bratton it meant dealing with small crimes to bring about big change. We think this principle is significant in its own right, so we'll consider it in more detail next.

Change can be a long and difficult path to take, but by thinking differently, it is possible to achieve significant change quickly. A tipping point is a point of in-balance. In seeking to think differently about leadership solutions, it's useful to think more about another principle that operates on a similar premise. This is sometimes referred to as 'the trivial many and the vital few'.

The trivial many and the vital few

Some things can have a far more significant impact than others. When the Sternins discovered that a vital few families had well-nourished children, amongst the many that were malnourished, they were finding the vital few that made a difference. Paying attention to these few families unlocked a solution for everyone. This was a phenomenon recognized by Peter Drucker when he argued that business is a social situation and therefore events tend not to be distributed according to the 'normal distribution.'[38] We often too readily assume that factors have an equal value or impact. More often, a very small number of events, at one extreme, will account for most of the results. According to Drucker, a few things in business matter more than most, and their impact can be profound.

The trivial many and the vital few go by many names. Based on the Pareto Principle, perhaps it's most commonly known as 'the 80/20 rule'. The basic premise is that, for many activities, the great majority of effects are generated from a relatively small number of causes. This idea might not be new but it's surprising how often it is overlooked by managers and leaders.

When routines become embedded, or there are periods of stability, it's all too easy to simply maintain the status quo. 'We do it this way because it's the way we've always done it.' Challenge this mindset by thinking about the trivial many and the vital few. Such an approach may be entirely new to your organization, in which case you will be finding the sense before it becomes common. Or it may stimulate fresh thinking, perhaps encouraging people to review the logic of a status quo that has been allowed to evolve. It may be that current practice is based on sound thinking, but thinking which is now just out of date. In that case, you'll be re-finding the sense, in order to make it common again!

The 80/20 rule

The numbers in the 80/20 rule are not necessarily fixed. It's the principle that's important. In using this approach to different thinking, there are two main points to remember:

1 A very small number of events, generally between 10–20 per cent, account for 80–90 per cent of all results.

2 Conversely, the great majority of events account for less than 10–20 per cent of the results.

The effects of this principle can be observed in several ways within organizations. What if for example:

- 80 per cent of your sales come from 20 per cent of your customers?

- 80 per cent of your complaints come from 20 per cent of your customers?

- 80 per cent of your productivity comes from 20 per cent of the time you spend working?

- 80 per cent of your problems come from 20 per cent of your work?

- 80 per cent of your problems come from 20 per cent of your people?

Even if these figures are only generalizations and the in-balance may vary, it still makes common sense to do something about them. Analysing these examples of the trivial many and the vital few can yield very worthwhile rewards. At the very least, making this sense common sense, can help your organization to make dramatic improvements.

If the typical pattern is for 80 per cent of your results to come from 20 per cent of your inputs, the great majority of your inputs have little, or marginal impact. We can either view this as a significant waste or look at it as a significant opportunity. And that might be the opportunity to do less but achieve more – a very timely thought in times of constrained business resource.

Do less, achieve more

In his book, *The 80/20 Principle*,[39] Richard Koch (2008) expands on the Pareto Principle. One aspect of his book clearly relates to finding the sense before it becomes common. Koch suggests that much of what we do, in life and in our organizations, can be re-purposed – perhaps far more than we realize. If this is indeed the case then there is very significant room for improvement. For example, it could be that, whilst you may feel your department is stretched for staffing, you actually have considerable capacity. Why? Because only 20 per cent of your input delivers 80 per cent of your results. That might seem hard to believe but thinking 80/20 could prompt an objective re-appraisal of your situation. Of course it won't be true in every case but often large improvements can be made by focusing on the important – the significant 'minority'.

80/20 people

There is nothing so useless as doing efficiently that which should not be done at all.

(Peter Drucker)

One of the most challenging aspects of the 80/20 principle arises when applying it with the people you lead or manage. What if the re-appraisal of your staff effectiveness does reveal that 20 per cent of your staff delivers 80 per cent of your results? This begs some fundamental questions. Such as:

- Have you got your staff doing the right things, and critically, are they working to their strengths?
- Are they doing what's necessary and important, or lapsing into Parkinson's Law – letting the tasks fill the time available?
- Are they doing something very well that isn't really worth the effort?
- Do you have your best people doing the most important things?

Be an 80/20 Leader

The 80/20 principle is about focus and simplicity. It prompts us to identify and address the important few things that matter. Here are some simple but effective questions to ask as an 80/20 leader:

- How could more be achieved by doing less?
- How can things be done better but in less time?

- Are there any small changes that would make a big difference to your organization?

- Do you focus on the 20 per cent of time that gives 80 per cent of results?

- Have you identified the things that are done which contribute least to the important parts of the organization? And stopped doing them?

Finding the vital few things that matter can be hard going, but it's just as important not to miss the obvious. Because sometimes that's the best place to look for the sense before it becomes common. Where it's most obvious!

The obvious in plain view

The striking lesson from the story of the Sternins' project was that the answer to their seemingly intractable problem was hidden in plain view. It was obvious. Yet only a very small number of the children and families seemed to have the answer. The obvious, it seems, isn't always that obvious!

Obvious Adams

In 1916 a US newspaper published a series of fictitious stories by Robert R Updegraff entitled, *Obvious Adams – The story of a successful businessman*. These told the story of a young boy named Adams following his career in an advertising agency – from 'periodicals filer' to president of the company. Adams's talent was his ability to discern the obvious solution to any problem. The story may be almost a hundred years old, but the ideas are as powerful now as they were then – arguably more so. Being able to find the obvious solution, especially in today's complex business world, is a skill all leaders should develop. It's especially important where others can't (or won't) see the obvious. Because this is when you are finding the sense before it becomes common. Just like the Sternins, noticing some healthy children in the midst of so much malnourishment. Or Steve Jobs's decision to simplify his product range based on an insight from what now seems an obvious comment from a relative – that Apple's customers were confused by too much choice.

In the *Obvious Adams* story, he was asked a question as he approached the end of his career: 'Why don't more business people do the obvious?' As questions go, this is almost as good as it gets! Though the prose style is dated, the reply makes interesting reading. According to Adams, people: '... look for a royal road through some short cut in the form of a clever scheme or stunt, which they call the obvious thing to do; but calling it doesn't make it so. They don't gather all the facts and then analyze them before deciding what really is the obvious thing.'[40]

The five tests of obviousness

Updegraff's little-known contribution to management literature didn't stop there. He later collated his newspaper series into a book, using the same name as the original articles.[41] Several years later he published a follow-up article entitled 'The Five Tests of Obviousness'.

We have adapted these tests to form a series of simple questions. When proposing or assessing any new idea, ask yourself these 'obvious' questions:

1   *Is it simple?* The obvious is nearly always simple, often hidden in plain view.

2   *Is it common sense?* Does it make sense to those around you?

3   *Is it easy to explain?* Can you put it down on paper and in a few words capture the essence of the idea?

4   *Is it striking?* Does the idea stand out and does it spark a response in people? Is the idea contagious?

5   *Is it timely?* If it's an idea whose time has come, you may need to take action, now. If it's not yet the right time, you'll need to be patient and watchful, so you are ready when its time does come. But however good the idea, if you're too late and its time has passed, you may need to just forget it.

Looking for in-balances (places where significant impact can be achieved), or making sure you don't miss the obvious are both powerful ways to find the sense before it becomes common sense. But these approaches are rooted in the present. Our final suggestion for finding the sense before it becomes common is to think about the future. And for this we return to thinking about vision – 'back to the future', one might say!

Three ways to look at the future

When the Sternins found children who were well-nourished amongst so many that were not, they were finding the seeds of the future solution in what was already present. It was just that nobody had recognized that yet. One of the ways to find the sense before it becomes common is to think about what is currently done well. Of course, the future is inherently unpredictable, which means it is best to try and think about it in different ways. The future that builds from what you currently do is only one way to think about the future. Two other ways of thinking about the future can provide us with some different but useful perspectives.

Renowned management thinker Peter Drucker[42] once said that there are two ways to look at the future: the future that is already happening and the future you want to create. So that gives us three helpful ways to look at the future:

1 The future that builds from what you are currently good at (ie what you have done well).

2 The future that is already happening (ie what is already happening around you).

3 The future you want to create.

To find the sense before it becomes common sense try thinking through each of these different views of the future.

The future that builds from what you are currently good at

Often the source of an idea that will make sense can be found within what you already do well. The strengths of the team or the organization can often be the source of new opportunities. Ask yourself:

● What do you do well now that can sow the seed for future success?

● Which of your past business goals have you successfully met? How? Why? What did you learn from those successes?

● What strengths exist in your current teams which, when stimulated, motivated or energized, can help you see the sense before it becomes common?

● Do you have the capacity and capability to realize the future you now see?

Deciding what you are going to do is important but it's often as useful to decide what you won't be doing. To give time to your 'future' ideas, perhaps some things need to stop. Part of your approach should be to review and perhaps stop some activities. Or try clarifying where you don't want your business to go, regardless of other pressures. Here are some more questions to begin with:

- What are you going to stop doing?

- What no longer fits your needs, or those of your customers, or markets?

- What products, markets, and areas for development will you definitely not be interested in?

The future that is already happening

There is much that we can try to make sense of, based on what we already know about the future. What Drucker calls 'the anticipation of a future that has already happened.' The future that is already happening might mean:[43]

- Population changes, eg changing demographics, attitudes, behaviours.

- Knowledge, what has changed or is changing that will impact on what you do?

- What has happened in other sectors or other countries that may happen here?

- What's happening in sectoral structures that may indicate a significant change?

- What assumptions have we made regarding society, the economy, our customers, knowledge and technology? Are they still valid?

The future you want to create

The third aspect is to imagine the future you want to create. Can you develop an idea that might give direction and shape to the future? In other words, can you make the future happen?

You might begin by thinking about conventional business proposals or market research here but that might not be enough. Don't discount your imagination or intuition when thinking about the future you want to create. Market research may be useful in testing or refining your ideas but in some respects it may not really tell you a lot. As Henry Ford famously once said: 'If I had asked customers what they wanted they would have said "a faster horse".'

And Anita Roddick graphically made the same point: 'Running a company on market research is like driving while looking in the rear view mirror.'

To these two entrepreneurs, spanning the generations, we can once again add the voice of Steve Jobs. You may remember how Apple's former CEO John Sculley recounts Jobs's response to a conversation with Edwin Land:

> *He said if I asked someone who had only used a personal calculator what a Macintosh should be like they couldn't have told me. There was no way to do consumer research on it so I had to go and create it and then show it to people and say 'now what do you think?'[44]*

Why? Because it's unlikely that people will realize they need or want a product or service, when it doesn't yet exist. Just as it might not be possible for others to see the future you want to create. So, create the future! Think about what you'd really like to be doing. Or in the words of another challenging Peter Drucker quote: 'What in our economy, our society, or our state of knowledge would give our business its greatest opportunity, if only we could make it happen?'[45]

Discussing how to find the sense before it becomes common leads us to a central point of our next chapter. How do you then *make* the sense you have found common sense? To help answer that question we will use an obvious combination: umbrellas, spaceships and bowling. Well, ok, perhaps it's not that obvious – yet!

Bibliography

1 Sternin, J (2010) [accessed 19 April 2013] Positive Deviance Case Studies (malnutrition, narrated by Jerry Sternin) (case study), *Positive Deviance Org* [Online] http://www.positivedeviance.org/about_pd/case_studies.html

2 Zeitlin, M, Ghassemi, H and Mansour, M (1990) Positive deviance in child nutrition: with emphasis on psychosocial and behavioural aspects and implications for development, *Food and Nutrition Bulletin*, Supplement 14

3 Pascale, R, Sternin, J and Sternin, M (2010) *The Power of Positive Deviance,* Boston, Harvard Business School Publishing

4   Pachon, H, Schroeder, D G, Marsh, D R, Dearden, K, Ha, T and Lang, T (2002) Effect of an integrated child nutrition intervention on the complementary food intake of young children in rural North Viet Nam, *Food Nutrition Bulletin*, **23** (4), pp 59–66

5   Mackintosh U A T, Marsh D R and Schroeder D G (2002) Sustained positive deviant child care practices and their effects on child growth in Viet Nam, *Food Nutrition Bulletin*, **3** (4), 16–25

6   Rumelt, R (2011) *Good Strategy Bad Strategy: The difference and why it matters,* New York, Random House

7   Isaacson, W (2012) [accessed 19 April 2013] The real leadership lessons of Steve Jobs, *HBR The Magazine* [Online] http://hbr.org/2012/04/the-real-leadership-lessons-of-steve-jobs/ar/2

8   Rumelt, R (2011) *Good Strategy Bad Strategy: The difference and why it matters,* New York, Random House

9   Fisher, L M (2003) [accessed on 28 March 2013] The paradox of Charles Handy, *Strategy+Business* [Online] http://www.strategy-business.com/article/03309?gko=f3861

10   Rosenzweig, P (2007) *The Halo Effect... and the Eight Other Business Delusions that Deceive Managers,* New York, Simon & Schuster

11   Weick, K (1996) Prepare your organization to fight fires, *Harvard Business Review*, May–June, pp 143–48

12   Rouleau, L (2005) Micro-practices of strategic sensemaking and sensegiving: how middle managers interpret and sell change every day, *Journal of Management Studies*, **42** (7), pp 1413–1441

13   Gioia, D and Chittipeddi, K (1991) Sensemaking and sensegiving in strategic change initiation, *Strategic Management Journal*, **12** (6), pp 433–446

14   Snook, S A, Nohria, N N and Khurana, R (2012) *The Handbook for Teaching Leadership: Knowing, doing, and being,* London, Sage Publications

15   Maclean, N (1992) *Young Men and Fire,* Chicago, University of Chicago Press

16   Weick, K (1996) Prepare your organization to fight fires, *Harvard Business Review*, May–June, pp 143–48

17   ibid

18   ibid

19   Buss Mitchell, H (2011) *Roots of Wisdom: A tapestry of philosophical traditions,* Boston, Wadsworth Cengage

20   Cooperrider, D L and Srivastva, S (1998) An invitation to organizational wisdom and executive courage, in (eds) S Srivastva and D L Cooperrider *Organizational Wisdom and Executive Courage*, San Francisco, New Lexington Press

21 Weick, K (1996) Prepare your organization to fight fires, *Harvard Business Review*, May–June, p148

22 Conger, J, cited in Gill, R (2011) *Theory and Practice of Leadership*, 2nd *edn*, London, Sage Publications, p 279

23 Kouzes, J M and Posner, B Z (2009) [accessed 19 April 2013] To lead, create a shared vision, *HBR blog* [Online] http://hbr.org/2009/01/to-lead-create-a-shared-vision/ar/1

24 Revans, R (1998) *ABC of Action Learning*, London, Lemon and Crane

25 Nahapiet, J and Ghoshal, S (1998) Social Capital, intellectual capital, and the organizational advantage, *Academy of Management Review*, 23, pp 242–66, in *How does leadership make a difference to organisational culture and effectiveness?* (2007) Northern Leadership Academy

26 Putnam, R (2000) *Bowling Alone: The collapse and revival of American community*, New York, Simon and Schuster

27 Senge, P (1990) *The Fifth Discipline: The art and practice of the learning organization*, London, Doubleday

28 Basadur, M (2001) *The Power of Innovation: How to make innovation a way of life and put creative solutions to work*, Toronto, Applied Creativity Press

29 Kahney, L (2010) [accessed 19 April 2013] John Sculley on Steve Jobs: the full interview transcript, *Cultofmac* [Online] http://www.cultofmac.com/63295/john-sculley-on-steve-jobs-the-full-interview-transcript/63295/

30 Linderman, M (2010) [accessed 19 April 2013] The story of Polaroid inventor Edwin Land, one of Steve Job's biggest heroes, *37signals* [Online] http://37signals.com/svn/posts/2666-the-story-of-polaroid-inventor-edwin-land-one-of-steve-jobs-biggest-heroes

31 Dodd, D and Favaro, K (2007) *The Three Tensions: Winning the struggle to perform without compromise*, San Francisco, Jossey-Bass

32 Kim, C and Mauborgne, R (2003) Tipping point leadership, *Harvard Business Review* March–April, pp 60–69

33 Kelling, G and Wilson, J (1982) [accessed 19 April 2013] Broken windows, *Atlantic Monthly* [Online] http://www.theatlantic.com/magazine/archive/1982/03/broken-windows/304465/2/

34 Kim, C and Mauborgne, R (2003) Tipping point leadership, *Harvard Business Review* March–April, pp 60–69

35 Nagy, A R and Podolny, J (2008) [accessed 19 April 2013] Yale School of Management case: William Bratton and the NYPD, *Yale School of Management* [Online] http://som.yale.edu/sites/default/files/files/Case_Bratton_2nd_ed_Final_and_Complete.pdf

36 Nagy, A R and Podolny, J (2008) [accessed 19 April 2013] Yale School of Management case: William Bratton and the NYPD, *Yale School of*

Management [Online] http://som.yale.edu/sites/default/files/files/Case_ Bratton_2nd_ed_Final_and_Complete.pdf

37 Gladwell, M (2000) *The Tipping Point: How little things can make a big difference,* London, Abacus

38 Drucker, P (1963) Managing for business effectiveness, in (ed) N Stone, *On the Profession of Management Drucker, P*, collection of articles published in the *Harvard Business Review,* (1998) Boston, Harvard Business School Publishing

39 Koch, R (2008) *The 80/20 Principle: The secret of achieving more with less,* New York, Doubleday

40 Archive organisation (no date) [accessed 19 April 2013] Obvious Adams: the story of a successful businessman, *Archive org* [Online] http://archive.org/ stream/obviousadamsstor00upderich/obviousadamsstor00upderich_djvu.txt

41 Updegraff, R R (2007) *Obvious Adams: The story of a successful businessman,* Minneapolis, Filiquarian Publishing, LLC

42 Drucker, P (1973) *Managing for Results,* London, Pan Books

43 ibid

44 Kahney, L (2010) [accessed 19 April 2013] John Sculley on Steve Jobs: the full interview transcript, *Cultofmac* [Online] http://www.cultofmac.com/63295/ john-sculley-on-steve-jobs-the-full-interview-transcript/63295/

45 Drucker, P (1964) The big power of little ideas, in (ed) N Stone, *On the Profession of Management Drucker, P*, collection of articles published in the *Harvard Business Review,* (1998) Boston, Harvard Business School Publishing

02

LEADING WITH ACTION

SHAPING THE ORGANIZATION BY TURNING SENSE INTO COMMON SENSE

KEY TOPICS

- Umbrellas and the secret to success.
- From sense-making to sense-giving.
- Bricolage – resourceful leadership.
- Culture eats strategy for breakfast.
- Shaping strategy.
- Getting into shape.

FIGURE 2.1 Shaping

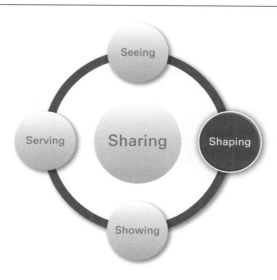

So how do leaders make the sense they have found common sense? We'll find out in this chapter by exploring the leader's role in shaping the way forward, and in doing so taking the sense-making we've just discussed one step further. Because leaders who shape the way forward do so by finding new ways to make sense of business. Then, they take the sense they've found, and turn it into common sense within their organizations.

It's often said that the trouble with common sense is that it's not that common. If this is true, then applying common sense in your organization could give you an advantage amongst so many others that don't. As the English poet Samuel Taylor Coleridge once reflected: 'Common sense in an uncommon degree is what the world calls wisdom.'

Interesting though that may be, does something as straightforward as common sense really belong in a discussion on leadership? Well one influential business leader certainly thought so.

Umbrellas and the secret to success

The business leader in question is Konosuke Matsushita (pronounced 'Matsoshta'). If you haven't heard of Matsushita before, then you're in good company. In 1990, renowned academic John Kotter was offered a prestigious Harvard professorial chair. But on being offered the position of 'Konosuke Matsushita Professor of Leadership', Kotter confessed that he'd never even heard of the influential Japanese businessman. Ironically, given that inauspicious start, if you *have* heard of Matsushita it may be through the award-winning book John Kotter later wrote about him.

Konosuke Matsushita was born in 1894, in a small farming community in western Japan. He started his working life with little money, few connections, a poor education, traumatic family issues and a constant battle with ill health. Yet by the time he died in April 1989, the company he founded, Matsushita Electric Industrial Co Ltd, had become a multi-national giant in the field of electrical appliances, with nearly 20,000 employees. You may not have heard of Matsushita but you'll almost certainly have heard of his business brands. Matsushita grew such household names as National, Panasonic and Technics. So what lies behind such phenomenal success, borne from such difficult beginnings?

Matsushita recounts a meeting with a young reporter who'd asked him a common but loaded question. What was the secret of his success? It was a question Matsushita had often been asked, but for which he never felt he had a satisfactory answer. On this occasion he said, he'd thought of a clever answer. He asked the reporter:

'What would you do if you were caught in a rainstorm?'

The reporter thought about the question and then replied:

'I would take out an umbrella.'

That, said Matsushita, was his answer to the reporter's question. The latter was rather bemused at such a glib reply, until Matsushita went on to explain: 'A natural response to a natural phenomenon – that is the secret of success in business and management. You will always win if you rely on common sense. This advice, I believe, also applies to the management of your own life. I can assure you however, it is not always easy to put into practice.'[1]

Uncommon common sense

Of course, what Matsushita thought of as common sense may not really have been as common as he made out. In his book, John Kotter (1997) described him as 'an uncommon leader in a time of great change in Japan.' His assessment of Matsushita is enlightening:

 By many standards, he didn't look like a great leader… Unlike most well-known western politicians, he didn't excel at public speaking… He rarely displayed speed-of-light intellectual skills or warmed an audience with hilarious anecdotes. Nevertheless, he did what all great leaders do – motivate large groups of individuals to improve the human condition.[2]

Right from starting his first business, Matsushita emphasized some common sense that at the time, wasn't very common – the importance of people. 'Matsushita Electric,' he told his staff, 'makes people before it makes appliances.' In doing so, Matsushita adopted a people-first philosophy long before such views became popular. His ground-breaking approach was backed up by practice, even during times of severe austerity. When his company struggled through post-war periods, he maintained his commitment to provide complete job security for his employees. During the worst crisis faced by the organization, the Great Depression of the late 1920s, not one single employee was made redundant. Perhaps just as impressively, the company halved production and working hours, but still managed to maintain the same wage levels. This was an approach to business crisis that would be considered enlightened even by today's standards!

It's also interesting that Matsushita's approach to business crisis wasn't a demand for longer hours in the office, or on the shop-floor. His views on the long-hour culture, now so common in many western workplaces, were typically forthright and straightforward, yet at the same time radical. For years he argued against long hours in the workplace, making the distinction between time and activity, and productivity. He argued that the critical issue is making *effective* use of the time spent at work: 'It is not how many hours you put in but how efficiently you get your work done that really matters.'

Without doubt, Matsushita was inventing business practices that were far ahead of his time. Some of his ideas, introduced in the 1930s, would later be advocated by Elton Mayo or Abraham Maslow. And according to Kotter, some of the ideas made famous by Tom Peters and Bob Waterman's *In Search of Excellence*, had actually been put into action by Matsushita decades before.[3]

What seemed common sense to Matsushita was only so because of the principles by which he lived. Fundamentally, he saw business as being concerned with enriching the whole of society. In 1932, using remarkably enlightened words, he explained to his employees that the mission of a manufacturer was 'to overcome poverty, to relieve society as a whole from the misery of poverty and bring it wealth'.[4]

Reflecting on his vast experience as a manager Matsushita, alluded to another key, underpinning principle of uncommon leadership: 'I am convinced that people really appreciate it when their merits are recognised… No one is perfect, but each person is good for something. If you are going to use personnel, why not utilize their talents instead of complaining about their faults.'[5]

This was an early approach to what is now sometimes called 'strengths-based management'. There is undoubted value in giving people work which uses their strengths. And on reflection, this may seem as obvious as putting up an umbrella when it rains. This common-sense approach to management was also obvious to Peter Drucker: 'It takes far less energy to move from first-rate performance to excellence than it does to move from incompetence to mediocrity.'[6]

But though such an approach might seem obvious, making common sense into common practice is not always so easy to do.

Common sense is not always common practice

Building a business on common sense may not seem very exciting but Stanford University professor Bob Sutton argues that if a business idea seems obvious, it's probably a good sign. Conversely, if an idea or a business model is complicated and difficult to understand, it's likely that most of us will struggle to implement or apply it. 'The most effective companies are masters of the mundane.'[7]

Common sense is not always common practice because it's one thing to see the sense, but quite another to do something with it. Seeing sense only begins to make sense when others can see it too. For that to happen, leaders need to move beyond sense-making towards *sense-giving*. They need to make the sense *they* have made of the situation into common sense for their organization. Why? Because there is little point in finding the right path if nobody is following. So the rest of this chapter is devoted to how leaders can make common sense more common in their organizations. It starts with that move from sense-making to sense-giving. This takes us first to the art and craft of persuasion, asking whether we can change behaviours without necessarily changing minds?

Shaping messages to influence others is a start but leaders also need to shape the organization, so that they can make the new sense a new reality. But how? To find out we turn to Jim Lovell's famously misquoted words when commanding the stricken Apollo 13 space flight: 'Houston we have a problem'. How does an aborted Moon-landing attempt provide insights into the way leaders might begin to shape their organizations? By shedding light on a generally overlooked leadership skill: bricolage. How can leaders craft and shape new ways forward with what they have, rather than with what they can only wish for? Perhaps by demonstrating bricolage leadership. This idea also prompts a warning against what leaders perhaps wished they *hadn't* done. For example it challenges the all too frequent tendency to make resource cuts a first course of action, especially when budgets are under pressure. Understandable though this may be, bricolage leadership helps us think about alternative ways forward – less predictable but possibly more effective. Alongside a skilful, considered redeployment of resources, leaders also shape an organization by developing its culture. We'll see how two very different organizations made culture central to their strategies. Then we'll discover why some argue that, whilst strategy should be flexible and responsive, it isn't necessarily the first thing a leader should think about. Shaping the organization is a demanding task, so we've put together some 'workouts' for you to use. These include tips and insights to help leaders think through how they can shape their organizations. First though, let's consider the magic of persuasion.

From sense-making to sense-giving

The first 'S' of uncommon leadership, *Seeing*, was about sense-making. The second, *Shaping*, is about how leaders persuade, influence and give sense to the team they lead. Sense-giving is the next logical step to sense-making. 'Sense-giving is concerned with their (the leader's) attempts to influence the outcome, to communicate their thoughts about the change to others, and to gain their support.'[8]

A key part of sense-giving is to communicate in a way that persuades. Persuasion can be defined as the act or process of convincing someone to do or believe something. But how do you set about persuading someone? This is by no means a new question – the art and importance of persuasion has been a source of debate for a very long time. Indeed, the ancient Greek philosopher Aristotle spent some considerable time developing what, even to this day, are still held as the core principles of effective persuasion. We'll explore these via an unusual stunt in a Washington subway.

Aristotle and Joshua Bell: lessons on subways, concert halls and the secrets of persuasion

What is this life if, full of care,
We have no time to stand and stare.
(from 'Leisure,' by W H Davies)

One January day in 2007, a young-looking man was busking during rush-hour in a Washington Metro subway station. With his violin case open to catch notes and coins from passers-by, the musician began to play his instrument. Plainly dressed in jeans, T-shirt and baseball cap, this was no ordinary busker. Joshua Bell was at the top of his game. He was one of the best classical musicians in the world. Only three days before, Bell had played to a full house and a rapturous audience at Boston's opera house, where average seat prices were $100 each. But on that January day, Bell was playing for anybody who passed by – for free. Why?

The idea came from *Washington Post* columnist Gene Weingarten. In 2008 he won a Pulitzer Prize for feature writing with his article based on the stunt. World-renowned violinist Joshua Bell agreed to participate in this unusual '... experiment in context, perception and priorities – as well as an unblinking assessment of public taste: in a banal setting at an inconvenient time, would beauty transcend?'

So what do you think happened? What was the reaction to a famous, classical violinist, with film-star good looks, playing some of the most moving and inspiring classical music ever written? How many busy subway commuters stopped to listen to his free performance, on a violin handcrafted by Antonio Stradivari in 1713? Surely a crowd formed quickly, full of people mesmeriszed by the wonderful music, mentally justifying their late arrival for work because of this unexpected treat? And of course, Bell must have ended the day with a violin case brimming with coins and notes. After all, his talents regularly filled concert halls all over the world. Indeed, the very next week Bell was to receive the Avery Fisher prize for being the best classical musician in the United States.

Well we know the answers to some of these questions because the *Washington Post* recorded the performance, and the reaction from passers-by.[9] So how many people stopped to listen, and how much money did Bell earn during the 43-minute spell? Here's how Gene Weingarten described it:

> In the three-quarters of an hour that Joshua Bell played, seven people stopped what they were doing to hang around and take in the performance, at least for a minute. Twenty-seven gave money, most of them on the run – for a total of $32 and change. That leaves the 1,070 people who hurried by, oblivious, many only three feet away, few even turning to look.[10]

This was an interesting experiment. A world-class virtuoso performed in two venues, demonstrating the same skill on the same violin. Yet while one performance held a packed audience in raptures, the other was virtually ignored. Why? And how does any of this relate to a book on leadership? The answer to the first question comes from an imaginative TEDEd[11] animation by entrepreneur and educator Conor Neill. The answer to the second question is that it helps us learn about persuasion, one of the most important of all leadership skills. In making his case, Neill drew on the work of the ancient Greek philosopher, Aristotle. So, before we explore what we can learn about persuasion from the *Washington Post* stunt, we'll take a look at Aristotle's version of persuasion.

Ethos, logos and pathos

Aristotle separated the means of persuading someone into three kinds of 'appeal':

1 An appeal to 'ethos' – the credibility of the person making the persuasive argument. How convinced are you by the person? How convincing are you to others?

2 An appeal to 'logos' – the use of logic to support a claim. Do the facts stack up?

3 An appeal to 'pathos' – the emotional or motivational appeal. Does the argument appeal to the emotions? Language choice can affect people's emotional response.

So why weren't passers-by in the Metro subway persuaded to stop and listen? For Conor Neill it boils down to the fact that two of Aristotle's appeals were missing. When an audience gathers in a concert hall, the very environment convinces them that the performance they anticipate will be credible. In contrast, people moving through a subway will have no expectation that they'll be hearing any great, musical performances. Ethos is missing.

Secondly, there is the issue of focus. At a concert hall, all attention is towards the artist. This can create an emotional bond as a communal appreciation is generated. But in a subway, as people rush by going about their business, there is little likelihood that any such bond can be created. In such situations there is little or no emotional connection. Pathos is missing. So while the music (that is the message or logos) might be the same, if ethos and pathos are absent then logos alone is unlikely to be persuasive.

Whilst all three of Aristotle's appeals are crucial in trying to persuade, one is potentially more influential than the others. For Aristotle, ethos mattered most. According to him, the speaker's 'character [ethos] is the most potent of all the means of persuasion'[12]

In order to persuade, we need to ensure that the message supports and builds our credibility. From the very start of any attempt to persuade, how do we connect with what our listeners find credible? As Aristotle implied, we are far more likely to believe someone whom we think is credible, whom we like and respect, even if their argument is weak. However, there may be an appeal that has a more significant effect on us, especially from a leader's perspective.

Two ways of thinking

It might be possible to manage or lead by getting staff to passively accept our ideas or wishes. Such an approach might encourage action and even some degree of progress or results. But, much like the three stonecutters we met in Chapter 1, it's far more beneficial to all concerned if we can foster deeper connections between organizations, people, and the work they are performing. In trying to communicate and instil the sense of such deeper engagement, it's tempting to use logical argument. But this assumes that people act, think or make decisions in a logical way. However there is very strong evidence to suggest that this is not the case.

Most people like to think they behave in a rational, self-interested way. This is perhaps understandable considering we've built numerous theories and models around the idea of humans as rational thinkers and decision-makers. Richard Thaler and Cass Sunstein call this: '...the notion that each of us thinks and chooses unfailingly well, and thus fits the textbook picture of human beings offered by economists.'[13]

Not surprisingly, this isn't the only way to explain how people behave. In fact, some would argue that thinking, choosing and acting in such a rational way is not even that common. For example, Thaler and Sunstein offer a powerfully contrasting viewpoint in their thought-provoking book, *Nudge – improving decisions about health, wealth and happiness*. They argue that there's much evidence to suggest 'serious questions about the rationality of many judgements and decisions that people make.'[14] So what if the more commonplace assumptions made about how people tick really are inaccurate? Are we less rational than we think, and perhaps more strongly influenced by subtle influences than we realize?

To answer these questions we need to think about the two distinct ways in which the brain operates. Firstly, there is the rational, deliberative way of thinking, where decisions are made in an orderly, step-by-step manner. Many people would recognize this process as it fits with that notion of humans as rational thinkers and decision-makers, which we've already mentioned. However, this isn't the only way the brain works. And, according to Nobel prize-winner and academic, Daniel Kahneman, neither is it the typical way. 'Most impressions and thoughts arise in your conscious experience without you knowing how they got there.'[15]

This means that we're far from being the logical, ordered thinkers many of us believe ourselves to be. In fact, our decisions come from a more automatic way of thinking, one that operates with far more subtlety and influence than we realize. Whilst we like to think that the rational brain dominates our thinking and decisions, it's really the *automatic system* that runs the show. Far from logic and rational thinking, this system is influenced by a complex range of feelings, emotions, memories and other subconscious stimuli.

So what does this mean for leaders? It means an emotive and motivational appeal to 'pathos' is likely to have far more impact than a logical argument. And when allied to 'ethos', where the person making the appeal has high credibility, we find the most effective combination of all. We'll return to these powerful ideas and uncommon insights in Chapter 5, where we look at ways to make you a more effective leader by making the most of the behavioural science ideas behind 'nudge'.

Do you need to be eloquent to be persuasive?

We often associate persuasion with people who are eloquent and practised orators. No doubt such skills would be useful but is it possible to be persuasive without being eloquent? Returning to the example of Konosuke Matsushita, earlier we found out that he was not known for his oratory skills. However, when reflecting on why others seemed to think of him as being persuasive, Matsushita attributed his ability to persuade to two things. The first was a simple truth: 'you have to believe in the idea you want to sell.' The second was the Japanese principle of 'honne', which means conveying true feelings and honest views.

Matsushita is a good example of how Aristotle's three appeals combine to help create a persuasive message, even without any natural eloquence in the speaker. The Japanese businessman clearly had credibility, and was therefore convincing (ethos). He connected with his audience through 'true feelings' (pathos), and his obvious belief in the ideas he held seemed contagious. He also conveyed honesty so, in the minds of his audience, the messages he purveyed clearly made sense (logos). Yet again, Matsushita is the source of a thought-provoking insight. Leaders don't necessarily need eloquence to be persuasive. It's far better to build your argument from logos, ethos and pathos.

Argue as if you're right, listen as if you're wrong

Sense-giving is an act of persuasion, but like any form of communication, it is also a two-way process. Effective sense-giving means having two-way conversations. Perhaps one key to unlocking communication is to adopt a skill advocated by Stanford professors, Bob Sutton and Jeffrey Pfeffer:[16] Argue as if you're right and listen as if you're wrong.

In Sutton's own words, this means 'the best leaders have the courage to act on what they know right now, and the humility to change their actions when they encounter new evidence. They advocate an 'attitude of wisdom'.[17] Sutton quotes former Intel CEO, Andy Grove as an elaboration of this point: 'I think it is very important for you to do two things: act on your temporary conviction as if it was a real conviction, and when you realize that you are wrong, correct course very quickly.'

So how do you go about arguing as if you're right, but listening as if you're wrong? It's done by balancing advocacy with inquiry.

Sense-giving a two-way conversation

Advocacy

Advocacy is about making your point. It means taking a position in an attempt to influence others, supporting your viewpoint by explaining how you came to hold it. But advocacy isn't just about getting your point across, although this is clearly important. It's also about making your thinking process more visible, whilst remaining open to alternative views. In expressing *how* you arrived at your view, it's useful to begin with any assumptions. Include information or data on which they are based, and the context in which they are set.

Effective advocacy will then include a detailed discussion of your view, including proposals, aims and desired outcomes. It's not unnatural to attempt to be persuasive whilst doing this, after all, we're advocating our view: what we see or want. However even at this point, the most effective leaders will be attuned to their audience as much as to their own advocacy. Stay aware of the impact you're creating in advocating your views. E M Forster's 'how do I know what I think until I see what I say?' may have referred to the written word, but it can just as easily relate to seeing the impact of a statement or argument on an audience. When you hear yourself talk, you see more clearly what matters and what you had hoped to say.

Such an approach is also a valuable mechanism for clarifying your own views. It can be useful to encourage comment and discussion about your underpinning assumptions and your own thought processes. Listening to comments and other views can help to confirm or refine your own position.

Listening is also the precursor to inquiry. As Lee Iacocca, the former CEO of Chrysler Corporation is reputed to have said: 'I only wish I could find an institute that teaches people how to listen. Business people need to listen at least as much as they need to talk. Too many people fail to realize that real communication goes in both directions.'[18]

Inquiry

The most obvious meaning of inquiry is to deliberately seek (or allow) views from others. But to be most effective, it also means asking them to make their thinking process visible. Used properly, inquiry allows people to explore one another's reasoning. Then it helps them to understand the conclusions they have reached.

Inquiry means asking questions such as: 'How does it sound to you?' and 'What makes sense to you and what doesn't?' Then exploring the answers more deeply with follow-up questions to find out why they might think or feel a particular way. It will help both in sense-making and in helping you to effectively implement your own plan of action. We've already explored the importance of 'ethos' in helping you to achieve your leadership aims. But in order to help you become respected, valued and trusted, you need to be understood. And if you want to be better understood, you need first to understand others better. In the words of Danish philosopher and theologian, Soren Kierkegard: 'In order to help another effectively, I must understand what he understands. If I do not know that, my greater understanding will be of no help to him… instruction begins when you put yourself in his place so that you may understand what he understands and in the way he understands it.'[19]

As with advocacy, inquiry means understanding 'what lies beneath.' It's important to discover the underlying assumptions, information, data and contexts on which others are basing their views. Inquiry thus involves exploring and testing their reasoning, in order to add new insights or understanding to your own position.

The importance of sense-giving conversations is that they start to shape the organization, so this is where we'll turn our attention now. Essentially, shaping is about creating the conditions for an organization and its people to grow. Specifically, this is done by shaping:

- the context;
- the culture;
- the strategy.

So in the next section we'll think about how to first shape the organization's context and culture. This will then enable us to create the right conditions for the organization and its people to grow, so that the seeds of a strategy can be sown.

Shaping context

Context is the environment, setting and situation of the business. As much as they can, leaders need to shape the environment in which their teams or organizations work. Although shaping is not just about making changes to the physical environment, Winston Churchill's words still resonate when applied to organizational leadership: 'We shape our buildings and then they shape us.'

There are any number of studies to support the impact a physical environment can have on well-being and efficiency at work. We can't help but be shaped by the environments in which we operate. But good leadership is about shaping that environment in as broad a sense as possible. To lead the way to greater effectiveness and growth, shaping the context involves:

- making good sense common sense;
- bringing people, resources, and knowledge together;
- creating the conditions to achieve the vision – structures, systems, processes, buildings, equipment;
- making the elements of culture visible – symbols, signs, routines, material;
- developing and encouraging resilience;
- combining planned (predictable) with emergent (unpredictable) change;
- seeing patterns and reconciling change with continuity;
- crafting change.

Shaping an organization on such a broad scale is no easy task, even when resources are plentiful. One of the most powerful ways leaders can shape context and the organization is by the use of the resources that are available to them. Frequently, however, leaders are expected to shape things when there are no new resources. Or worse still, when they are faced with serious resource constraints. In such circumstances, it's all too easy to resort to a form of shaping that involves cutbacks. But this needn't be the only or the default option, however tempting that might be. How can you refrain from jumping to predictable (though understandable) resource cuts, when budgets are under pressure? Even in the face of fierce pressure on resources, the answer might come from a closer examination of the last point in the list above – crafting change.

Shaping by bricolage

The idea of crafting brings sense-making and sense-giving together, to help create tangible outcomes. Crafting suggests the role of an artisan, skilfully combining any necessary materials to create something worthwhile, valuable or meaningful. But crafting can also suggest the ability to make the most of whatever is to hand, creatively using existing resources. One might argue that there is more skill in creating something practical from scarce resources, than there is in creating sublime works of art from an abundant supply of materials.

One interesting way to think about this view of crafting is the idea of bricolage. *Bricolage* is the French word meaning: 'to make creative and resourceful use of whatever materials are at hand (regardless of their original purpose).' It's an especially important idea for any manager or leader trying to shape success in times of constrained resources. Successful bricolage requires:

- intimate knowledge of resources;
- careful observation and listening;
- trusting one's ideas;
- confidence that any structures can be self-correcting.[20]

If bricolage means each of these things, how do we bring them all together to make something happen from the resources and capabilities we have to hand? The answer is by developing bricolage leadership.

Bricolage leadership

Life is not a matter of having good cards, but of playing a poor hand well.
(Robert Louis Stevenson)

Tough choices are often a part of organizational life. For example, how do you cope with severe constraints on budgets and resources? Especially if you're given less than you had before, but need to achieve the same – or more. Tough choices indeed. Yet tough choices aren't all negative, whatever the connotations. They should also lead us to think more creatively and resourcefully about our options. This type of thinking is what we call 'bricolage leadership'.

Bricolage leadership means taking the lead in times of crisis or constraint by crafting something out of what is available. It can be applied in several ways. For example:

- finding different uses for scarce resources;
- releasing trapped resources;
- re-purposing resources which are being used ineffectively.

Think for a moment about how bricolage leadership can help you challenge underlying assumptions and craft solutions creatively, but within your resource constraints. This kind of leadership is nowhere better illustrated than in a well-known film.

One of modern cinema's iconic screen moments comes from the film *Apollo 13*, starring Tom Hanks. Portraying flight commander Jim Lovell, Hanks delivered that famous, misquoted sentence of classic understatement: 'Houston we have a problem...'

'Houston we have a problem...'

Many management courses have illustrated problem-solving techniques by using some of the scenes that follow Hanks's line. Back at mission control in Houston, the support team had to solve Apollo 13's problem. Without warning, an explosion in the command module blew a hole in the side of the vessel, causing vital oxygen to leak into space. This meant the mission had to be aborted but in reality there was an even bigger problem still. Instead of landing on the Moon, the crippling loss of oxygen meant focusing on a new, much more critical mission – to bring the three-man crew safely back to Earth.

With guidance from mission control, the crew of Apollo 13 worked frantically to save their lives. They moved everything they would need for survival from the damaged command module into the relative safety of the lunar landing module. No longer needed for its original purpose, this became their 'lifeboat' for the long, tense journey home. But just when they thought they were safely on their way, both crew and mission control became aware of another deadly development.

The lunar landing module had been designed to detach from the command module, once this had settled into an orbit around the Moon. Its original purpose was to transport just two of the crew to the surface of the Moon. To do this, the lunar landing module was designed and equipped to keep two men alive, for two days. But the problem facing the crew was that the 'lifeboat' would now need to support the lives of all three crew-members, over the next four days. Having secured and conserved their oxygen supply, the crew soon realized they faced another, completely unexpected problem. The real danger wasn't shortage of oxygen, it was an unexpected excess of carbon dioxide.

The cause soon became apparent. The CO_2 filters in the lunar module had been designed to filter the breathing of two men, not three. With every breath, CO_2 levels in the lunar module were rising to dangerous levels. The frantic work to stabilize the stricken space-ship, and to re-focus the mission, would all be wasted if this problem couldn't be solved. Without proper CO_2 filtration, the crew of Apollo 13 would all be dead long before they returned to Earth.

There were plenty of additional filters in the (now shut-down) command module but the ground support team soon realized this was no easy solution. The problem was even worse than it seemed. The command module filters were square-shaped. But those in the lunar module, having been designed and built by a different supplier, were round. In the film, members of the support team were assembled in a room and presented with the problem by a team leader: 'You have 24 hours to find a way to get this (the square-shaped, command module filter), to fit into the hole for this (the round-shaped, landing module filter), using only that.'

At this stage he points towards an assortment of items emptied onto a table – among them plastic moon rock bags, cardboard, suit hoses, and duct tape. They had to tell the astronauts how to make a square peg fit into a round hole, by using only what they had with them in space. Quickly! The challenge was to solve a problem by:

- Using only what was available to them – they could not have any new or extra resource.
- Thinking differently – about how the resources they had could be used for alternate purposes.
- Piecing together what might work.
- Addressing a compelling need to make it happen.
- Communicating the solution effectively.

The rest, as they say, was history!

Based on a true story, this is not just an example of problem-solving, it's an example of bricolage leadership. The metaphor of bricolage has its roots in the work of French anthropologist Claude Levi Strauss, during the 1960s. He suggested that the bricoleur 'acquires and assembles tools and materials as he or she goes, keeping them until they might be useful.'

UK academics Gerry Stoker and Alice Moseley argued that bricolage was about 'making sense of things as they go along and finding out what is useful as the need to bring something into use comes into focus.'[21]

Finding creative ways to use available resources is one way to shape the organization. Developing a culture where such creativity and resourcefulness is the norm is another. Our next theme will help you with that most complex but critical of topics – culture.

Culture eats strategy for breakfast

There is a well-known saying, often attributed to Peter Drucker, that: 'Culture eats strategy for breakfast.'

If this statement is true then we shouldn't underestimate the importance of having a culture that *enables* vision and strategy. By all accounts, there is one online shoe retailer which 'eats, sleeps and drinks' culture – Zappos. This successful US company started out with a primary business aim of delivering 'WOW'. We'll have a more detailed look at the Zappos success story in the next chapter but for the time being it's worth focusing on what makes them stand out – their culture. Here's how they describe themselves on their website: 'We've been asked by a lot of people how we've grown so quickly, and the answer is actually really simple... We've aligned the entire organization around one mission: to provide the best customer service possible. Internally, we call this our WOW philosophy.'[22]

Interestingly, Zappos has now changed its emphasis to the importance of 'delivering happiness'. Perhaps even more interesting is the fact that they've been very successful at doing this whilst, at the same time, delivering some pretty good profits too. Professor John Kotter, whom we talked about earlier in this chapter, refers to Zappos in a thought-provoking article for *Forbes* magazine. Here is Kotter's take on the Zappos approach to building a strong culture: 'Zappos believes that their fun traditions, their mission, and their attitude towards customers create a culture that is a key driver of their growth. It could be true.'[23]

This is by no means an anecdotal assessment. Kotter connects the Zappos focus on culture to his own extensive study of culture and performance. Back in 1992, Kotter and Harvard colleague Professor John Heskett demonstrated some startling findings about how culture impacts on performance. In their book, *Corporate Culture and Performance*, Kotter and Heskett argued that 'strong corporate cultures that facilitate adaptation to a changing world are associated with strong financial results.'[24]

But they also found something else about cultures that delivered performance. Typically, these tended to 'highly value employees, customers, and owners and... encouraged... leadership from everyone in the firm.' This approach empowers employees to adapt their practices to meet customer needs, with notable success.

At Zappos you'll hear plenty of talk about what they do and how they do it. But you'll also find plenty of evidence to demonstrate that the company doesn't just 'talk the talk, it walks the walk'. This is a topic we'll return to in the next chapter. One way Zappos keep its focus on a performance culture is by producing an annual culture book. Here's how they describe the need for the book and the purpose it serves:

> *As we started to grow, we asked ourselves, how we can sustain this culture? How can we remember it while simultaneously inspiring ourselves for the next year? Our answer was the culture book. It's packed with each employee's idea about our culture, as well as photos, our core values and more.*[25]

It might surprise you to know that Zappos don't keep this competitive advantage a secret. In fact they do the reverse. The Zappos organizational culture is not just for internal consumption. Not only does the company make its culture visible to employees, it also welcomes outsiders to come and see how they work. Zappos has won accolades for being a great place to work and they readily make their culture book available for any business to request, expressing the hope '... that it will inspire you to create a workplace where everyone loves to be.' For Zappos, shaping their culture is core to delivering their strategy.

Shaping culture

We introduced an earlier section with a quote from Winston Churchill: 'We shape our buildings and then they shape us'. This was intended to focus attention on the importance of shaping the right environment in our organizations. Although he was talking about buildings, Churchill's words relate equally well to a critical element of an organization's environment – culture. So we're going to explore two key questions:

- To what extent do leaders shape an organization's culture?

- And to what extent are they themselves shaped by the culture they inherit?

These are crucial questions to answer, a point well made by Peter Drucker *(see publication cited in endnote 6).* He pointedly suggested that all organizations develop people, '…they either form them or deform them.'[26]

First though, some definitions. Whilst organizational culture is something we all talk about, it's not always easy to define. Culture can be all-pervading and influential, but also intangible and difficult to discern or understand. But one thing is certain: it's critically important. Because, in the words of Peter Senge: 'Every organization is the product of the way its members think and interact. Change the way people think and interact, and you can change the world.'[27]

Webs, icebergs and onions

Culture is often defined as 'the way things are done' in an organization. Although culture is crucial in enabling change, changing culture itself is no easy thing. This is partly because of the difficulty in identifying, influencing and managing culture. This complexity is sometimes described as a 'cultural web'. Adapted from the well-known work of Johnson and Scholes,[28] the idea of a web suggests that culture is all-pervasive. Similarly, complexity is illustrated by a common distinction between visible and hidden levels of culture. Not only is culture all-pervasive, but much of it is often hidden.

This point is illustrated by another popular metaphor, Schein's 'iceberg model'. Whilst many of the tangible elements of the cultural web may be visible, it's the hidden aspects of culture that are perhaps the most important. This is often represented as the 'cultural iceberg'. Visible signs of culture, such as customer service statements or job titles and organizational structures are above the surface, and relatively easy to see. However, these are just the tip of the iceberg. And, as any ship's captain knows, it's what lies beneath the iceberg that's most important. In organizations, cultural indicators, such as accepted, sub-conscious beliefs, are hidden beneath the surface. Although these might be the least-visible aspects of culture, it's these underlying assumptions that are the most important. They are the real source of values, attitudes, beliefs – and resultant activity – within the organization.

To get to some of these important cultural aspects you may well need to 'peel' some outer layers away. This view of culture places special emphasis on its depth, comparing it to the layers of an onion. With this metaphor, the inner layers of the onion represent the organization's values, norms and belief systems. The middle layers represent routines, rituals and processes, while the outer layers represent the tangible, visible signs of culture.

These three images of culture provide us with helpful ways to recognize it. This is useful because culture can be both subtle and all pervasive. Many of the important aspects of culture are hidden. They are multi-layered, requiring leaders to 'peel away' some of the outer layers in order to reveal the hidden underlying assumptions.

Thinking about culture

Thinking about culture through these metaphors has several implications. Firstly, they clearly illustrate that the visible elements of culture need to be built upon appropriate underpinning assumptions. Visible cultural indicators need to match what lies beneath. Where this is not the case, there can be serious discord in the workforce, making it far less likely that organizational aims and objectives will be met easily, if at all.

Secondly, if the most important part of culture is 'what lies beneath', then it can be difficult to change. Especially given that these hidden elements are likely to be deeply embedded, often at the very heart of the organization. If this is the case, the issue for leaders is how can they connect their vision with those existing values and beliefs held within the organization?

A crucial implication for leaders, especially those new to an organization, is their own relationship with an existing organizational culture. If culture is both embedded and pervasive, to what extent are leaders themselves *shaped by* the organizational culture? This is especially important when leaders are trying to shape the culture they want or envisage.

Being conscious that leaders can be significantly influenced by existing culture is a good starting point, and one often overlooked. The power of culture is hidden in the underlying assumptions to which we subconsciously conform. So becoming more aware of these assumptions helps us to begin the process of changing them. However, real progress only begins when we realize the full impact of a leader's actions and behaviours in shaping culture.

Changing culture

Noted culture expert Edgar Schein sees leadership and organizational culture as 'two sides of the same coin'. He suggested that, 'the unique and essential function of leadership is the manipulation of the culture'.[29]

That's a view which Zappos CEO, Tony Hsieh (pronounced Shay), would agree with. In an article for *Forbes* magazine, he was once asked: 'As CEO, what's your primary focus?' Hsieh's answer was both succinct and telling: 'Company culture. We focus on making sure we have a great service-focused culture. If you get the culture right, then a lot of really amazing things happen on their own.'[30]

If an essential part of leadership is to shape the organization, then the ability to influence and change culture is critical. Later in this chapter we'll return to discuss one of the most powerful ways that leaders can change cultures. We'll also find out the two questions that Sir Terry Leahy asked staff at UK supermarket Tesco. Questions that helped shape a culture that was crucial to that business's exceptional performance.

Shaping strategy

How do sense-making and bricolage leadership relate to strategy? Regardless of what an organization plans to do, success is only likely when change is supported by an appropriate strategy. We think there are some vital questions about leadership and strategy that are often overlooked. For example:

- What are the essentials of strategy?
- Has leadership been lost in a conventional view of strategy?
- Is strategy too slow?
- Is strategy the right place for leaders to start?

Our starting point is to suggest that strategy and leadership have too often been separated, with a body of thinking and a field of study developed for both. Whilst there is much to be gained from recognizing the differences and developing ideas, tools and techniques for each, failing to think of them together can result in significant problems. That said, first we'll get to grips with the meaning of strategy.

The essentials of strategy

Having written comprehensive academic texts on strategy, US professor and strategy expert Richard Rumelt (2001) decided to try and strip strategy down to its essentials. What he concluded connects with the thrust of our discussion to date. Strategy is: 'a focusing of energy and resources on a few key objectives whose accomplishment will make a real difference.'[31]

This definition echoes the approach adopted by Bratton and the Sternins, and it especially reflects some of the key factors in a tipping point. Each of these examples illustrated this focus, of energy and concentration of resources where they had the most impact. It also captures something of the bricolage leader, as someone who is resourceful with the resources at hand. This is a point that has some significance to strategy, as we shall see shortly. Rumelt's definition also reflects another key theme we have already discussed, the idea of those few, vital things that really matter. What's also striking about this stripped-down definition of strategy is a notion that Matsushita would no doubt identify with immediately. This is the idea that leaders focus on where they can make a real difference.

Energy, resource, the vital few and making a difference – these echo much of our earlier discussion about leadership. A strategy puts these elements together to help the organization achieve a few key objectives. For Rumelt 'the heart of a good strategy is insight into the hidden power in a situation, and into an appropriate response.'[32]

Notice the stress on insight. Seeing what others don't see is a critical part of strategy. Rumelt describes strategy as applying strength to the most promising opportunity. In many cases it will be relative strength that is applied, and will often have most benefit where competitors have a relative weakness. That is: finding an advantage or a difference that means your organization is able to compete in a way that others can't.

However, vital as these points are to good strategy, Rumelt argues that there is still something missing. He suggests that business should be about much more than making a profit. In words reminiscent of Matsushita's ideas from the 1930s, Rumelt proposes that business organizations should have a big vision, of how a business contributes to society and to the good of others. The danger with strategy is that it can lose its connection with leadership. This can mean it loses the sense of purpose, the bigger purpose that organizations can make a difference.

The strategy–leadership divide

There has been a tendency to separate strategy from leadership to the detriment of both but we think strategy needs leadership, just as leadership needs strategy. Strategy has developed into a discipline in itself, with well-established models and theories. Whilst this development has resulted in a wide range of useful and important tools to help the process of developing a strategy, it could be argued that this has also led to the separation of strategy from the discipline of leadership.

The two fields of strategy and leadership are often taught separately in our business schools, when in practice they should go hand-in-hand. One view of strategy is that it is just a glorified plan, albeit a vital one needed to help take an organization forward. However, this is only part of the picture. But strategy is certainly more than just a plan. You could say it is a plan with a difference. It is about putting a plan together that differentiates, finding an advantage. But the plan should not only find a difference and advantage, it should also make a real difference, an impact. The purpose of a strategic plan is to produce directions for change. These should be about positive, desired, ideal futures, answers to critical problems not current problems, negative reactions or mitigation of past failures. A strategy needs vision and purpose, a 'why' to bring life to the 'what' of a strategic plan. There is a danger that over-emphasis on models, tools and resources can create an analytical focus on strategy, which may overshadow the crucial role of leadership. Or worse still, ignore it altogether.

Leadership is needed to bring vision, purpose and life to any strategic plan. A powerful vision is important because it is one way of linking the realities of the present to the desirability of the future. The role of strategic planning is to map out a path to achieve that vision. As Canadian academic Henry Mintzberg said: 'If you have no vision, but only formal plans, then every unpredicted change in the environment makes you feel your sky is falling in.'[33]

There's a risk that strategy and leadership may become separated, or at least be perceived to be separate. But just as serious is the possibility that an over-emphasis on the tools of strategic analysis might result in problems. It might mean that developing strategy just takes too long!

Is strategy being developed too slowly?

Trying to apply strategy without leadership vision runs the risk that organizations can lose direction, or at least be easily knocked off course. But there is also another risk with traditional strategic processes – they can make setting that course a slow or cumbersome operation. Two INSEAD academics, Yves Doz and former Nokia senior manager, Mikko Kosonen make this point. Firstly, they characterize mainstream approaches to strategy as being focused on the bigger picture, with perhaps too much focus on planning and looking ahead. They contrast this view with what they consider a more realistic approach to emerging situations, where 'fast pattern recognition, rather than accurate scenarios becomes key.'[34] They go on to make the salient point that 'the world around us keeps emerging, and our perception of it keeps reshaping it as we play.'

This responsive, dynamic world of strategy, calls for a significant change in how we approach strategy. As with Rumelt, Doz and Kosonen note the importance of insight, specifically proposing that 'insight needs to replace foresight.'

Insight is the spark of clarity that can be gained through sense-making, as leaders and organizations try to connect and make sense of what is emerging. Insight is about gaining clearer, deeper perceptions of any given situation. It's what happens when ideas, experience, context and practice are brought together. Taking time to think, and to see things afresh, can help you realize the possibilities and benefits that insight can bring.

So interpreting what is emerging, in order to gain insight, implies some changes to the way we think about strategy. It means strategy needs to be crafted to be adaptive and responsive, with more emphasis on insight than on foresight. All of which suggests there is a need for a more speedy response to developments, which may have been missing from traditional approaches. But how can you speed up the process of strategy?

That is exactly what Doz and Kosonen explored in their 2008 book, *Fast Strategy*. They asked the question: How can leaders radically accelerate changes in their business? Based on an empirical study of over a dozen information technology companies, Doz and Kosonen argued that many organizations failed to do this for an interesting reason. It wasn't because they were doing something wrong or mediocre, but because they persevered too long with methods that were inappropriate or out of date. These organizations fell victim to reliance on the status quo, or on the rigidity of the way they'd always delivered their services. Specifically, they lacked agility.

Doz and Kosonen describe agility as the 'thoughtful and purposive interplay' of leaders between three capabilities:

1 seeing and framing things differently with constant alertness, awareness of what's going on, high-quality dialogue;

2 re-connecting departmental silos and polarized views – leaders working well together rather than being pulled apart – and *crucially;*

3 ability to redeploy resources fast. Increasing an organization's capacity – resource fluidity.

These ideas clearly resonate with the themes we have so far explored in *Uncommon Leadership*. The first capability echoes some of our discussions on sense-making and uncommon sense. The second is the subject of our subsequent chapter on shared leadership, whilst the third capability fits well with the notion of bricolage leadership.

We would suggest building on these three capabilities in order to reflect the insights of uncommon leadership with these five steps to a responsive strategy:

1 Strategic sense-making – seeing things differently, having sense making conversations.

2 Insight – finding the uncommon sense before it becomes common sense.

3 Advantage – using uncommon sense to create a strategic advantage. This idea builds on Rumelt's essential idea on strategy – finding an insight that can give you relative advantage.

4 Shared leadership – building a broader base of leaders, working collaboratively without the barriers of organizational silos and

polarized views. This is the theme of the fifth 'S' in our leadership framework and is the subject of Chapter 5: Shared Leadership.

5 Resourceful leadership – using a bricolage approach to resource use. Perhaps the critical element of a responsive strategy is to be able to commit resources to the activities that will deliver the strategy. That often means unlocking trapped resources or adapting and re-purposing resources to realize an advantage, and to enable delivery of the strategy. In our 'getting into shape' section later in this chapter, we'll discuss six resource strategies that will help increase the flexibility and responsiveness of resources.

Strategy needs leadership, it needs to be responsive but surprisingly, perhaps it's not necessarily the first thing a leader should think about.

How to start a strategy? Don't start with a strategy!

Jim Collins is well known for asking and seeking answers to some very challenging questions. One of these: 'Why do some companies seem to be able to sustain success?' was the key question he addressed with his colleague Jim Porras, in their best-selling book *Built to Last*, Collins's more recent best-seller asks another intriguing question: how do some companies manage to jump from being just good to being great?

In this book, *Good to Great: Why some companies make the leap... and others don't*,[35] Collins and his team made a surprising finding. In discussing the team's early assumptions, Collins expected to find organizations starting out with a clear vision and strategy, which shaped the direction of the organization. What they actually found surprised them. In fact, the organizations that moved from good to great did the exact opposite to what the team considered conventional wisdom. 'The executives who ignited the transformation from good to great did not first figure out where to drive the bus and then get people to take it there. No, they first got the right people on the bus and in the right place... and then figured out where to drive it.'

It's a counter-intuitive approach to strategy, yet one that makes perfect sense when you think about it. Collins certainly did just that, concluding that assembling the right team *before* making strategy means they can all help to make sense of where they are going. In his view, strategy is what comes after you 'get the right people on the bus'. This will result in a coming together of sense-making, insight and resource flexibility built on a bricolage approach. If success in business is often about seeking an advantage, then one of the most important advantages is to have the right people, in the right place, at the right time, doing the things they are good at.

Getting into shape

Shaping organizations is no easy task, so we've put together some thought-provoking ways that leaders can develop approaches and practices that will help to shape their organizations.

Bricolage and being resourceful

The key to doing more with less is to be resourceful. That is, being mindful of the resource situation, developing a strategy to manage it, and being resourceful in the process. We've already discussed the importance of adopting a bricolage approach. This encourages people to think differently about the resources currently available, rather than wishing there were more or that they'd been dealt a different hand. As we saw earlier, if strategy is to be responsive then leaders need to view resources as being flexible and adaptable.

So before committing to resource cutbacks, first make sure you have made the most of what you have got. Given the innate ingenuity of the human mind, it's surprising just how much extra can be done, even with resources that are limited or diminished. Try:

- *Restricting* – some resources are high-value and costly so they need to be used very carefully. Make sure that high-value resources are used where they have the greatest impact for you and take care to assess their use. Misuse or wasted use of high-value resources can be extremely costly.

- *Releasing* – one of the common problems with resources is that they get stuck. They get trapped in unproductive, inefficient or inappropriate activities. Sometimes it can be surprising how much resource is trapped in this way. Releasing it and re-purposing on high-value activities can have dramatic effects.

- *Focusing* – concentrate current resources on areas most needing change, or where the impact is likely to be the greatest. This is the approach that Bill Bratton found so useful when taking over the New York City Transit Police.

- *Sharing* – find ways in which outcomes can be met by resources that are shared across parts of an organization, and crucially across other organizations.

- *Shifting* – using the resources of customers as a means of delivering aspects of a service. It is often the case that customers can actually become more engaged with your business when they take on more responsibility.

- *Synergizing* – by combining resources so that they deliver more together than they do apart, and in ways that make sense for the customer.

A straightforward process to review organizational resources is to take the ABC approach. This spells out three relatively simple steps to take, before identifying some more detailed steps for implementation. Firstly, assess

FIGURE 2.2 The 'ABC' of resourceful leadership

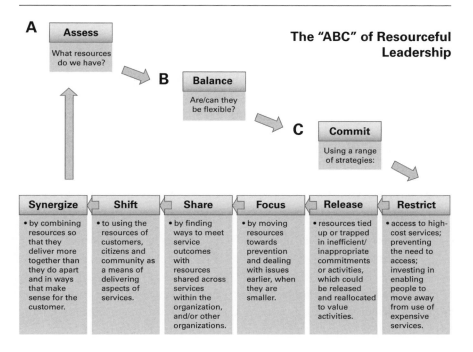

Synergize	Shift	Share	Focus	Release	Restrict
• by combining resources so that they deliver more together than they do apart and in ways that make sense for the customer.	• to using the resources of customers, citizens and community as a means of delivering aspects of services.	• by finding ways to meet service outcomes with resources shared across services within the organization, and/or other organizations.	• by moving resources towards prevention and dealing with issues earlier, when they are smaller.	• resources tied up or trapped in inefficient/ inappropriate commitments or activities, which could be released and reallocated to value activities.	• access to high-cost services; preventing the need to access; investing in enabling people to move away from use of expensive services.

what resources you have. Then ask how well balanced they are, especially in relation to the way they are deployed. For example, are they in the right place, or could they be better used elsewhere? Then, when you have balanced your resources, commit to a mix of resource strategies, which will help you, lead resourcefully.

Taking some time to think about resources may reveal some useful possibilities. These may help to shape what you do differently. Next we'll consider how to create the right conditions in the workplace by shaping culture.

Conveying what you care about

If a leader wants to change the culture in an organization, perhaps they need to shape it first. A key element of this is to communicate what you believe in and care about. According to Edgar Schein, a leading expert on culture, one of the most powerful ways to do this is quite simple: it's what you systematically pay attention to. Colleagues note what we consider important by observing what we emphasize, and how we spend our time. Overwhelmingly, people will pay attention to where their leaders pay attention. Think about your own leadership. How much time do you spend on the things you care about? How do you signal that something is important to you?

Let's take a couple of examples. If you believe in the importance of a strong customer focus in your organization, then you should be thinking about how you pay attention to this, or in how your beliefs manifest themselves. Promoting a customer-focused culture might mean:

- thinking about how you enthusiastically emphasize a focus on customer service quality;
- ensuring your time is spent visiting customers and listening to them regularly;
- promoting customer needs and expectations as a core part of meetings.

Or perhaps you care about building a performance culture (probably in addition to customer focus, rather than instead of!). This means paying attention to performance and conveying its importance, perhaps by:

- supporting and encouraging high performance;

- praising people for performance;

- being an example with your own performance;

- refusing to accept mediocre or poor performance;

- dealing quickly with genuine poor performance issues;

- getting colleagues to experience the consequences of poor performance as your customer does.

Often it's actions that communicate intent far more effectively than words, which is something we discuss in more detail in the next chapter. Stop and think about what you're paying particular attention to at the moment. It's possible that your colleagues are noticing your actions far more than you realize. This can have a profound effect on both how they interpret what they see, and how it affects their actions. Whether intentionally or not, the way you act is constantly shaping the culture in your organization.

Questioning culture

When Sir Terry Leahy became CEO of the UK retailer Tesco in February 1997, he knew he needed to create a strong sense of identity if he was to deliver his ambitious strategy. He asked his workforce two questions, which helped to shape a culture that sparked a startling transformation in Tesco's fortunes. Within a decade Tesco has grown from the UK's third-largest supermarket chain to the position of number one retailer in the UK, and a global force in retailing. Although the questions were simple and straightforward, the process to embed them was anything but. Leahy made the point that you can't create a culture overnight. In a disarmingly honest reflection, Leahy said:

The process is never-ending and relentless. Wherever I went, I would talk about the values. Fourteen years of speeches... I always referred to them. That bored me to death – but only by repeating simple things, time and again, do you drive your message home: 'this matters'.[36]

With these words, Leahy also captures the essence of Schein's belief in conveying what you care about. So what were the two questions? Well, as we said, they were incredibly simple:

1 What does Tesco stand for?

2 What would you like it to stand for?

Simple – but powerful when properly answered and applied. Of course *asking* the questions was not quite so simple. Leahy's initiative meant tens of thousands of people were asked these two simple questions, over the course of an entire year. But the immediate results proved well worth the effort. The two questions encouraged everyone to get involved, determining the values they all felt the organization should stand for. Perhaps these people were already on Jim Collins's bus, but the questions certainly got them involved in deciding where they were going!

Developing the values at Tesco may have been demanding enough but it was nothing compared to the challenge of making them come to life. We'll return to Leahy's own words to explain what he considered crucial to making values work: 'To create that culture leadership is crucial. A team needs to be told, 'This is important' by the leader. And they need to see the leader not merely talking about values, but using them and making decisions on the basis of them.'[37]

This is reminiscent of one chief executive who referred to what he called the 'stellar test'. He asked another simple question of his staff: 'If someone asked you... where you worked, what response would you get?'

Think about what you would say. Ask yourself: would you reply that you work in a stellar organization? Would your staff? How can you build an organization that will make you and your colleagues its advocates? What would you like your organization to stand for? Clarifying what you stand for, your values and underpinning beliefs can be an interesting and fruitful exercise. Often, this kind of exercise can surface some interesting underlying assumptions.

An elephant never forgets...

It's said that in circuses and in India, baby elephants are tethered by a rope to a stake driven deep into the ground. The stake is too strong for the baby elephant to pull up, and it eventually comes to believe escape is impossible, no matter how hard it tries. This learned behaviour stays with the elephant. Even when fully-grown and strong enough to easily escape its shackles, the elephant doesn't try to pull up the stake. It remains trapped in a limiting belief formed by a past experience.

Underlying assumptions, by their very nature, are hidden but hidden doesn't mean innocuous. Underlying assumptions can have a very powerful effect on so much of organizational life. For example bricolage leadership is often best seen in the crucible of need – when compelling reasons clash with implacable constraints. The essence of bricolage leadership can be expressed quite simply. It's the challenging of underlying assumptions, and beliefs that are limiting, in order to release and use resources creatively. One area where limiting beliefs are particularly prevalent is in an organization's culture. Shaping the right culture can be one of the most critical things any leader can do. And achieving this can often require leaders to challenge some embedded limiting beliefs. Here are some questions to ask that will help you to challenge limiting beliefs:

1 What are some of the lessons that we could learn from experience?

2 What are the constraints of the current situation?

3 What assumptions have we made about this situation?

4 How can we assess whether the constraints are fixed or perceived?

5 Which constraints could be challenged or removed?

6 How would you do this?

7 What's stopping you achieving your team/organization goals?

Head, hand and heart

One particularly useful tool to help leaders encourage cultural change is the head, heart and hand metaphor. This approach means looking at change through three lenses, but with the aim of making cultural change personal – as something that is personally engaging. For example, whilst it's important to think rationally about change, by using your head, this alone is not enough. To encourage a fuller commitment to change you need to engage the heart as well. The heart relates to feelings and emotions, and these are often far more influential than any simple, rational response to change. It's no coincidence that attempts to make change sustainable are often based on the concept of winning both hearts and minds. The third lens relates to the hands. This means trying to gain an early experience or sense of what the change looks like, what it is likely to do. Trying to visualize the change and making it tangible are powerful ways to engage people and to make the changes seem more personal.

Of the three lenses, organizations often focus much of their effort on the head – making the 'case' for change by facts and figures. But we've already seen how people aren't necessarily the rational thinkers we believe them to be. So there can be a fundamental problem with relying too much on this

FIGURE 2.3   Changing culture with head, heart and hand

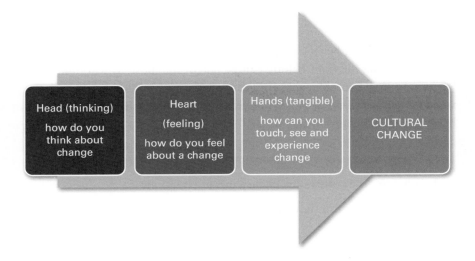

approach. Often, the case that's made misses what some might consider the two most important factors: how people *feel* about culture change, and whether the change is being made tangible and real for them.

Organizations, just like athletes, need to get into shape if they are to perform at their best. Leaders shape organizations by the way they deploy resources, create the right conditions, and then build an appropriate culture. This is a culture that can help shape a direction by using adaptable strategies. Leaders do this so that organizations can perform: doing the common things uncommonly well. That's the subject of our next chapter in which we'll pose some more interesting questions. Questions such as:

- How does a packed lunch relate to uncommon leadership?

- What's a prawn sandwich got to do with authentic leadership?

- Would people pay to see your work team perform?

Bibliography

1   Matsushita, K (1989) *As I See It*, Tokyo, PHP Institute

2   Kotter, J (1997) *Matsushita Leadership*, New York, Simon & Schuster

3   Peters, T and Waterman, R, In Search of Excellence, in J Kotter (1997) *Matsushita Leadership* New York, Simon & Schuster

4   Kotter, J (1997) *Matsushita Leadership*, New York, Simon & Schuster

5   Matsushita, K (1989) *As I See It*, Tokyo, PHP Institute

6   Drucker, P (2005) *The Daily Drucker: 366 days of insight and motivation for getting the right things done,* London, HarperCollins

7   Sutton, R (2006) [accessed 10 June 2013] Management advice: which 90% is crap? *Change This* [Online] http://changethis.com/manifesto/23.90Percent Crap/pdf/23.90PercentCrap.pdf

8   Rouleau, L (2005) Micro-practices of strategic sensemaking and sensegiving: how middle managers interpret and sell change every day, *Journal of Management Studies*, **42** (7), pp 1413–1441

9   *Washington Post* (2007) [accessed 10 June 2013] Stop and hear the music, *YouTube* [Online] http://www.youtube.com/watch?v=hnOPu0_YWhw

10 Weingarten G (2007) [accessed 10 June 2013] Pearls before breakfast: can one of the nation's great musicians cut through the fog of a DC rush hour? Let's find out, *Washington Post* [Online] http://www.washingtonpost.com/wp-dyn/content/article/2007/04/04/AR2007040401721.html

11 Neill, C (No date) [accessed 10 June 2013] What Aristotle and Joshua Bell can teach us about persuasion, *TEDEd* [Online] http://ed.ted.com/lessons/what-aristotle-and-joshua-bell-can-teach-us-about-persuasion-conor-neill

12 Cooper, L (1960) *The rhetoric of Aristotle*, New York, Appleton-Century-Crofts

13 Thaler, R and Sunstein, C (2009) *Nudge: Improving decisions about health, wealth and happiness*, London, Penguin Books

14 ibid

15 Kahneman, D (2011) *Thinking, Fast and Slow*, London, Allen Lane

16 Pfeffer, J and Sutton, R (2006) *Hard Facts, Dangerous Half-Truths, and Total Nonsense: Profiting from evidence-based nanagement*, Boston, Harvard Business Press

17 Sutton, R (2006) [accessed 10 June 2013] Management advice: which 90% is crap? *Change This* [Online] http://changethis.com/manifesto/23.90PercentCrap/pdf/23.90PercentCrap.pdf

18 Purdy, M and Borisoff, D (eds) (1997) *Listening in Everyday Life: A personal and professional approach*, Lanham, University Press of America Inc.

19 Kierkegaard, S A (No date) [accessed 21 February 2014, online] http://en.wikiquote.org/wiki/S%C3%B8ren_Kierkegaard

20 Weick, K (2004) *Making Sense of the Organisation*, Oxford, Blackwell Publishing

21 Stoker, G and Moseley, A (2010) *Motivation, Behaviour and the Micro-foundations of Public Services 2020*, London Public Services Trust

22 Zappos (No date) [accessed 10 June 2013] Customer Service Isn't Just A Department! *Zappos* [Online] http://about.zappos.com/

23 Kotter, J (2011) [accessed 10 June 2013] Does corporate culture drive financial performance? *Forbes* [Online] http://www.forbes.com/sites/johnkotter/2011/02/10/does-corporate-culture-drive-financial-performance/

24 ibid

25 Zappos (No date) [accessed 10 June 2013] The Zappos Family Culture Book, *Zappos* [Online] http://www.zapposinsights.com/culture-book

26 Drucker, P (2005) *The Daily Drucker: 366 days of insight and motivation for getting the right things done*, London, HarperCollins

27 Senge, P (1990) *The Fifth Discipline: The art & practice of the learning organization*, London, Doubleday

28 Johnson, G, Scholes, K and Whittington, R (2007) *Exploring Corporate Strategy*, 8th edn, London, Financial Times Prentice Hall

29 Schein, E (1992) *Organizational Culture and Leadership: A dynamic view*, San Francisco, Jossey-Bass

30 Reiss, R (2010) [accessed 10 June 2013] Tony Hsieh on his secrets of success, *Forbes* [Online] http://www.forbes.com/2010/07/01/tony-hsieh-zappos-leadership-managing-interview.html

31 Rumelt, R (2011) *Good Strategy/Bad Strategy: The difference and why it matters,* New York, Random House

32 ibid

33 Mintzberg, H (2000) *The Rise and Fall of Strategic Planning*, Harlow, Pearson Education

34 Doz, Y L and Kosonen, M (2008) *Fast Strategy: How strategic agility will help you stay ahead of the game,* Harlow, Pearson Education

35 Collins, J (2001) *Good to Great: Why some companies make the leap... and others don't* New York, Random House

36 Leahy, T (2010) *Management in Ten Words*, New York, Random House Business Books

37 ibid

LEADING WITH PURPOSE

SHOWING THE WAY BY DOING THE COMMON THINGS UNCOMMONLY WELL

KEY TOPICS

- Service, sandwiches and simple messages.
- The quickest route to bankruptcy?
- Memorable businesses and memorable performances.
- Walking the talk.
- Mirror leadership.
- The stonecutter revisited.
- Crafting a calling.
- Uncommon sense in practice.

FIGURE 3.1 Showing

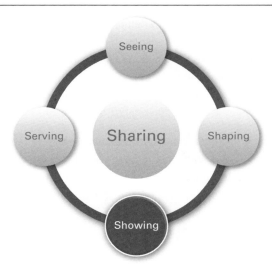

t's not just what you do that matters: it's *how* you do what you do. Influencing and shaping the organization are both critical, but each must be backed up and matched by something equally important – the way leaders act and behave. This means *showing* the way, taking purposeful action that ensures the habit of excellence becomes a natural part of what the organization does.

Service, sandwiches and simple messages

How do you deal with a customer who is consistently complaining and never happy with the service you provide? Recently we delivered a series of workshops to several hundred leaders and managers. One day we were facilitating a session on something that is not often addressed as a leadership topic – the impact of small actions. One delegate, a school catering manager, related an experience which got everyone thinking. This story, of sandwiches and simple messages, nicely illustrates one of the main themes of this chapter – doing the common things uncommonly well.

Serving sandwiches

Pupils at this school normally received lunch in the school cafeteria, except when they were out on trips. The day of one such trip, catering staff prepared packed-lunches for each pupil to take with them. One child didn't like school food at the best of times, and was particularly unimpressed with packed lunches. Aware of this, one of the catering staff packed a normal lunch but included an unusual addition. She put a short note in with the packed food. The note simply wished the child a good day, and expressed the hope that he enjoyed the lunch, packed 'especially' for him. Later in the day, when the boy opened his lunch and saw the note, he not only ate the meal but thoroughly enjoyed it. Even more importantly, he went home and told his mum.

This incident is significant for two reasons. Firstly because, unknown to the school's catering staff, this mother was a regular visitor to the head teacher's office. And these visits were invariably to lodge a complaint. In one way or another, she always felt the school wasn't meeting the needs of her child. Immediately after the packed lunch note, the parent went to see the head teacher yet again. But this time the meeting was totally different. Speaking with the head teacher, the mother was full of praise for what the school had done for her child. Expecting another criticism, the stunned head teacher listened to the parent's glowing comments with equal measures of relief and disbelief! Of course, the head teacher could have simply savoured the moment and left it at that. But she didn't, which is the second significant point about this story. The head teacher immediately went to see the catering team in person. She told them about the parent's visit and her complimentary comments. She added to this something they hadn't known about, of the frequent difficult conversations she'd had with this parent over the preceding years. Then she told her staff one final thing. She thanked them for doing that little bit extra, one little act, by one of the team, which had made such a big difference to a customer's experience, perception and attitude.

Simple messages

That story provoked a lively discussion with the managers at our workshop. Some thought, this was a very interesting little story but hardly significant enough to make much difference to a large organization. But others agreed with our interpretation: that what many might see (or overlook) as relatively small acts, can often have a significant impact for others. The act may have seemed small and insignificant to the organization, but it was clearly far more than that for the parent and child. And if such a small act had such a dramatic impact on its customers, surely the lesson to be learned is the impact *many* such acts can have on the organization as a whole. This is something we'll come back to in the next chapter, where we consider the hidden power of small actions and defining moments.

But the impact of small acts isn't the only key message in this simple story – let's reflect on two others. The second comes from what the story tells us about the dinner-lady, in particular how she viewed her work. In her place, it would have been all too easy to see the job in very straightforward terms. She was simply paid to prepare food and serve it to her customers. However it's obvious that she clearly thought of her job as more than that – she was *caring* for the children, not just catering for them. She had no idea that the parent of the child was regularly complaining about many aspects of the child's experience at the school. She did however know the child, and understood that he didn't like school dinners. *How* she viewed her job had a big impact on *what* she did. As we shall see later in this chapter, how we frame our work has a dramatic impact on whether we do the common things uncommonly well. A common task became part of an uncommon act of care.

The third key message in this story can be seen from the head teacher's reaction. It's unlikely any of the points discussed would have become public unless she had chosen to personally visit the catering team. It would have been very easy for this head teacher to simply bask in the relief of a compliment, instead of the angst of an expected complaint. And then, what busy senior manager wouldn't be tempted to simply move on to the next pressing task? But because she acted promptly to share what she'd seen and heard, a seemingly insignificant event became very significant to the organization and the people in it. This action did two things: it highlighted the positive effect of her staff member's action, in turning an adversary into an advocate with one, small, thoughtful act. The head teacher also demonstrated the power of positive feedback, something we'll explore later in this chapter. As we'll see, catching the right behaviours, and praising people for them both quickly and publicly, can be far more powerful than we realize.

This story had a surprising and unexpectedly successful outcome. This was largely because two people did their jobs well – uncommonly well. It's easy to overlook the benefits of doing things well, especially in the constant clamour to be trying something new. And there is significant benefit in doing what you do *really* well. This is something echoed in the words of one of the most successful entrepreneurs of his time. At the turn of last century, J D Rockefeller was asked a similar question to that asked of Konosuke Matsushita. Whereas Matsushita's answer made us think about common sense differently, Rockefeller gave us a different insight: 'The secret of success is to do the common thing uncommonly well.'

One way to be a successful leader then, is to do something really well, better than anyone else. To do it uncommonly well! As we shall now see, there are other, more contemporary entrepreneurs who would probably agree with J D Rockefeller's assessment of success. So let's now look at other successful leaders who have built on Rockefeller's secret.

The quickest route to bankruptcy?

Many great businesses have been started or built upon the conviction that someone could do a better job than the organizations currently delivering a particular service or product. One of the UK's great entrepreneurs, Sir Richard Branson, once described why he decided to enter the airline industry. Put simply, he was fed up with the poor service he got when flying and knew he could do a better job. This, it turns out, is an approach he has adopted for his other businesses too.

My businesses grow out of my experiences, usually my bad experiences. I see something done badly which I know that we could do better – like the airline. No one was offering their customers a decent service. I was sure that whoever did so would not only have a successful company but would also change the whole industry.[1]

For Branson, it wasn't enough to just spot something he could do better. He also saw the potential for being a game-changer on a much larger scale – to change the whole industry. As he went on to explain: 'I knew within a minute that this new airline was for me. I had travelled in other people's airlines and the experience had been ghastly. I could do it better.'

Combining uncommon sense and vision

Once Branson had made up his mind, what came next? It's interesting to see how he explains his next steps: 'I've always said that you don't need to do lots of expensive research... Mostly, you need common sense and vision.'[2]

Common sense and vision are often realized by seeing what others have missed, such as the opportunity in a problem, and in taking counter-intuitive action. These are lessons, clearly apparent in Branson's approach, which we've already discussed in relation to uncommon leadership. Although he calls it common sense, in reality his was an idea based on uncommon sense. So much so that many of those around him counselled against the move: 'Everyone told me that the quickest way to bankruptcy was to make a million and then start an airline.'[3]

Branson's use of 'uncommon sense' was also illustrated by the way his airline would operate. Moving into the airline business was risky enough but Branson envisioned success by also bucking industry trends. At a time when so many airlines were turning to the increasingly successful low-cost, no-frills business model, Branson actually wanted to offer *increased* service. The fact that he not only did this, but made a longstanding success in doing so, clearly illustrates the power of uncommon leadership.

The language of uncommon leadership

Another important lesson we shouldn't overlook from this example, is the language Branson used when taking action on his idea. Though so much of the initiative was due to Branson's own opportunism and drive, he nonetheless used an inclusive language when discussing the plan. Always seeing the importance of what his people did, and the potential in what they could do – Branson preferred the word 'we' rather than 'I'. This doesn't seem to be an isolated instance, or a slip of the tongue on Branson's part. Using the word 'we' seems to be fundamental to the way he sees and runs his businesses. In the epilogue to his book: *Screw it, Let's do it*, Branson explained his approach to his relationship with his employees: 'If you look for the best in your employees, they'll flourish. If you criticize or look for the worst, they'll shrivel up. We all need lots of watering. We have a really wonderful team of people and I feel that whatever happens, Virgin is in good hands.'[4]

Memorable businesses and memorable performances

Innovation isn't always about having a new product or service. It can often relate to doing what others already do, but doing it better. Especially if better means doing something extraordinarily well. So how can you make your business memorable in the minds of your customers? And how do you give them a memorable experience? Well one way is to think of what you do as a performance. And best of all, by trying to deliver memorable experiences through memorable performances.

Service as a performance?

Is it time to think of service as a performance? Thinking about service as a show, and your role in it as a performer, can put a whole new light on how you manage. But how many of us would think of their service in that way? Virgin Atlantic certainly does. Here's what Sarah Miller, editor of *Condé Nast Traveller* and industry insider, makes of Virgin Atlantic: 'Virgin transformed the idea of a journey – from lounge, through inflight, to landing – into a glamorous experience.'[5]

So what makes for a good performance from the viewer's perspective? Is it as simple as a perception of enjoyment? Or is it a more complex combination of satisfaction, wonder, fulfilment of expectation, or value for money? When we witness a great performance we are often enthralled, appreciative of the skill involved. Perhaps we are fully engaged and involved in the moment. But could such a view of performance really apply to some of the more down-to-earth, everyday activities, which most of us experience at work? It's easy enough to envisage great performances that are artistic and dramatic in the worlds of art, drama and sport, but can we really use similar language to describe the workplace?

Before answering that point, think for a moment about the different ways we use the word *performance*. It can be defined in a number of ways, each of which conveys a number of meanings. One useful way to think about workplace performance is to take some of these different definitions and bring them together.

Firstly, performing is often described as accomplishing something, and often to do so with great skill. The word 'accomplish' has the sense of doing something significant, often overcoming difficulties in the process. Being accomplished in what you do has the sense of expertise, competently and expertly applied.

Secondly, performing is often associated with meeting requirements: to fulfil a promise or undertaking. To fulfil is to live up to expectations, or to satisfy demands or wishes. Fulfilling promises has the sense of personal commitment to customers.

Our third interpretation of the word is to give a performance of something. Great performances are recognized by everybody. This is the notion of a performance being a show, put on for the benefit of the audience, or customer.

Combining these three definitions reveals a fascinating insight. Working backwards through each definition produces a new, interesting definition: 'Great performances fulfil a promise and do so with great skill.'

Memorable service performances

If your business was more like a performance on a stage, what might it be like, and why would this be a good idea? Chris Voss and Leonieke Zomerdijk, from London Business School, offer some interesting ideas about service as performance. They investigated 'experiential services', where customer interaction with the organization matters most. What stands out is a sense that all kinds of organizations are now realizing the importance of customer experience as part of the service. And for good reasons. According to Voss and Zomerdijk,[6] building the customer experience:

- improves service levels;
- acts as a point of difference between you and your competitors;
- is important in influencing customer loyalty;
- encourages positive word-of-mouth recommendations from customers;
- creates emotional connection.

Regardless of whether your organization offers mainly products or services, there is a growing trend to address the importance of the customer experience. Increasingly, all businesses are evaluating those aspects of the business that are about service, and deciding how these can be made into great experiences for their customers. Even organizations that are more focused on manufacturing are thinking more about the customer experience in relation to their service activities. For example, car manufacturer Land Rover has developed their 'Land Rover Experience Centres'. Here customers can test drive the range of Land Rover vehicles, experiencing the products over some challenging, outdoor terrain.

All the (business) world is a stage!

Some businesses even use theatrical terminology when referring to some of their activities. For example, Disney parks and resorts employees are called 'cast members' and they don't serve customers, they look after 'guests'. So for Disney, service clearly is seen as a performance, one that involves a stage, performers, scripts, off-stage areas and, of course, an audience. To help you think about your service in such terms, try thinking differently about some of the things you do, and the language you use to describe it. For example, using Voss and Zomerdijk's 'five distinct design areas':

1 physical environment ('stage');
2 service employees ('actors');

3 service delivery process ('scripts');

4 fellow customers ('audience');

5 back office support ('back stage').[7]

To reinforce the notion of service as a performance, Voss and Zomerdijk refer to other interesting research from the behavioural sciences. This suggests that when trying to create memorable performances, we should remember what customers remember. Namely: beginnings; peaks and conclusions. Specifically:

- Beginnings – customers tend to remember how things begin, so try to start on a high.

- Peaks – it's high points throughout the service that are particularly memorable, contributing to overall customer satisfaction levels.

- Conclusions – ends matter even more than beginnings so it's important to concentrate on good goodbyes!

So making your service memorable means starting with a good impression, creating high points and then, most of important of all, ending well. But don't make the mistake of over-emphasis on any one of these aspects. Evidence suggests that customers say they're more satisfied with services that do well in all three phases.

Some businesses are clearly acting on these insights. Perhaps unsurprisingly, one used by Voss and Zomerdijk to illustrate their arguments is Virgin Atlantic. Building on their work, here's how you might describe the key features of Virgin's customer experience:

When you travel Upper class with Virgin you begin a journey that is a 'glamorous experience'. Gone is the usual check-in. Upper class customers can be picked up by a limousine and chauffeured to the airport. Not for you the queues and delays at check-in. Instead you are whisked away to a unique drive-thru check-in. You start with a memorable experience. Then the clubhouse has a wide range of services for you, from restaurant and bar to a spa with facial and massage facilities. On board you have flatbed seats, bar, facilities to work if you have to. Plenty of peak experiences in the middle of your customer journey. Then when you arrive, Virgin again makes sure that your experience ends really well. Look out for the aptly named revivals lounge. In the words of

Virgin Atlantic: 'After a long flight, what could be better than a refreshing shower, or a freshly prepared complimentary breakfast[8] *You can freshen up with some spa treatment or have your clothes pressed for you. When you're ready to continue your journey your chauffer is awaiting you, ending on a noteworthy high.*

But let's bring you back down to earth and return to whether it's appropriate, desirable or even possible to think of your service as a show. Perhaps the quick way to address that point is to answer a question: Would people pay to come and watch your team perform?

Would people pay to see your team perform?

This may seem a strange question to ask. Your team probably doesn't do anything that would inspire many people to come and watch. And never mind any hint of paying for the privilege! Yet asking that question might prompt you to think differently about what you do, and how you do it. It might give you cause to reflect on the quality of *performance* in your organization, rather than viewing quality from the usual perspectives. And that might not be a bad thing at all.

With this question in mind, it may surprise you to know that some organizations do just this. They routinely think about their service activities as performances. And it may surprise you even more to hear that these organizations actually *do* charge people to come and see how they perform in their work. What they do, and/or how they do it, is so interesting that other organizations come to watch, listen and learn.

One such organization is the UK-based company Happy Ltd. This is a relatively small but successful business, which started life as a provider of computer skills training. At first thought, this doesn't sound like the kind of organization people might queue up to watch in action. Yet Happy Ltd has repeatedly earned a very high ranking in surveys that list great places to work. This success has prompted Happy Ltd to diversify its operation. Alongside an expanded computer skills training division, the company has now developed a successful business, which helps other organizations become great places to work. Here's what they say about their approach:

Imagine a workplace where people are energized and motivated by being in control of the work they do. Imagine they are trusted and given freedom, within clear guidelines, to decide how to achieve their results.

Imagine they are able to get the life balance they want. Imagine they are valued according to the work they do, rather than the number of hours they spend at their desk. Wouldn't you want to work there?[9]

Henry Stewart is the engaging CEO of Happy Ltd. He is a popular corporate speaker, freely talking about how to create great places to work. Stewart has also written about how to create a happy workplace in his book, *The Happy Manifesto*. This book outlines the values he has successfully applied to his own business. He built this business around a simple principle: people work best when they're happy, so managers should focus on creating the environment were people are happy and feel good.

Another organization worth mentioning here is one we discussed in the last chapter. US-based, Zappos.com, is an established online shoe retailer. In contrast to Happy Ltd, Zappos is a very large organization. So large that in 2009 Amazon bought it for $1.2 billion. Zappos is known for its great customer service, free shipping and very favourable returns policy. However, it's also well-known for something else. Zappos has such a distinctive organizational culture that this company too has diversified from its original business activity. The company now offers services to help other organizations create their own version of the Zappos 'WOW' culture. These services include a dedicated 'Zappos Insights' website, a 'Zappos Tour Experience', and a range of training events. As Zappos goes from strength to strength, it seems that large numbers of people clearly *are* prepared to watch that company perform! Zappos Insights, has grown to be so successful that it now operates as its own legal entity, within the parent Zappos company. 'So many businesses not only wanted to learn the 'what,' they wanted to learn 'how' we do what we do.'[10]

Tony Hsieh is the successful CEO of Zappos and, like Henry Stewart, he too has written a book. Interestingly, both of these successful businessmen have chosen to write books about happiness at work. Hsieh's book, *Delivering Happiness*, makes the case that happiness *can* be a profitable business model. Originally Hsieh set out to create a business that, first and foremost, delivered outstanding customer service and experience. Now, he says, the business delivers happiness – for their customers and their employees.

So why have we dwelt on these two examples in a book on leadership? Well, because there is much to be learnt from the way these two very different companies work. Henry Stewart of Happy Ltd and Tony Hsieh of

Zappos have demonstrated some uncommon leadership. And in the process, they have made the way they run their businesses clear for all to see. But they have done more than just attract attention. They've managed to build part of their business on the demand for watching other teams and people perform at work. Would you be willing to invite other businesses to come and see how you do things? And if they did, what do you think they'd say? Take a closer look at the examples set by Stewart and Hsieh. Then consider what you might need to do in order to get visitors queuing (and paying) to watch your teams perform!

Walking the talk

Arguably, there is no greater sign of a leader's commitment than when actions back up words. Conversely, there is no greater disconnect than when leaders' words don't match their actions. As Stephen Covey says in *The Seven Habits of Highly Effective People*, 'You can't talk your way out of something you behaved your way into.'[11]

For many organizations there are gaps to be bridged. Gaps between the present and the desired future, or between what a leader sees and what is currently happening. How can others be helped to see what a leader sees? That gap is certainly addressed by what leaders 'say' but more than anything it needs to be bridged by what leaders do. Leading with action is about *showing* the way. *Showing* is a powerful way to lead because it:

- signals and reinforces change;

- helps to make planned changes tangible;

- creates movement and momentum;

- counteracts the tendency to lead by 'saying' (too much talk) rather than by action.

This is important because people tend to notice *what we do* as much as, if not more, than *what we say*. The ideas conveyed from making sense of the situation (seeing), begin to make even more sense as leaders begin to let these ideas take shape. However, if these ideas really are to have impact, they need to be acted on, so that they become common sense within the organization. That's why it's so critical that what leaders say is congruent with what they do.

The authenticity of action

There are many things in life that are 'caught' as much as they are 'taught' but it's easy to overlook the power of example. We tend to understand things far better when we see them being done. There is something authentic about words that match actions. But there can also be something deeply disconcerting when they don't. And in some exceptional circumstances, the results can be far worse than just disconcerting. Take Gerald Ratner as an example.

Gerald had finally made it to the top table. His retail business was one of the most successful in the UK. With 2,500 shops, it was also, at the time, the biggest jeweller in the world. Invited to speak at a private dinner, Gerald Ratner addressed some of the top directors in the country. At the peak of his success, he was speaking to some 5,000 members of the Institute of Directors, crowded into London's prestigious Royal Albert Hall. This event was the pinnacle of his profession. Some of the top business leaders in the country were there to hear what he had to say. Gerald prepared his speech, adding a couple of throw-away jokes for good measure. After all, who didn't enjoy a little bit of humour on such occasions? Indeed, many public speaking coaches would insist on it. Well, perhaps until this most infamous of business speeches!

Within a few weeks of the speech, sales in the Ratner Group were plummeting, as was the value of the business, down by £500 million. The business very nearly went bust and directors were forced to resort to a name change in order to salvage credibility, value and sales. Within a year of making his speech, Gerald Ratner, was asked to step aside and leave the business he had founded and nurtured. The name of Ratner disappeared from the high street but not from the business lexicon. There is still a healthy respect for the 'Ratner Effect' in boardrooms across the business world.

CASE STUDY   Prawn sandwiches and authenticity

Ratner made his most famous speech in 1991, with the UK in (another) economic recession. In spite of this, or perhaps because of it, Ratner was doing well – extremely well. So what could Ratner have said that so profoundly affected a relatively healthy business? Not a business on the edge of viability, his was a business that seemed stable and was growing successfully. Neither had Ratner stretched himself financially, or taken on a risky growth strategy, or expanded into new markets. Ratner was a secure, successful high-street brand. But businesses, it seems, are far less stable than we might think. So what was it that shook this organization to the core? It took just two short jokes.

The first, referred to sets of six cut-glass sherry decanters, complete with a silver serving tray. These sold for a bargain price, in the dozens of Ratners shops across the UK. 'People say how can you sell this for such a low price?' quipped Ratner happily. '... because it is total crap,' he went on, before pausing for laughter. The auditorium did indeed fill with laughter, but it was nervous and unconvincing. Then Ratner's second joke hit home. 'We even sell a pair of earrings for under £1... which is cheaper than a prawn sandwich from Marks & Spencers. But I have to say that the sandwich will probably last longer than the earrings.'[12] The rest, as they say, is history. The newspaper headlines, which followed the speech, were indignant and damning. The *Sun* led with 'ROTNERS', the *Mirror* with 'You 22-carat gold mugs' and the *Guardian* with 'Millionaire rough diamond cashes in on poor taste'.[13]

No longer synonymous with cut-price, bargain jewellery, the name Ratner is now more identified with classic business gaffes. Not many people realize that Ratner has since overcome this high-profile calamity. He built and sold a successful fitness business before going on to develop another jewellery business, this time online rather than on the high street. But in 'doing a Ratner', he will no doubt always be remembered for those few minutes, and those two jokes. This story has been widely used to highlight the importance both of respecting your customers, and of not taking them for granted. Or worse still, of suggesting that you are taking them for a ride. Yet it does more than that. It also reinforces the underpinning rule that words must match actions, and vice versa.

There is no doubt that Ratners offered value for money. The company's business success was longstanding and built on solid foundations. Yet these few, glib words from the CEO didn't match the reality of the business. They gave no sense of a business that sourced good value products with a determination to offer them at affordable prices. Instead, the words gave the impression of a complete disconnect. Nothing changed physically with the products in Ratner's shops, but they were devalued overnight. This wasn't just because of Ratner's ill-chosen words, there was much more at play here. It was because those words created a disconnect between him and his products, and stripped both of their authenticity in the eyes of his customers. We all know and sense when someone is being authentic, we know it when we see and hear it. Authenticity resonates. But, unfortunately for Gerald Ratner, we also know when it doesn't!

The search for coffee, books and tax

Mistakes such as Ratner's may seem almost unbelievable but they are far from isolated incidents. To this day, sound business reputations can be easily damaged, especially when people perceive that disconnect between word and deed. Even the biggest organizations aren't totally safe from at least some damage, when 'talk' and 'walk' don't match.

In the UK, there has recently been a public outcry over very large and successful businesses that seem to be paying little or no corporation tax. None of this is illegal, but given the relative financial pain faced by the population because of a persistent economic recession, it's not surprising the public weren't too happy. Perhaps the public also senses that disconnect between words and action. Executives from some of these companies have had to explain why they seem to be saying one thing yet, in the eyes of the UK public, they're clearly doing something else.

Margaret Hodge, chair of a UK parliamentary Public Accounts Committee, inquired into corporate tax avoidance. She reflected on Google's position on its UK tax liability. She pulled no punches when suggesting that Google were being 'devious, calculated and, in my view, unethical'. Referring to Google's corporate motto, Hodge went on to say: 'You are a company that says you 'do no evil'. And I think that you do do evil.'[14]

And Google aren't the only multi-national giant to cause a storm in a tea-cup. Well, coffee cup! According to Reuters,[15] over a three-year period, coffee giant Starbucks didn't pay any UK corporation tax at all. Although its UK sales reached £398 million in 2011,[16] the company's corporation tax liability for that year was zero. In fact, the company had only reported taxable profit once during the 15 years of operation in the UK. This was in rather stark contrast to the UK-owned Costa Coffee, which turned over £377 million and paid £15 million in corporation tax. And a recent BBC report revealed that it's not just Google and Starbucks under scrutiny in such matters. The global internet giant Amazon 'had sales in the UK of £3.35 billion in 2011, but only reported a 'tax expense' of £1.8 million.'[17]

So how can expanding businesses with multi-national corporate backing and excellent sales figures, make a tax loss? And with no suggestion of illegality? In the case of Starbucks, it was done by taking advantage of perfectly legal tax loopholes. By paying other parts of the Starbucks business, usually situated in more favourable tax regimes, for licence rights, etc., the UK business was able to minimize profit or even show a loss. But the issue here is one of authenticity. Take a quick look at the Starbucks mission statement and the anomaly with its corporate tax arrangements becomes apparent. Starbucks states that its mission is, 'to inspire and nurture the human spirit – one person, one cup and one neighbourhood at a time.'[18] In explaining the company's commitment to the neighbourhoods in which their cafés are based, Starbucks says:

> *We can be a force for positive action – bringing together our partners, customers, and the community to contribute every day. Now we see that our responsibility – and our potential for good – is even larger. The world is looking to Starbucks to set the new standard. We will lead.*

This is another clear example of that disconnect between the talk and the walk. Although in this case, there have been steps to bridge that gap. In a bid to redress the bad publicity, Starbucks paid £5 million in UK corporation tax, with the promise to pay another £5 million later the same year. 'We listened to our customers in December and so decided to forgo certain deductions which would make us liable to pay £10 million in corporation tax this year and a further £10 million in 2014'.[19]

Regardless of public outcries, it could be argued that these businesses are doing what they are expected to do. In fact they could argue that it's their duty to find the best ways to make a profitable return for their shareholders. They are simply using the fact that they are big multi-nationals to their advantage. Why not manage their operations so that their tax burden is shifted to countries with more favourable tax regimes? As they rightly point out, they don't make the tax laws, governments do. This is what Google UK boss Matt Brittin had to say on the subject: 'Google plays by the rules set by politicians; the only people who really have choices are politicians who set the tax rates.'[20]

Of course these organizations can point to numerous ways in which they make a very real and considerable contribution in the communities in which they operate. Yet their values and vision statements, and their notion of being ethical contributors to society, clearly jar with public perception on the issue. And it's difficult to support their case when the public's notion of fairness seems to be so at odds with their tax practices. Especially during such a challenging period for the countries and communities within which they work. Many people are asking why, with austerity biting, are the biggest businesses able to pay the lowest contributions?

Does this point to a changing public focus on organizations and their leadership? It certainly feels that way, following the crisis of leadership in the financial business community, most notably the banking sector. Now that leaders in these organizations are having their ethics, integrity and motives challenged by the public, are we seeing a similar disconnect with big business more broadly? As we shall see shortly, this disconnect has in turn prompted a re-think of leadership, with an emphasis on such ideas as authentic leadership.

The UK's BBC[21] recently quoted the director-general of the Confederation of British Industry. John Cridland agreed that the heart of the debate comes down to fairness.

> *A company may be making good revenues but pay lower amounts of tax for completely legitimate business reasons. But if it's doing this by using so-called 'black-box' arrangements, where transactions are designed for no commercial purpose at all, other than to avoid tax, then the CBI does not condone it, even if it is legal.*

Starbucks is not alone in discovering just how much perception matters. There is evidence of an emerging need for leaders in businesses to be 'authentic', true to their mission statements, with actions matching words, and demonstrating a sense of fairness and integrity. But important as this may be for organizations, it's also crucial for individuals. It applies to anyone with leadership responsibility within organizations. But how can we do this? Well one key to being an authentic leader is being true to yourself. We are all different, with diverse strengths, so to be authentic is to be yourself – using your strengths to help you lead, and to improve yourself. '… to be a more effective leader, you must be yourself – more – with skill.'[22]

Of course, being authentic is not always easy. As we have seen, it is often built upon the small things we do.

> *We are what we repeatedly do. Excellence, then, is not an act, but a habit.*

> *(Aristotle)*

So how can we make authenticity more a part of how we lead? If Aristotle has a point then we need to take a good look at what we are doing. Remember the argument made by Edgar Schein, that leaders create a culture. And what's the best way do this? Lead by showing what you pay attention to – people *notice* what leaders spend their time on. And perhaps the best place to begin is by taking a good look in the mirror.

Mirror leadership

As this chapter is about how leaders *show* the way, it's timely to think about the power of mirrors to help improve leadership skills. Perhaps the most obvious use for a mirror is to ensure we look good but, worthwhile though that may be, mirror leadership goes far deeper than helping us to keep up appearances. Here we consider three ways for leaders to think about mirrors. Mirror leadership can mean:

- Looking in a mirror – taking a good, objective look at yourself.

- Being a mirror – setting the example you want others to follow.

- Building a satisfaction mirror – so that positive actions and attitudes can be replicated.

Looking in the mirror

We ended the last section with a quote from two UK academics, Rob Goffee and Gareth Jones: '... to be a more effective leader, you must be yourself – more – with skill.' This was taken from their provocatively titled book, *Why Should Anyone Be Led By You?* The book was based on a question the two London Business School academics have asked countless managers and leaders. It's a good question to ask!

Interestingly, the strap-line to Goffee and Jones's book is, 'What it takes to be an authentic leader'. To a large extent, the idea of authentic leadership has gained prominence as a reaction to the crisis of leadership prompted by the global financial crisis. This has resulted in deep and widespread misgivings across society, prompting questions about the integrity, ethics and motives of business leaders.

Authentic (and ethical) leadership can be seen as part of a values-based approach to leadership. This requires leaders to develop their self-awareness in such a way that they understand the impact of their behaviour on those around them. So authentic leaders are those who have a good 'moral compass', and are capable of both self-awareness and of understanding the impact they have on other people. Such leaders develop 'an understanding of self, including strengths, weaknesses, values, drivers and how all of these affect behavior and outcomes'.[23]

So what better way to reflect on your self-awareness than by looking in the mirror? Of course this might be a good place to start but it's not necessarily the easiest. As anyone who has tried some serious introspection, an objective look in a mirror can be more revealing than you think. But it will certainly be worth the effort. Mirror leadership means asking yourself questions, such as:

- How do others see you?

- How self-aware are you? How well do you understand what motivates you, and why you do what you do?

- How do your actions and attitudes affect those around you?

Once you've begun to look at yourself, and to provide your own answers to some of the questions, think about asking other people. Seek out the opinions of people you value and respect. Ask them for their honest views about the questions above, and whether you fit the bill as an authentic or ethical leader.

Being a mirror – golden rules and insufficient mandates

Just as important as looking in a mirror is the idea of leaders *being* a mirror, by setting the examples that they want others to follow. This can be especially useful where leaders are trying to deal with problems or instigate change. So thinking of yourself as a mirror may help you make positive changes within your organization, and to encourage the behaviour you *want or expect* to see. What does this mean in practice? Well, there is nothing wrong or old-fashioned in leading by example. The golden rule applies as much in organizations as it does elsewhere in life: 'Do unto others as you would have them do unto you.'

This approach to mirror leadership, reflecting what you wish to see in others, is particularly important in the context of change. This quote from Confucius expresses a variant of the golden rule: 'What you do not wish for yourself, do not do to others.' Or, as Eleanor Roosevelt once argued, in her typically straightforward manner: 'It is not fair to ask of others what you are not willing to do yourself.'

To do so is unfair but there is another, related reason why such leadership approaches are likely to fail – the principle of insufficient mandate. This expression is much less well-known than the golden rule, but perhaps just as powerful. It was first coined by Reg Revans, the founder of 'action learning' who argued that: 'Those unable to change themselves cannot change those around them.'[24]

This highlights a key challenge for all leaders involved in trying to implement change. If we ourselves are not willing to be changed, then how can we have sufficient mandate to ask for change in others?

Perhaps mirror leadership also means using the mirror to look for evidence that we ourselves are being changed by the situations we encounter. This can be especially useful in ensuring that such change is for the better! So let's look at an example, based on findings published in the *Journal of Service Research*,[25] of how mirror leadership might be put to good use. In a situation where a leader is trying to create a truly customer-focused organization, the following actions by senior managers would be crucial:

- Putting an enthusiastic emphasis on quality of service and customer relations, with occasional direct interventions.

- Spending time visiting customers, listening eagerly for customer points of view, and insisting that colleagues do the same.

- Placing an emphasis on customer needs and requirements, and embedding this into strategic reviews.

In doing so, managers and leaders in this organization would be seen acting in a way that was consistent with the desired change. They would also then mirror the change of attitude and behaviour expected of everyone in the organization.

The mirror of satisfaction

Is there a link between employee engagement and customer satisfaction? If you were to ask Henry Stewart or Tony Hsieh that question there would be only one answer. We would go even further by suggesting there is more than a link. Managed properly, each can mirror the other, leading to a virtuous circle, or a mirror of satisfaction. To begin with, listen to how Hsieh explains his approach at Zappos:

> *Over the years, the number one driver of our growth at Zappos has been repeat customers and word of mouth. Our philosophy has been to take*

most of the money we would have spent on paid advertising and invest it into customer service and the customer experience instead, letting our customers do the marketing for us through word of mouth.[26]

Does the Hsieh approach really pay off? It would certainly seem so as 75 per cent of Zappos sales come from repeat business. Not only that, repeat customers order 2.5 times over the next 12 months. What's more they spend more with a higher average order size.[27]

Zappos aren't spending the lion's share of their marketing on advertising to attract new customers. Instead they are growing their business by focusing on existing customers, who spend more with them, and who become their best advocates. But what's really different about the Zappos approach is the lengths to which they will go to maintain or develop their customer relationships. For example, if your organization couldn't supply something to a customer because you were out of stock, what would you do? Apologize? Try to sell them something else? Offer them a late or discounted delivery? All of these might be standard responses but how many organizations would advise the customer to go to a competitor, *after* taking the trouble to ensure they had the item in stock? Not many!

Another example of us using the telephone as a branding device is what happens when a customer calls looking for a specific style of shoes in a specific size that we're out of stock on. In those instances, every rep is trained to research at least three competitors' web sites, and if the shoe is found in stock to direct the customer to the competitor. Obviously, in those situations, we lose the sale. But we're not trying to maximize each and every transaction. Instead, we're trying to build a lifelong relationship with each customer, one phone call at a time.

In their influential book, *The Service Profit Chain*, James Heskett, Earl Sasser and Leonard Schlesinger make a point which goes some way towards explaining the success of Zappos. They state that for over a decade, the private sector (particularly the service industry) has demonstrated the link between employee engagement, customer satisfaction and financial results. Heskett and his co-authors go even further, making this telling claim: 'Show us an operating unit with higher employee satisfaction than another and we can predict with a high degree of reliability that its customers will also be more satisfied.'[28]

And there is strong evidence that such a relationship is not confined to the private sector. Ralph Heintzman and Brian Marson built their research into the Canadian public sector on the work of Heskett and his colleagues. Even

FIGURE 3.2 The mirror of satisfaction

in this sector, Heintzman and Marson found a strong link, between employee engagement and customer satisfaction. They concluded that: 'The two-way link between employee satisfaction and client satisfaction is so strong that it has been called the "satisfaction mirror"... employee satisfaction yielded the most consistent information about customer satisfaction'.[29]

Their findings illustrate the satisfaction mirror, our third element of mirror leadership. Most notably they found that engaged employees and customer satisfaction is a two-way mirror. Engaged employees feed customer satisfaction, and satisfied customers improve the engagement of employees. The satisfaction mirror suggests a reciprocal and mutual reinforcement – a virtuous circle of engagement. So leaders would do well to think about the importance of these findings. Spending time fostering a sense of engagement within the organization will reap considerable rewards in customer satisfaction. And being a virtuous circle, this will be mirrored in reciprocal benefits amongst staff engagement. A win-win situation for any leader! But just how engaged are your staff and how do they show it? One key indicator is what they say about the job when they're not at work. Are they proud to be an employee or pleased not to be there! In the next section we'll look at some surprising findings about what people say about their organizations.

Would you recommend your service/organization to your friends?

This is an interesting question but not just because of what the answer says about you and your organization. It also indicates the link between staff engagement with the organization, and their willingness to be advocates of its services. Why does that matter? It's because there is credible research evidence to suggest that more engaged staff deliver much better services, with higher resultant levels of customer satisfaction. This is borne out by a challenging report for the UK's National Health Service, which found that: 'Patient satisfaction is significantly higher in [Hospital] Trusts with higher levels of employee engagement.'[30]

Heintzman and Marson's research into the Canadian public sector found that employee engagement scores accounted for 20 per cent of the difference in service satisfaction scores. In general, service satisfaction scores improved by one point when employee engagement increased by approximately two points.

But what is employee engagement? One report for the UK's National Health Service uses the following three perspectives:

1 Motivation (intrinsic – dedication and energy).

2 Involvement (contributing to decisions).

3 Advocacy (recommending your organization as a place to work or to receive a service from).[31]

These have been developed and adapted by the NHS, from an established body of research into engagement. So which of these perspectives do you think has the greatest impact on customer satisfaction? According to the report, the evidence is quite clear – advocacy:

> *Patient satisfaction is significantly higher in trusts with higher levels of employee engagement. The main driver for this is the 'advocacy' element of engagement, which has by far the highest correlation with patient satisfaction.[32]*

When employees are advocates of their organization, then customers tend to be more satisfied. So in order to capitalize on the power of the satisfaction mirror, the fast-track route is to focus on employee engagement.

Mirrors can be very powerful. They can help leaders show the way from several perspectives. Mirror leadership can tell you more about yourself, it can exemplify behaviour and attitudes, and it can illustrate a virtuous circle of employee and customer engagement.

The stonecutter revisited

So far we have discussed some interesting ideas on how to do the common things uncommonly well. We started with the impact of small acts, then moved on to something much bigger – a bold decision to start a business, simply because you think you can do better than the opposition. We've discussed the value in thinking of your business as a performance, highlighting two organizations where people pay to see how they work. To do this, inviting others into your organization, you need to be confident that you 'walk the talk'. This introduced a fundamental principle for all leaders who want to show the way – the need for authenticity. Leaders must walk the talk or risk paying the price of disconnection, so dramatically paid by Gerald Ratner. All of which led us to some thoughts about the power of mirrors, as tools to check authenticity and to promote that most precious of relationships – employee engagement and customer satisfaction.

In this second part of the chapter we'll get to grips with *why* we do what we do at work. We'll approach this by considering three very different ways people tend to *think* about work, and the impact this has on how we *feel* about work. Then we'll look at some practical ways to help you do the common things uncommonly well. We'll begin by returning to a story we told you earlier.

I am building another cathedral

Our second version of the stonecutter story is a version told by Peter Drucker. As one might expect from a thinker of his stature, Drucker's interpretation draws out lessons that go well beyond the obvious. In Drucker's version, when asked what they were doing, the first stonecutter replied: 'I am making a living'. The second kept on hammering while he said:

'I am doing the best job of stone cutting in the entire country.'

The third stonecutter, when asked the same question said: 'I am building a cathedral.'

As with the earlier version, the first stonecutter knew what he wanted to get from his work, and was doing so. He was giving a fair day's work for a fair day's pay. The third stonecutter obviously had a positive attitude to his work, perhaps because he saw the bigger picture. But what about the second stonecutter? Drucker suggested this was a potential problem area, perhaps the opposite of the third stonecutter's view of the bigger picture. Here was someone focusing on his or her own narrow view of work. A desire to do 'the best job of stone-cutting' was perhaps laudable but could also be to the detriment of the project as a whole. Having a functional or professional view may have been at the expense of the overall contribution to the task in hand or to the organization.[33]

But what do Drucker's lessons mean to us in general terms? Perhaps it's worth reflecting on how we see ourselves at work. Try asking these questions of your own attitude to work:

- Has work become simply a means of earning a living?

- Are we too focused on our individual performance or achievements?

- Do we have a sense of the bigger picture in what we do?

But I'm not building a cathedral!

Of course, that's all well and good if you're leading people who are creating something as rare, great and noble as a cathedral. But what if they're not? What if they're cleaning floors, or sweeping streets, or serving at a checkout? As it happens, Amy Wrzesniewski, a professor of business at New York University, has asked just these kinds of questions. In speaking to people working in all sorts of jobs and organizations, she found some very surprising results.

Crafting a calling

At the beginning of this chapter we found a dinner-lady whose job was to prepare and serve food for children at school. Yet that doesn't appear to be how she defined her work. Leaving a note for the little boy suggests that she saw her work as more than simple food service. Did that one, simple, caring act reveal that she viewed her work as more than just a job?

How do you see your work?

The stonecutter story revealed three different responses to how those men saw their work. One thought he was simply earning a day's pay. The second thought he was cutting stones. The third thought he was building a cathedral. Each indicated a very different view of the workplace and his role in it. Wrzesniewski[34] and other writers have tended to distinguish between three kinds of 'work orientation'. These are people who see their work as:

- A job – earning a day's pay
- A career – such as stonecutters, cutting stones
- A calling or vocation – building a cathedral

You may do a job just to earn a weekly pay cheque. Perhaps you're not looking for other rewards and it's simply a way to support yourself or your family. Or maybe you do it because it enables you to do other things in your life, such as leisure interests, study or community work. Your job may be an interim step until you find something else, or a necessity, which you feel you can't leave at the moment.

Feeling you're engaged in a career, rather than just a job, suggests a more personal and committed investment in work. You'll probably (but not necessarily) also be keen to achieve promotion, status indicators and increased salary. You'll almost certainly be interested in personal and professional development.

However, when it comes to a calling, you'll have a passionate commitment to your work for its own sake. You'll probably be doing what you love, or seeing how what you do contributes to the greater good. Like the third stonecutter, you may feel you're building something of social worth. Being engaged in a calling tends to be fulfilling in its own right.

Thinking about these 'work orientations' may help you to think differently about your workplace. However, wouldn't it be better, in an ideal world, to do something we really loved for a living? To pursue a calling?

Can you make your work more like a calling?

Some argue that we can regard any job as a calling if we re-frame how we see it. Perhaps this is what the dinner-lady did, when serving the schoolboy in our packed-lunch story. This is one of the surprising findings that Amy Wrzesniewski discovered when she interviewed cleaners at a hospital. Whilst she found that many only regarded their work as a job, others saw the greater good in what they did. They viewed their work as making a vital contribution to the well-being of sick people, perhaps even considering their work as a calling. And it wasn't necessarily the nature of the job that determined such a perception. Surprisingly, Wrzesniewski also found doctors who didn't see their work in this light.[35] Some regarded their work as simply a job, perhaps contrary to the expectation that such people would be most likely to view their work as a calling. So, Wrzesniewski found that it's not the work you are doing that matters, it's the way you view it. Regardless of whether you are curing cancer or polishing bedpans, it's still possible to see what you do as a calling rather than as a job or chore.

Re-framing work – the business benefit

The Royal Automobile Club (RAC) is one of the UK's leading roadside assistance companies. But if you think RAC patrolmen fix cars, then you might be in for a surprise. The RAC is one of five leading companies included in Professor Robert Johnson's report for the Institute of Customer Service. Johnson and his team from Warwick Business School conducted research into how some of the world's best companies manage to deliver service excellence. Based on interviews with frontline staff, the report clearly illustrates the importance of how they view their work. Consider this typical response from an RAC patrolman: 'That is the difference – we class the customer first. The customer is first, not the car. I think that is the secret to our success – we are treating the person, not the vehicle. Everybody is a trained mechanic so everyone can treat the vehicle but what matters is how you deal with the person.'[36]

The benefit to the business is that service excellence is delivered. And the key to that? Front-line staff who view their work differently. What's also significant in Johnson's report is that he found similar responses from staff in five very different service organizations. When asked how they would describe their jobs, staff in high-performing, service organizations all saw their jobs in exactly the same way – helping people. What makes all the difference is the way in which they frame and interpret their jobs.

Uncommon sense in practice

This chapter is about showing the way to doing the common things uncommonly well. And this means taking action, so in this next section we'll think of some insights and tips to help leaders do just that – put ideas into action. We'll discuss some ideas that, although perhaps common, often aren't practised particularly well. These are approaches that require neither capital investment nor commitment to significant spending. These approaches are wholly within the power and remit of leaders and better still, cost little or nothing to use. And despite offering a competitive advantage, these ideas don't have patent or copyright protection inhibiting their use. Does that sound too good to be true? Possibly, but we prefer to think of it as simply doing the common things uncommonly well.

Learning from mistakes or leading with successes?

If you want to improve performance, which of these might be more helpful: being told what you've done wrong or being told what you're doing right? That's the question sports psychologist Dr Daniel Kirschenbaum set about answering in a fascinating experiment with a group of bowlers.

Kirschenbaum made video recordings of the group's bowling techniques then divided the group into two. One group viewed an edited version of the recording, which only highlighted good bowling techniques. They were advised to observe what was working well, and to build on that. The second group watched another version of the tape, which contained only images of poor bowling style. This group were asked to take note of what they were doing wrong, and to make improvements. Both groups showed some improvement to their technique but which group improved the most – those who learned from their mistakes or those who learned from successful performance? Interestingly, those bowlers who viewed examples of proper bowling techniques showed significant improvement in bowling scores, far more than the other group. 'The evidence...' Kirschenbaum argued:

> ... suggests that performance often improves when people believe they will succeed (positive expectancies), and when they keep track of examples of their successes (positive self-monitoring). Positive expectancies and positive self-monitoring generally improve performance when the tasks being performed are difficult and poorly mastered.[37]

However, Kirschenbaum did qualify his findings when conducting a similar experiment which found comparable improvements to golf swings.[38] When we are performing tasks which are easy, or which we're good at, he found it was actually better to focus on the negatives, rather than the positives. On these occasions, it's more helpful for people to monitor their relative ineffectiveness, with a focus on improving what was done poorly.

Given that qualification to some interesting research observations, what can leaders learn from this? It certainly begs some thought-provoking questions. Could it be that the route to more effective performance improvement lies in a focus on strengths and successes? This would certainly seem to be the case where complex or difficult activities are concerned. Although a focus on what's wrong might be appropriate for some tasks, do we have the balance right? Overall, do we focus too much on weaknesses and pointing out what is wrong, and not enough on what is right and what is working?

Do we get what we expect?

At the beginning of the chapter we asked you a question about our dinner-lady story. Did the child change his behaviour because of the way he was treated? This prompts an interesting question: To what extent people behave in the way others *expect* them to behave?

Perhaps the answer to these questions lies in the Pygmalion Effect. This well-known phenomenon was initially identified after ground-breaking research by Robert Rosenthal and Lenore Jacobson.[39] They conducted an experiment on teachers and two groups of schoolchildren. At the beginning of the experiment, the teachers were told that one group contained some (named) students, of whom they could expect better than average results. The other group contained students from whom teachers could expect standard results. It came as no surprise to the teachers that at the end of the year, the students of whom they had higher expectations did indeed perform much better than the other (control) group. Except that the results actually were surprising! That's because the researchers had misled the teachers and, in reality, both groups contained a random selection of children. So there really should have been no difference between the two sets of results. As the teachers were unaware that they were treating the two groups differently, the conclusions were both clear and profound. When teachers have higher expectations of their students, the students perform better!

Similar results have been found in organizational research.[40] In a test conducted at an Israeli army training centre, trainers were told that the group they were working with contained individuals who had already demonstrated their potential to lead. Other trainers were not given information on the (so-called) potential of their trainees. This research was published by Ross Business School professor, Dov Eden. His findings supported Rosenthal and Jacobson's work that higher expectations often result in better performance. But intriguingly his research pointed to something else. Dov Eden found that when leaders have higher expectations of those they lead, they themselves provide better leadership. In Eden's own words: 'Leaders lead best when they expect success.'[41]

Does the Pygmalion Effect work in reverse? When we have low expectations do people perform poorly? Although not as widely researched, there is evidence to support what has been called the Golem Effect. Coincidentally, one early example of this came from research conducted in another military organization, the US Air Force Academy. In two separate experiments with cadets, Wilburn Shrank[42] concluded that student performance was influenced by the 'labelling effect' of allocating them to groups ranked by perceived ability level. Shrank found that negative behaviours and poorer grades from students were the clear result of negative expectations from their instructors. There is no doubt that this effect relates equally to the workplace. Jean-François Manzoni and Jean-Louis Barsoux, two INSEAD researchers, found evidence of the 'self-fulfilling and self-reinforcing dynamic which ensues for subordinates perceived as 'lower performers'.[43]

Both Pygmalion and Golem echo the famous work of Douglas McGregor.[44] Behind his 'Theory X/Theory Y' approach to management is the notion that managers have different expectations of their staff, based on underlying assumptions. McGregor suggested that Theory X managers tend to think that people don't really want to do a good job, they only come to work for the pay cheque. Such managers will then treat their staff accordingly, being generally mistrustful and reluctant to delegate. On the other hand, managers with a Theory Y outlook tend to assume people come to work to do a great job, and that they are enthusiastic about what they do. These leaders also act in accordance with their beliefs. They generally trust people, allow them to get on with their work, delegate more often and encourage people to expand their capabilities. McGregor's characterizations may paint extreme positions but how we think about our colleagues *does* shape the way we act. And that in turn shapes how *they* tend to act in response.

So if it can be argued that Theory Y managers have higher expectations of their staff, assuming that they will perform better if empowered and trusted, there are several clear messages here:

- The greater the expectations placed on people the better they perform.

- When expectations are low so is performance.

- We get better as leaders when we have higher expectations of others.

- Your underlying assumptions about your work colleagues may be influencing workplace performance more than you think.

- Leaders can show the way forward by having the right expectations of their colleagues.

Do we get what we believe?

As we've seen, having high expectations of others not only raises their game but can also improve the leader's performance. We tend to get what we expect. But how dependent might this be on what we *believe*, about both our own capabilities and those of our colleagues? Henry Ford is reputed to have said: 'If you think you can, or you think you can't you're right.'

To what extent does our confidence in our own abilities influence how successful we are? One leading expert in this area is Albert Bandura from Stanford University. He describes one of the most pervasive mechanisms with which we influence ourselves: 'When faced with obstacles, setbacks, and failures, those who doubt their capabilities slacken their efforts, give up, or settle for mediocre solutions. Those who have a strong belief in their capabilities redouble their effort to master the challenges.'[45]

This is what academics refer to as self-efficacy. This means *affirming* a capability level but with a sense of *how strongly* the belief is held. In simple and practical terms, it means if we believe in our capability to achieve something we are far more likely to be motivated to act. But self-efficacy is not just self-belief. Simply saying something with self-confidence doesn't amount to self-efficacy. This is developed through more robust mechanisms, what Bandura refers to as *sources of self-efficacy*. The kind of confidence implied by self-efficacy is that built on realism, a firm platform from which confidence can be justified. In other words there is a good level of confidence that someone's assessment of their confidence is realistic.

So what are Bandura's four ways to build self-efficacy?[46] In order of importance, they can be summarized as: mastery, modelling, words and senses.

1 The most powerful way to build self-efficacy is through what he termed mastery experiences. Successful performance has the strongest influence on self-efficacy 'because seeing yourself succeed at a job is incontrovertible evidence of one's ability to do the job.'[47] This is best done when the tasks are challenging but achievable and require perseverance.

2 The next best thing to experiencing something yourself, is to observe success in others, especially someone you can relate to. This is referred to as modelling or vicarious success. Seeing someone you can identify with may convince you that such success is within your own grasp: 'If they can do it so can I.'

3 It's also important to hear words of assurance, asserting that you are capable of success. These are most effective when the person providing feedback also helps to structure situations so that the person is more likely to succeed (for example setting tasks that are more often achievable than likely to result in failure).

4 The least effective way to build self-efficacy is through our physiological senses. The way we respond to the threat of failure or the exhilaration of success, can help us draw inferences about our self-efficacy. If we identify certain feelings with success then when we have those feelings they are more likely to raise our perception of our self-efficacy.

It's useful to think through each of Bandura's sources of self-efficacy, firstly from your own perspective as a leader. Having confidence in your own abilities is an important leadership capability. It's equally important that such confidence comes from secure foundations. When confidence is misplaced or over-egged, perhaps even verging on arrogance, then what can quickly emerge is a lack of authenticity or authority. Secondly, building the confidence of others around you, to help them realize their potential, is equally important for any leaders. Understanding and building self-efficacy is an essential skill for any leader seeking to do the common things uncommonly well.

From expectation to efficacy

There is a clear relationship between expectations, self-efficacy and performance. Combining high expectations and self-belief will undoubtedly help raise performance but that might be easier said than done. Dov Eden argues that 'the most practicable way for a leader to create productive, self-fulfilling prophecies (Pygmalion effect) wilfully is to communicate high-performance expectations to followers, in a way that augments their self-efficacy.'[48]

Bandura's self-efficacy is not about misplaced confidence or anything bordering on arrogance. It is built on solid foundations. This view of confidence matters because, as Bandura points out:

Among the mechanisms of agency, none is more central or pervasive than people's beliefs about their capabilities to exercise control over their own level of functioning and over events that affect their lives. Efficacy beliefs influence how people feel, think, motivate themselves, and behave.[49]

If both of these quotes are true, then perhaps the first thing leaders need to consider is how they encourage the people they lead.

Praising is amazing

Kind words do not cost much. They never blister the tongue or lips. They make other people good-natured. They also produce their own image on men's souls, and a beautiful image it is.

(Blaise Pascal)

Referring to our dinner-lady story one more time, there is a final practical lesson to be learned from the tale. It's clear that, regardless of how positive the incident, nothing more would have come of it without the head teacher's action. By taking the time and effort to speak to her team, she demonstrated one of the most powerful of leadership actions. Praising people is one of the simplest yet most under-used motivational tools available to managers and leaders. How strange that regardless of the benefits of praise, and the relative ease with which it can be applied, it seems to happen so rarely. In essence, giving praise is a straightforward, two-step process. It's not, as they say, rocket science!

FIGURE 3.3   Praising is amazing

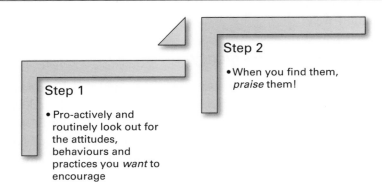

Step 2

•When you find them,
praise them!

Step 1

• Pro-actively and
routinely look out for
the attitudes,
behaviours and
practices you *want* to
encourage

Don't be quick to blame and slow to praise. Typically, praise for what is done well is far more powerful than criticism of what is done poorly. Making the simple act of praising a part of your routine is a prime example of doing the common things uncommonly well. If you want to see performance levels in your organization increase, then learning how to praise effectively is one of the simplest and most powerful things you can do. Of course, however simple the essence of praise may be, praising effectively may not always be so easy. For example, although it needs to be given regularly, it must also be done appropriately and in proportion to what has been achieved. Otherwise its value may eventually be diluted, or it may lose its (and with it your own) credibility and validity. Here are some suggestions to help you make effective praising a part of your daily routine:

● Proactively try to 'catch' people doing the things you want to reinforce.

● Immediately inform people of why you're praising them and what you value in their actions, attitudes or behaviours.

● Be specific about the reasons for the praise.

● Make your praise public.

● Be fair, consistent and even-handed.

● Praise often but appropriately.

● Mean it.

● Encourage others to recognize and praise the people they work with.

● Start praising people today!

Entrepreneur Tim Waterstone has some strong views on the value of praise. Founder of Waterstones, the UK's leading high-street book store business, he has clearly grasped the importance of doing common things uncommonly well: 'I believe that the mindset that allows you to spend your working life thanking and congratulating people rather than being unpleasant to them is the mainstay of good leadership.'[50]

Feedback: the fuel of performance

It's good to know your boss is pleased with progress but when working towards a particular goal, what really helps performance is to know some specifics. Praise is encouraging but we also like to know *how* we're doing and *why*. So if praising is amazing, feedback is the fuel of performance. There is much research which points to the motivational benefits of giving feedback on how people are performing. But not just any kind of feedback.

To be really effective feedback needs to be timely and it needs to be specific. It is also a good idea to separate feedback that is motivational from that which is corrective or formative. That means the so-called 'praise sandwich', a popular way of giving negative feedback sandwiched between two positive comments, is off the menu! If you mix the two, there is a natural tendency for people to only hear what they might perceive as criticism. The same could be said about another popular feedback technique: the 'but' sandwich where praise is given, then followed by criticism introduced with a 'but'. It's been jokingly said that you should ignore everything that's said before the word 'but', as that's when the real message starts!

So, giving feedback might seem a common-sense thing to do, but the secret of showing the way is to do the common things uncommonly well. And that might mean practicing the art of effective feedback. We'll explore the impact of positive and negative feedback more deeply in Chapter 5 but for now, here are some tips on how to make feedback the fuel of your uncommonly good performance:

- Praising is amazing but people also want to know *how* they are doing, and *why*.

- Positive feedback is crucial to increasing motivation, so practice praising more than criticizing.

- The reason for giving feedback is to motivate and to improve performance.

- Separate motivational feedback from corrective feedback.

- Do not underestimate the power of motivational feedback.

- Make your corrective feedback future-oriented.

- Make your feedback specific and clear.

- Avoid feedback overload.

Giving effective feedback is a good example of doing the common things uncommonly well, but a chapter about showing the way can't end there. It's perhaps more appropriate to end with advice on how to take steps towards a vision, even when this may seem daunting or beyond reach. Curiously, one of the biggest barriers to leadership can be *too much* focus on the bigger picture.

Small steps and next-mile leadership?

It's one thing to set a challenging, worthwhile goal, it's quite another to achieve it. Sometimes, what we desire can seem too far away or just too hard to reach. In a counter-intuitive way, what may be needed is a focus on the small steps that can get you on your way.

During the Second World War, author and correspondent Eric Sevareid was forced to parachute from a damaged transport plane into the jungle on the Burma-India border. Sevareid and the other survivors knew that any rescue attempt would take several weeks so they had no option but to start walking. They faced a daunting task – tropical heat, monsoon rains and a painful, 140-mile march over mountainous terrain. The torturous route to civilised India seemed almost impassable – the dream of salvation almost impossible. As Sevareid recounts:

> *In the first hour of the march I rammed a boot nail deep into one foot: by evening I had bleeding blisters... on both feet. Could I hobble 140 miles? Could the others, some in worse shape than I, complete such a distance? We were convinced we could not. But we could hobble to that ridge; we could make the next friendly village for the night. And that, of course, was all we had to do...*

This story is adapted from David Schwartz's: *Magic of Thinking Big*.[51] Although taken from a classic self-help book, the story is also useful for any leader trying to do the common things uncommonly well. Taking things one step at a time is common sense but it's all too easy for leaders to lose sight of how important that is, especially when they are charged with turning a bigger vision into a practical reality. In such cases, it's easy for people to feel that the current reality is hopelessly far from your vision. The bigger the perceived gap between reality and vision, the more likelihood of tension until something has to give. Either your vision or your reality has to change. You can lower your vision and make your goals less challenging, and perhaps less worthwhile. Or you could raise your own game, bringing yourself closer to your goals.

Too often we lower our vision, convinced that the task is just too much. Yet, in reality all we have to do is take things step by step. Perhaps we need to be more like Eric Sevareid and just get to that next ridge or that next village, day by day. Walk that next mile. Central to Schwartz's argument is the importance of belief. Having well-founded confidence can affect motivation and the willingness to persevere, even in the face of big changes or seemingly intractable problems. If you believe something is possible, your mind gets to work for you – finding a way to achieve it. Leading the way with small steps, or 'next-mile leadership', can be one way of building that confidence.

Whereas leadership is often thought of in terms of strategic vision, there will be times when leaders need to adopt a more tactical approach. Next-mile leadership may be needed when your focus needs to be on achieving smaller goals, which then build towards your overall aim. It helps to build belief in what can be done by focusing on short steps, taken one at a time. This is a very effective way of overcoming barriers, which sometimes arise from too much emphasis on the bigger picture, or the long haul. Next-mile leadership puts much more emphasis on the importance of reaching the next achievable goal. What may seem impossible, or extremely difficult, is less so when you break it down to the next step, the next mile. Of course, stretching and worthwhile goals are important and should not be easily given up. Yet, when facing serious difficulty, it's all too easy to aim for less. Next-mile leadership is a useful way to counter this tendency, encouraging shorter, purposeful steps towards goals that can be more easily achieved.

How do you become a next-mile leader? Awareness of the need for a more tactical approach to leadership is the first step, so keep your eyes out for too much emphasis on bigger issues or problems. Developing your own ability to take the next mile on your journey is only the start. Think about how you can encourage next-mile focus in your staff, as and when that's needed. Remind them that each day, each step may be all that's needed to get them closer to these goals. This can become a powerful means of building self-belief and confidence. Reminding people that ambitious goals are usually achieved by hitting smaller targets will help them both believe and succeed.

 People become really quite remarkable when they start thinking that they can do things. When they believe in themselves they have the first secret of success.

(Norman Vincent Peale).

Big leaps and long-jump leadership?

Taking a series of small steps can help us to bridge the gap between bigger visions and current reality but taking the *right* steps can lead us to big gains. Focusing on the best small steps to take can result in big leaps! This is the kind of leadership that we would hope to see more of – leadership that transforms things for the better, and does so in a significant way. Someone once said: 'All improvement is change, but not all change is improvement.'

Leadership should be about change that improves things – transformational change. We usually associate transformational change with radical or significant change, but what if leaders can transform situations without the upheaval of big changes? What if we thought of ways to transform outcomes by taking the right small steps? We've already discussed one example of how relatively small changes can yield big results: tipping point leadership. As we've seen, a tipping point occurs when you are able to achieve major change by altering a few small but very significant things. The New York City Transit Authority story clearly shows how taking the right small steps can gain the benefits of a big leap.

Similarly, smaller changes implemented by a large number of people can also have a significant effect. For example, the power of a positive, enthusiastic personality can be infectious to any team. When a team of people *decides* to think and act positively, the collective benefit of such a relatively small attitude change can be dramatic to the organization and customers alike.

 Never doubt that a small group of thoughtful, concerned citizens can change the world. Indeed it is the only thing that ever has.

(Margaret Mead, 2000)

But there is also no doubting that sometimes what's really needed is a genuine 'big leap'. This may come when paradigm or fundamental change is needed, such as the critical situation facing Apple when Steve Jobs re-took the reins in 1997. Or it may be as a result of a perceived opportunity or from a leader's own instinct, as evidenced by our earlier discussion of Sir Richard Branson's decision to start his own airline. On such occasions simply taking those small or next steps aren't enough. As former British prime minister David Lloyd George once famously said: 'Don't be afraid to take a big step when one is indicated. You can't cross a chasm in two small steps.'

Of course, in reality even big leaps require a run up! However large or fundamental the changes proposed by the likes of Jobs and Branson, they could only succeed by combining the right small steps, with the impact of a big leap. So, perhaps it's worthwhile thinking of leaders who do the common things uncommonly well as long-jumpers. Running is a common activity for most people and most of us can jump, to one extent or another. But putting it all together, so the steps are just right, and the leap at the end is well-timed and executed, means doing something uncommonly well. Could that be called 'long-jump leadership'?

In the next chapter we'll explore some more examples of small, seemingly insignificant changes that can have a big impact. The key to doing the common things uncommonly well is to have the common touch. To demonstrate the power of the common touch we'll find out how one simple act of courtesy transformed a young boy and his nation. We'll see how one small change on a sandwich barcode saved half a million pounds. And we'll also discuss a surprising insight from one well-known leader, talking about 'the best leadership I ever gave'.

Bibliography

1   Handy, C (1999) *The New Alchemists: How visionary people make something out of nothing*, New York, Random House Group

2   Branson, R (2007) *Screw It, Let's Do It: Expanded lessons in life and business*, London, Virgin Books

3   Handy, C (1999) *The New Alchemists: How visionary people make something out of nothing*, New York, Random House Group

4   Branson, R (2007) *Screw It, Let's Do It: Expanded lessons in life and business*, London, Virgin Books

5   Calder, S (2009) [accessed 24 June 2013] Branson's flights of fancy: the highs and lows of Virgin Atlantic, *The Independent* [Online] http://www

.independent.co.uk/travel/news-and-advice/bransons-flights-of-fancy-the-highs-and-lows-of-virgin-atlantic-1697795.html

6   Voss, C and L Zomerdijk (2007) Innovation in experiential services – an empirical view, in DTI (ed) *Innovation in Services* London, DTI, pp 97–134

7   ibid

8   Virgin Atlantic.com [accessed 30 June 2013] [Online] http://www.virgin-atlantic.com/gb/en/the-virgin-experience/our-clubhouses/revivals-lounge.html

9   Stewart, H (2013) *The Happy Manifesto: Make your organization a great workplace*, London, Kogan Page

10   Zappos Insights Inc (2013) [accessed 17 November 2013] *Zappos Insights* [Online] http://www.zapposinsights.com/about

11   Covey, S (1989) *The Seven Habits of Highly Effective People*, New York, Simon and Schuster

12   Institute of Directors (2013) [accessed 20 November 2013] Gerald Ratner speaking at the 1991 Institute of Directors Annual Convention [Online] http://www.youtube.com/watch?v=Nj9BZz71yQE

13   Hattenstone, S (2009) [accessed 20 November 2013] Gerald Ratner Interview, *The Guardian,* News, Business [Online] http://www.theguardian.com/business/2009/mar/07/gerald-ratner-interview

14   Bowers, S and Rajeev, S (2013) [accessed 17 November 2013] *The Guardian,* News, Technology [Online] http://www.theguardian.com/technology/2013/may/16/google-told-by-mp-you-do-do-evil

15   Bergin, T (2012) [accessed 17 November 2013] Special Report: how Starbucks avoids UK taxes, *Reuters Edition UK* [Online] http://uk.reuters.com/article/2012/10/15/us-britain-starbucks-tax-idUKBRE89E0EX20121015

16   D'Arcy, C (2012) [accessed 17 November 2013] What If You Were Taxed Like Starbucks? *Yahoo! Finance: UK & Ireland* [Online] http://uk.finance.yahoo.com/news/what-if-you-were-taxed-like-starbucks.html

17   Barford, V and Holt, G (2013) [accessed 20 June 2013] Google, Amazon, Starbucks: the rise of 'tax shaming', *BBC News Magazine* [Online] http://www.bbc.co.uk/news/magazine-20560359

18   Starbucks.co.uk/about-us/company-information/mission-statement. (2013) [accessed 17 November 2013] Starbucks Corporation. [Online] http://www.starbucks.co.uk/about-us/company-information/mission-statement

19   Starbucks pays UK corporation tax for first time since 2009 (2013) [accessed 20 June 2013] *BBC News/Politics* [Online] http://www.bbc.co.uk/news/uk-politics-23019514

20   Google's tax avoidance is called 'capitalism', says chairman Eric Schmidt (2012) [accessed 20 June 2013] The Daily Telegraph [Online] http://www

.telegraph.co.uk/technology/google/9739039/Googles-tax-avoidance-is-called-capitalism-says-chairman-Eric-Schmidt.html

21 Barford, V and Holt, G (2013) [accessed on 20 June 2013] Google, Amazon, Starbucks: the rise of 'tax shaming' *BBC News Magazine* [Online] http://www.bbc.co.uk/news/magazine-20560359

22 Jones, G and Goffee, R (2003) *The character of a Corporation: How your company's culture can make or break your business*, 2nd edn London, Profile Books Ltd

23 Lewis, R (2012) *Perspectives on Leadership in 2012 and Implications for HR*, London, CIPD

24 Revans, R W (1998) *ABC of Action Learning*, London, Lemos & Crane

25 Shah, D, Rust, R T, Parasuraman, A, Staelin, R and Day, G S (2006) The path to customer centricity, *Journal of Service Research*, **9** (2) pp 113–124

26 Hsieh, T (2010) [accessed 20 June 2013] Branding through customer service, *Huffington Post* [Online] http://www.huffingtonpost.com/tony-hsieh/branding-through-customer_b_799316.html

27 Hsieh, T (2009) [accessed on 27 June 2013] Delivering Happiness [Online] http://www.slideshare.net/hein2006/zappos-tony-hsieh-3580169

28 Heskett, J L, Sasser, W E and Schlesinger, L A (1997) *The Service Profit Chain*, New York, Simon & Schuster

29 Heintzman and Marson (2006) in Employee Engagement in the Public Sector: a review of literature, *Scottish Executive Social Research*, May 2007

30 West, M, Dawson, J, Admasachew, L and Topakas, A (2011) *NHS Staff Management and Health Service Quality: Results from the NHS staff survey and related data*, London, Department of Health

31 ibid

32 ibid

33 Drucker, P (1968) *The Practice of Management*, London, Pan Books Ltd

34 Wrzesniewski, A and Dutton, J E (2001) Crafting a job: re-visioning employees as active crafters of their work, *Academy of Management Review* **26** (2) pp 179–201

35 Wrzesniewski, A, in Achor, S (2011) *The Happiness Advantage*, London, Virgin Books

36 Johnston, R (2003) *Delivering Service Excellence: The view from the front line*, London, Institute of Customer Service

37 Kirschenbaum, D S (1987) Self-regulation of sport performance, *Medicine and Science in Sports and Exercise*, **19** (15), p 108

38 Johnston-O'Connor, E J and Kirschenbaum, D S (1986) Something succeeds like success: positive self-monitoring for unskilled golfers, *Cognitive Therapy and Research*, **10** (1)

39 Eden, D (1992) Leadership and Expectations: Pygmalion effects and other self-fulfilling prophecies in organisations, *Leadership Quarterly* **3** (4)

40 Sutton, R I and Pfeffer, J (2006) *Hard Facts Dangerous Half-Truths and Total Nonsense*, Boston, Harvard Business School Press

41 Eden, D (1992) Leadership and Expectations: Pygmalion effects and other self-fulfilling prophecies in organisations, *Leadership Quarterly* **3** (4)

42 Wilburn, R and Schrank, A (1970) Further study of the labelling effect of ability grouping, *The Journal of Educational Research*, **63** (8), pp 358–60, London, Taylor & Francis, Ltd

43 Manzoni, J F and Barsoux, J L (1998) *Inside the Golem Effect: How bosses can kill their subordinates' motivation*, Fontainebleau, INSEAD

44 McGregor, D (2006) *The Human Side of the Enterprise*, New York, McGraw-Hill

45 Bandura, A (2000) Cultivate self-efficacy for personal and organizational effectiveness in E A Locke (ed) *The Blackwell Handbook of Principles of Organizational Behavior*, pp 120–36, Oxford, Blackwell

46 ibid

47 Eden, D (1992) Leadership and Expectations: Pygmalion effects and other self-fulfilling prophecies in organisations, *Leadership Quarterly*, **3** (4)

48 ibid

49 Bandura, A (1993) Self-efficacy in cognitive development and functioning, *Educational Psychologist*, **28** (2), p 118

50 Waterstone, T (2006) *Swimming Against the Stream*, London, Pan Macmillan

51 Schwartz, D J (2006) *The Magic of Thinking Big*, London, Simon and Schuster UK Ltd

LEADING WITH SERVICE

SERVING COLLEAGUES AND CUSTOMERS THROUGH COMMON TOUCH LEADERSHIP

KEY TOPICS

- The poor aren't creditworthy.
- Upside-down leadership.
- Upside-down thinking.
- A simple thank-you.
- Talking with crowds, walking with kings.

FIGURE 4.1 Serving

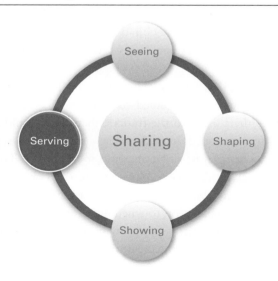

Banks don't lend to the poor. Bad debt can be hard enough to manage, even in the best of circumstances. And if there is one lesson we've learned from the 2008 banking crisis, when even the wealthy West was struggling, surely it's that the poor aren't creditworthy. Or is it? Back in the early 1970s, one man had already proved that this conventional wisdom could be turned on its head. He created a flourishing bank for the poor, in one of the world's poorest countries, in the midst of an unprecedented humanitarian and economic crisis. In doing so, this man applied uncommon sense to create a quite remarkable business. How he challenged conventional wisdom makes a resounding statement about the power of leading with service.

The poor aren't creditworthy

In 1974, Bangladesh was in the midst of a terrible famine. With no money and unable to borrow from conventional banks, the people were suffering. Seeing the plight of hardworking but impoverished villagers, economics professor Muhammad Yunus decided things needed to change. For Yunus, the economics of the poor simply did not add up. One woman he met epitomized the debt spiral that appeared so commonplace to him. She earned a living weaving beautiful baskets, which she sold back to the very trader who had lent her money for the raw materials needed to do her work. This one-sided transaction left her with barely enough money to live on. These traders kept women like this trapped in a cycle of economic dependency. Yet how could such beautiful work be worth so little? Yunus made a list of all the people in her village who were trapped in a similar spiral of debt and poverty. He found that 42 villagers had borrowed a total of $27 between them.[1] How could such a small amount of money create so much misery?

Yunus did something that was to change both his life, and that of millions of people in his country. He decided to lend that $27 to the villagers so they could repay their debts to the traders, then they would be free to sell their products for a good, fair price. 'When should they repay you?' his assistant asked. 'Whenever it is advantageous for them to sell their products,' Yunus replied. 'They don't have to pay any interest. I am not in the money business.'[2] But this was about to change. 'The excitement that was created in the village by this small action touched me deeply. I thought, 'If this little action makes so many people so happy, why shouldn't I do more of this?'[3] That simple question heralded the creation of what was to later become the Grameen Bank, a new bank for the poor of Bangladesh. Reflecting on how this experience changed his life, Professor Yunus expressed a view of work which we will come back to later in this chapter: 'In my case what began in a time of crisis became a lifelong calling. I gave up my academic position and founded a bank – a bank for the poor.'[4]

But trying to start a bank with a difference was fraught with difficulty. Yunus tried to convince his university campus bank to lend to the poor. But all he received was the same reply he was to hear many times over: the poor aren't creditworthy. So initially Yunus acted as guarantor for loans authorized by a hesitant bank manager. Although the bankers were worried about the loans, his plan worked: 'People paid back the loans on time, every time.' Echoing the Sternins' positive deviance approach, which we discussed in at the start of Chapter 1, Yunus saw what was working and backed it.

Working on trust

The Grameen Bank is not a charity but a profitable business, which charges interest and uses profits to grow its range of services. Unusually, the bank is set up as trust, with 94 per cent owned by borrowers and 6 per cent owned by the government. It pays a dividend to its owners but its purpose is very different to conventional banks. Whereas these normally aim to maximize profits, Grameen's stated aim is: 'To bring financial services to the poor, particularly women and the poorest — to help them fight poverty, stay profitable and financially sound.'[5]

If you're going to lend to the poor, many normal banking practices need to change. For example, there's no requirement to put up collateral to guarantee Grameen Bank loans, which average around $200. Yet the repayment rate for these loans is an impressive 98 per cent, especially considering that the bank even lends to beggars. What Grameen does has become known as microfinance, something that has spread around the world. How it works is very different too. Each branch of the bank is self-contained, with its own community of borrowers. This builds a relationship of trust, which encourages repayment. Grameen Bank pioneered what has also become known as solidarity lending. Grameen lends to individuals, but they have to be a part of a five-member group which benefits both bank and borrowers alike because: 'Repayment responsibility solely rests on the individual borrower, while the group and the centre oversee that everyone behaves in a responsible way and none gets into repayment problem.' The group doesn't have to guarantee the loans of its members, but because Grameen does not extend credit to a group in which a member defaults, the group as a whole works hard to ensure that they all meet their repayments. In fact they will often help each other out if one person gets into financial difficulty. There is no written contract between Grameen bank and its borrowers – the system works on trust.[6]

In 2006, Yunus and the bank he founded won the Nobel Peace Prize. By 2011, the Grameen Bank had 8 million borrowers, of which 97 per cent were women.[7] This striking statistic was no accident and it illustrated another common-sense approach that few put into action. Targeting women was an early, deliberate choice. Initially Yunus had focused on women partly as a protest against the refusal of conventional banks to lend them money, even when some applicants were relatively affluent. But he also did so because he saw women had the potential to become income earners. As it turned out, women borrowers brought much more benefit to their communities than most realized. Lending to them became a powerful way to combat poverty, as children in particular saw immediate benefit from their mothers' income.

Who is creditworthy now?

As radical as when he first started, Yunus argues that micro-financing endured the ravages of the 2008 banking crisis because, unlike the major banks, Grameen wasn't propped-up with collateral that suddenly lost its value. He believes that the crisis should be seen as an opportunity – to rethink banking. 'Nobody should be refused access to financial services. Because these services are so vital for people's self-realization, I strongly feel that credit should be given the status of a human right.'[8]

And he's got a point. In a 2009 interview with the University of Pennsylvania's Wharton School, Yunus made a provocative challenge. Thirty-three years after starting his bank for the poor, Yunus asked: 'Who is creditworthy? It is the poor who turned out to be more creditworthy than the other category of people, because microcredit programmes all over the world still function very well. Their repayment is very high, whereas the big banks and their big lending operations are [near] collapse. They are falling down.'[9]

What did Professor Muhammad Yunus do that sheds light on leading with service? Without doubt he demonstrated the common touch. The Grameen Bank started because he was in touch with what was happening around him. Seeing the plight of the hardworking poor sparked a watershed response. As we shall see, the common touch often begins by being in touch with your colleagues and customers, and then being moved enough to respond – to do something. Next Yunus used upside-down thinking. Ignoring the perceived wisdom of the time, he was confident that the poor both *could* and *would* repay their loans. He also quickly found that lending to women in particular yielded much greater community benefit than just helping local business to survive and grow. Two other themes emerge from the story, which we will explore in more depth shortly – legacy and loyalty. The bank is owned by its customers, and it aims to exist for the long term, building a legacy of support for the poor. It's also built on trust and loyalty. The communities of borrowers become support groups, committed to helping each other. The bank is structured so that it remains local and responsive to the needs of the locality, building that sense of loyalty.

The Grameen Bank operates without complex contracts, working primarily on trust. This illustrates another strand of thinking which we will develop later in this chapter – the importance of simplicity. As we shall see, simplicity is more important to leading with service than we might first think. Leading with service is about leaders who serve first and lead second, demonstrating the power of the common touch. And it's surprising how often this power is revealed from the impact of seemingly small acts. It's not just small loans from the Grameen Bank that prove this point. The power of small acts can sometimes become defining moments in the lives of others.

Defining moments

In South Africa during the 1940s, a nine-year-old black boy saw something which astounded him. He saw a white priest doff his cap as a mark of respect to the boy's mother – a black domestic worker. The boy couldn't believe his eyes. At that time and in that place, it was almost unheard of for a white person to do such a thing for a black servant.

That boy, Desmond Tutu, grew up to become the Archbishop of Cape Town and a leading figure in the anti-apartheid movement. In later life, when speaking on a BBC World Service programme,[10] Tutu described this incident as a turning point in his life – a defining moment.

And what about the priest, Trevor Huddleston? Did he realize that his simple action, no more than a small gesture, would have such longstanding significance? Probably not but it's likely that such a simple act was not an isolated gesture. It was the mark of someone who deliberately made such behaviour – the common touch – central to his leadership. Desmond Tutu, the boy who became an archbishop, summed up the impact of Trevor Huddleston: 'If you could say that anyone single-handedly made apartheid a world issue then that person was Trevor Huddleston.' And in the words of the late Nelson Mandela, that other great anti-apartheid statesman: 'No white person has done more for South Africa than Trevor Huddleston.'[11]

It's not uncommon to think that life's defining moments come from major events. However, this story illustrates a point made by sociology professor Frank Furedi. He suggests that it's the small and personal moments that are more likely to really shape our lives: 'Sometimes very minor personal events that you don't notice at the time, sneak up on you and a week later, or a month or a year later, you realize you're never the same person again.'[12]

Furthermore, Furedi sees such acts as being counter-intuitive, something different from the normal experience of our day-to-day lives: 'The key element here is that it is always something that goes against the grain of your life, something that you've never really experienced before, that opens your eyes to new possibilities – and life is never the same after that.'

So what do stories such as Desmond Tutu's tell us? They illustrate the power of simple, straightforward acts that show others you care. They encourage us to:

- Think about the things you may consider small or irrelevant, yet which others might feel to be quite significant.

- Reflect on the potential impact of some of the simple things we do. Attention to the small things can have an impact far beyond our initial comprehension.

Small actions, big events

At the beginning of the last chapter we considered the story of how a small act by a school dinner-lady had a profound impact on a problem situation. That story shows how small things can make a difference in any context, business or personal. But it also illustrates the importance of encouraging such seemingly insignificant acts, especially when we never know when they might become 'defining moments'. As we saw, that story actually contained two small, thoughtful acts which, when combined, produced a potent effect. It was the head teacher's act, personally informing and praising the catering team, which really made the original act so effective. Both dinner-lady and head teacher demonstrated the power of the common touch. But this is not the only lesson to draw from this story. It's easy to miss another key idea. Leaders can benefit as much from 'catching' such behaviour as they can from modelling it. There is much to be gained by demonstrating the common touch, but there just as much from encouraging it in others.

We have thought about how doing the common things uncommonly well can set leaders and their organizations apart from the rest. But for such ideas to take root and spread within an organization, leaders need to have that common touch. That is, they need to engage and connect with colleagues as people, not just as employees. The common touch means leading with service. As we saw with Desmond Tutu's defining moment, the common touch is often seen in the small things, so we'll start by looking further at how small things can have a big impact. Like the small change to a take-away sandwich barcode that was worth half a million pounds, or how a seemingly insignificant measurement cost a CEO his job. In contrast, we'll discuss another CEO's intuitive take on leadership and service when he described 'the best leadership I ever gave'.

As we shall see, it's not enough for leaders to exercise the common touch with the people they lead. It's as important to engage and connect with your customers. We'll see how two organizations bring the concept of leading with service to life. Firstly, a well-known UK retailer shows how servant leadership can successfully challenge the very fundamentals that underpin the way others do business. In contrast, the second example comes from a relatively unknown business. Although you may not have heard of them, they may well know about you! Bringing some uncommon sense to the idea of customer loyalty, this highly successful company has transformed the fortunes of businesses around the world.

Finally, we'll introduce some surprising findings about what businesses that excel at service are doing differently. We'll see how Apple, despite 'expert' predictions of failure, built a retail store-business which returned some of the highest profit-per-square-feet anywhere in the world. What was the Apple secret? Keeping it simple and putting their customers at centre-stage.

First we'll return to the idea of small things having a big impact. Leading with the common touch often begins through being in touch with the realities of your business. Such leadership means being close to colleagues, listening and responding. It also means being close to customers, being in tune with their needs. In contrast, all too often a distant leader may seem to be an absent leader. But leaders who are in touch are better able to demonstrate the common touch. The phrase 'common touch' conveys a sense of leaders keeping their connection with colleagues and customers. These leaders still connect with the ordinary, everyday activities around them. Those who do connect can bring about some surprising outcomes. Those who don't may find the cost of losing touch can be considerable, as we are about to see in two very different stories.

The half-million pound sandwiches

Small acts with major impacts aren't necessarily confined to political or social leaders, such as Desmond Tutu's life-changing experience. As we have already seen with our dinner-lady story, small things can have a big impact on organizations. But this next example illustrates that, however simple, such acts can do more than motivate staff, or change the attitude of individual customers. They can also yield considerable financial benefits.

Sir Terry Leahy, the former CEO of Tesco, recounts one simple idea that came from a member of staff. It's another sandwich story but this time on a completely different scale to one schoolboy's packed lunch. The UK's pre-packed sandwich market is worth about £6.5bn per annum. That means the production and sale of around 3.25 billion sandwiches per year.[13] It's probably not surprising that Tesco sells around a million of these sandwiches every year but what *is* surprising is that one simple change in the way these products were labelled resulted in savings of half a million pounds. How? Some simple but back-to-front thinking.

As with any short-dated product, Tesco staff discounted sandwiches as these neared the end of their shelf life. Staff drew attention to these cheaper sandwiches by placing a 'reduced price' label on the front of the package, whilst at the same time removing the original barcode from the back. This all took time. Placed there to ensure the pack's presentation wasn't spoiled, these barcodes were actually spoiling profits. Of course the solution was obvious – simply put barcodes on the front, then cover them with new labels when discounting. So this is what Tesco did. Neither the problem nor the solution was rocket-science. The real reason this story warrants a mention is the bigger picture. This task was repeated on thousands of products, in hundreds of stores, by hundreds of staff, every single day. Which means the simple act of moving a sandwich barcode saved Tesco both time and money: according to Leahy, around half a million pounds.[14] Sometimes, the small things can have a big financial impact too.

As it turns out, this isn't the only example of how Leahy encouraged his staff to make the small changes that could have a big impact. He also advocated a sense of discipline aimed at: '... picking up on small failures before they become big ones, and before an "I can get away with it" culture begins to spread.'[15] In some ways echoing Bill Bratton's 'broken window' principle, Leahy stressed the importance of not letting even apparently trivial incidents or details go unchecked. As we saw in the previous chapter, excellence is a habit not an act. And excellence in the small things can be just as important as anywhere else.

Making things simple is a critical yet often under-estimated leadership skill, one that we'll return to later. But for now it's useful to note how simplicity can make a big difference to leading with the common touch. This means more than simply staying in touch, or listening, or saying the right things. It's about simplifying in order to make it easier to serve. It means taking action, especially action that shows leaders are serving both their employees and their customers. Without action, seemingly small things can have a huge detrimental effect.

The multi-million pound pellets

When you think of the nuclear industry you might reasonably expect the highest possible degree of quality assurance. After all, surely no nuclear business would gain a licence to operate if it didn't comply with every essential safety standard. So how did an established organization in this industry find itself in serious trouble due to an error in one, simple, precautionary measurement? If you're still not convinced about the benefits or implications of small things, this next story might cause you to think again.

CASE STUDY British Nuclear Fuels

British Nuclear Fuels (BNFL) was a UK-based international supplier of nuclear fuel. One of their facilities manufactured fuel pellets, used in fuel assemblies for nuclear-powered reactors. On one occasion, BNFL had shipped an order for four fuel assemblies to Japan. This required an 18,000-mile sea-journey with an armed escort to minimize the dangers of piracy or terrorist attack. No sooner had the shipment arrived than controversy struck. BNFL quality staff found that shift workers at their plant had falsified a simple measurement of the pellet's diameter. These workers had been 'cutting and pasting' previous results into the spreadsheet records, in order to avoid the boring task of re-measuring the sample.[16] Although this was a straightforward check of something already measured in the process, the omission had a profound impact on the business. The Japanese were furious that BNFL had admitted 'falsifying records about safety checks on the consignment.' They insisted the company bore the cost of returning the faulty shipment to the UK for disposal.[17]

The initial response of management was to point to the process workers as the cause of the problem. But far from just finding fault with the shift workers, the UK's Nuclear Inspectorate focused on a much more fundamental issue. They pointed out that management supervision of the process was 'virtually non-existent'. In fact, they went further, arguing that management in the work area lacked both presence and a questioning attitude to what was happening. This sent entirely the wrong message to staff, who consequently had no sense of the importance of the routine task.

The fall-out from this 'small' action was profound. Relationships between Japan and the UK were strained and the Japanese company insisted that the shipment be returned to the UK. At a significant cost and risk, radioactive materials were again shipped under armed escort. Governments expressed reluctance to allow the cargo through their waters, and environmentalists protested against the 18,000-mile journey.[18] The financial cost to BNFL was also enormous, costing the company between £113–£133 million in compensation to their customer. The CEO resigned and, as you might expect, the shift workers responsible were sacked.[19]

These few measurements of a diameter were not an especially crucial part of the process, and might seem to be small and insignificant. Small – yes, but far from insignificant. As the Nuclear Inspectorate concluded, these small acts indicated a much bigger issue. This story is a powerful reminder that leaders need to convey *why* things matter and find ways to create the right conditions for people to feel motivated. In other words, rather than being distant, disengaged, ineffectual and out of touch, leaders need to be grounded in the reality of their business. But what does 'being grounded in the reality of a business' mean for leaders? We'll explore how one CEO answered this question by what he considered to be the best leadership he ever gave!

'The best leadership I ever gave...'

The fundamental importance of being grounded in a business is illustrated in this story about Sir Terry Leahy (from his own, insightful book, *Management in 10 Words*). Under his leadership, Tesco grew to become the UK's leading retailer. In fact the company was so successful that by the year 2013, £1 out of every £8 spent on British high-streets went through Tesco's cash registers.[20] Leahy acknowledges that he learnt much from his background, growing up in working-class Liverpool. His upbringing taught him the value of good manners, education, hard work, and common sense. It also instilled in him the desire to succeed in some way and to help everybody, no matter what their background, to have a better life. Perhaps such a background helps us understand his determination to keep things simple and to maintain a discipline. And, of course, it might help to explain how he maintained the common touch. Leahy's approach at Tesco was both powerful and arresting. When he became CEO, he committed to working one week a year as a general assistant, performing every job in the store. Then he challenged his senior managers to do the same. Leahy argued that, unless they spent more time on the 'front-line', there was no way these senior managers could get 'under the skin of the business'. This approach has some similarities to that adopted by both Bill Bratton and the Sternins, as they experienced their customers' problems first hand.

This grounding in the reality of the business was matched by an uncompromising approach to listening to his customers – for Leahy, the best leadership he ever gave. Not only is this an interesting contrast to the view of leaders taking centre stage, it also suggests an upside-down view of leadership: 'The best leadership I ever gave was to be in the background, listening, and allowing the customer to be the leader instead'.[21]

Leahy's idea of letting the *customer* lead came from the customer panels that he set up with Tesco. Here customers were encouraged to talk about their needs, wishes and any problems they faced at Tesco's stores. According to Leahy,[22] Tesco were willing to 'do the things that other people (or conventional wisdom) said wouldn't work. We did these things because customers like them.' He suggests it was this discipline, of listening to customers, that answers questions about how Tesco grew so spectacularly. No doubt phrases like 'listening to the customer' will sound familiar to most organizations, but given the scale of their success, there was something clearly different about what this meant to Tesco. Perhaps the answer can be found in Leahy's own words once again. He suggested that: 'Out of all the things we did, the most important change was in how we thought. In simple terms we reversed the flow of the company: instead of our work ending with the customer, it started with the customer.'[23]

This implies that these panels were more than standard, marketing focus groups. After all, how many businesses would have their CEO at dozens of focus groups and customer meetings? Perhaps they are more indicative of an inverted approach to leadership, which is illustrated by the concept of leading with service. Leahy went to 'dozens' of the customer panels 'sitting anonymously at the back'.[24] He listened to customers providing insights worth acting upon, defining moments, which helped to show how Tesco could make significant changes.

One of these was to prove a game-changer for Leahy and for Tesco. It was a counter-intuitive idea and one that seemed very risky on face value. Risking losses of up to 25 per cent of profits and any initial advantage if copied by competitors, the idea perhaps didn't sound the most attractive of propositions. But Leahy felt it offered the prospect of something special for customers and for Tesco. The idea? We'll return to it a little later. But first let's talk about 'reversing the flow' within an organization. Some of the ideas Leahy considered required a real leap of faith. And the commitment to implement these ideas required a faith in what customers were saying – a belief that they themselves knew best what they needed in their lives. This too could be called an upside-down view of leadership.

Upside-down leadership

Many traditional organization charts depict leaders at the top. The concept of leading with service inverts this common perception of the way organizations are led. Rather than showing an organization which is led from the 'top-down', an inverted leadership pyramid puts leaders at the bottom. It thus depicts and helps to reinforce the leader's role as one of supporting or serving people, which as we shall see shortly, is at the core of the idea of servant leadership.

FIGURE 4.2 Upside-down leadership

Inverting the normal organizational structure in this way can have several benefits. In many organizations, complex structures and layers of management can force employees to deal with dual priorities. Often they must juggle the immediate priority of serving customers with demands placed on them by the organization's bureaucracy. And all too often, such demands on frontline staff are loaded too heavily towards looking inward, meeting the internal needs of the organization. This often comes at the expense of a true customer focus.

The inverted leadership pyramid is a useful tool to help change that focus. It illustrates how leaders serve their people and how together, they can all better serve their customers. Such an upside-down view of leadership can become a catalyst for leaders, encouraging them to ask some fundamental questions about their approach to leadership. Not unlike one such challenging question which Benjamin Disraeli, the 19th-century British prime minister, asked of himself: 'I must follow the people. Am I not their leader?'

In an interesting twist, he answers his question before he asks it, and in so doing captures three key themes of leading with service. The idea that to lead you must follow is certainly upside-down thinking. There is definitely a feeling of leadership with the common touch about his words. And Disraeli nicely introduces the ideas of servant leadership and stewardship.

Servant leadership

The concept of servant leadership was developed and popularized by Robert Greenleaf. As a manager in the United States through the 1950s and 60s, Greenleaf became increasingly frustrated by what he saw as the dominant, authoritarian approach to leadership. So he thought it was time to think differently about the way we lead – starting with motives. He asked two basic questions: 'Why should someone want to be a leader?'; and 'What makes a good leader?' His answers were both thought-provoking and instructive.

Firstly Greenleaf turns the motive for leading upside-down, arguing: 'Leadership must first and foremost meet the needs of others.' A leader's primary motive should therefore be to serve. Secondly, he proposed that if you want to know what makes a good leader, look for people who know how to serve others: 'Good leaders must first become good servants.'

In 1970, Greenleaf published his thoughts on leadership in an essay: 'The servant as leader'. This expressed and elaborated on his views that leaders should be servants first, and then leaders. This has clear echoes of the inverted leadership pyramid – turning the view, role and philosophy of leadership upside-down. Greenleaf felt that there was a sharp difference between people who seek to serve first, compared to those who see themselves as a leader first.

 The difference manifests itself in the care taken by the servant first to make sure that other people's highest priority needs are being served. The best test, and the most difficult to administer, is this: do those served grow as persons? Do they, while being served, become healthier, wiser, freer, more autonomous, more likely themselves to become servants?[25]

Leaders as stewards

Closely related to the idea of servant leadership is the notion of stewardship. A steward is someone entrusted with the care of something – as custodian, guardian or caretaker. Viewing leaders as stewards implies they have a responsibility to look after an organization, leaving it in better shape than when they took over. Thinking about leadership as a form of stewardship may mean changing your perspective, perhaps even turning it upside down. It will certainly mean a refusal to compromise when facing competing tensions.

Cathedral thinkers

A constant tension in life and in business is to ensure that satisfying current demands on the organization doesn't result in longer-term loss or damage. This is the conflict between expediency today at the expense of security in the future. Put another way: you kill the goose that lays the golden eggs. This was one of the most famous of Aesop's fables – the cottager who found he owned a goose that could lay golden eggs. Assuming that the goose must be full of gold inside, the cottager killed the goose, only to find it was no different to any other.

The temptation is always there to make decisions which may work well in the short term, but which can prove to be costly in the future. We need leaders who see stewardship as a key part of what they do, leaving their organizations better than when they found them. Leadership that includes a sense of creation – building something that will last and that will make a difference. This idea is captured in this thought-provoking passage from Charles Handy's insightful book, *The Hungry Spirit*:[26]

> *Cathedrals are incredible testaments to human endeavour. It is not only their grandeur or splendour, but the thought that they often took more than 50 years to build. Those who designed them, those who first worked on them, knew for certain that they would never see them finished. They knew only that they were creating something glorious which would stand for centuries, long after their own names had been forgotten... We may not need any more cathedrals but we do need cathedral thinkers, people who can think beyond their own lifetimes.*

The notion of stewardship is about caring for something that is of worth, then striving to increase that value. The word suggests an inspirational take on leadership. Stewardship means ensuring that the organization and its people are equipped to create value for the present, and for the longer term. Here are some tips to help you master servant leadership and stewardship:

- Remember the power of the common touch.
- Re-discover the meaning of a service ethos.
- Ask what you need to do in order to help others to contribute, achieve and grow.
- Serve first, and from a motive of service, then seek to lead.
- Take good care of what you have been entrusted with.
- Adopt a leadership style that creates value, by investing and improving.
- Use resources wisely, not wastefully.
- Think of the long term as much as the short term.

- Turn loyalty on its head, be a loyal company to your customers.
- Create a sense of legacy – building something that will be there for others.

It could be argued that the last point is what really differentiates stewardship from any other approach to leadership. Walter Isaacson, author of the authorized biography of Steve Jobs, once asked Jobs a revealing question about stewardship. He asked what Jobs thought was his most important creation. Isaacson assumed the answer would be one of Apple's flagship products, such as the iPad or the Macintosh. 'Instead he said it was Apple the company. Making an enduring company, he said, was both far harder and more important than making a great product.'[27]

Stewardship is an interesting way to think about leadership. It often means that leaders need to hold competing tensions. To be a steward means holding the tension between expediency today and actions that secure the long-term survival and health of the organization. But what do servant leadership and stewardship look like in practice? Two contrasting businesses offer differing perspectives on these approaches. One focuses on legacy and how leaders serve employees, the other on loyalty and how leaders serve customers. In the next section we'll see how a well-known business turns the meaning of business upside-down, through its focus on leaving a legacy. Then, we examine a surprising truth about loyalty, which demonstrates another upside-down approach to doing business.

Upside-down thinking: what's the meaning of business?

One organization that has made legacy central to the way it operates is the UK retailer John Lewis. The John Lewis chain of upmarket department stores is well respected by the British public. But this is not just because of the store's reputation for quality products and quality service. It's because John Lewis does business differently, and it's a very startling difference. To begin with, how many businesses can you name that put the happiness of their employees (or partners) at the core of everything they do? And how many of those incorporate that aim as part of a mission statement?

> *The John Lewis Partnership is a visionary and successful way of doing business, boldly putting the happiness of partners at the centre of everything it does. It's the embodiment of an ideal, the outcome of nearly a century of endeavour to create a different sort of company, owned by partners dedicated to serving customers with flair and fairness.*[28]

In a reversal of how most businesses tend to describe themselves, the John Lewis philosophy doesn't start with business success as its principal aim. Instead, the partnership puts staff happiness at the core of its operations, which they believe will *then* lead to a profitable business. Compare this approach with the declared aim of one of their main rivals – Debenhams. This retailer is run as a conventional department store business, for the primary benefit of its shareholders. This approach is made clear in the Debenhams mission statement, with its stated aim to: 'drive profitability and grow market share.'[29] But though the John Lewis approach to business is different, it's still based on sound, practical principles:

> *The John Lewis Partnership's reputation is founded on the uniqueness of our ownership structure and our commercial success. Our purpose is 'the happiness of all our members, through their worthwhile, satisfying employment in a successful business', with success measured on our ability to sustain and enhance our position both as an outstanding retailer and as a thriving example of employee ownership. With this in mind, our strategy is based on three interdependent objectives – partners, customers and profit.*[30]

A visionary and successful way of doing business

In reversing the emphasis of their business, the John Lewis Partnership stands out as a challenge to the real purpose of a business. We'll return to this idea shortly but first let's consider how their philosophy contributes to their success. John Lewis is renowned for its high levels of customer service and satisfaction, and for being a great place to work. The partnership claims that this is because they put the happiness of their partners first. This relationship, between happy customers and happy staff, echoes the 'satisfaction mirror's' virtuous circle, as we discussed in the last chapter. But what has this to do with legacy? Well, the John Lewis philosophy gives them a long-term perspective, driving them to survive and succeed, making a difference for future employees/partners. This long-term approach might be called the legacy of leadership.

Former chairman Sir Stuart Hampson contrasts the John Lewis approach with other, prevailing business views: 'If more businesses could act longer-term, we would have a stronger British economy'. A more recent chairman, Charlie Mayfield, referred to the extreme resilience of the partnership model. 'We're not vulnerable to short-term thinking. Our model means we are absolutely committed to long-term plans. Probably the key element of our resilience long-term is the continuity we establish with our people.'

This focus on the long-term was also identified by a report produced by CASS Business School for the UK government.[31] The report captured some of the key differences that seemed to set employee-owned businesses apart from the rest, during times of recession. It found such businesses created jobs faster and planned more for the long-term. Not only were they more resilient than conventionally run businesses; they also delivered far better customer satisfaction, significantly higher value-added-per-employee and typically higher profits. It's not surprising that the success of the John Lewis philosophy is prompting governments, academics and other businesses to take notice, suggesting a realistic alternative to current business models.

Since the global financial crisis there has been renewed interest in business models such as that of John Lewis. As their chairman suggests, there is a:

> *need to look again at the way that businesses are owned and managed – because the decisions taken in the boardrooms of banks and other companies affect all of us... We need to create a balanced economy that supports long-term sustainable growth and a fairer society. That requires us to rethink what companies are for, asking not simply about the wealth they produce, but how they create value and for whom.[32]*

Perhaps the ideas of the John Lewis Partnership are as relevant today as when they first challenged capitalism and conventional business models, some 80 years ago. And to illustrate this, it's worth a brief look at how the John Lewis Partnership began.

Knowledge, power and profit

The man responsible for the partnership vision was John Spedan Lewis. His 'experiment in industrial democracy' started in the early 1900s and became a success both economically and socially. Lewis's radical business innovations ranged from a profit-sharing scheme, a third week's paid holiday (unheard of in retailing, at that time) and the recruitment of university graduates, including women. Showing an insight still very relevant to this day, Lewis felt that, if businesses were to be really successful, they needed to attract the same well-qualified candidates as the professions.[33]

Much more of Lewis's radical thinking is still relevant to modern businesses. For example, he was also interested in another key business relationship – the link between knowledge, power and profit. He insisted that partnership schemes needed a balance between all three if they were to be effective. Perhaps even more radical and insightful, he further argued that *sharing* knowledge was the most important of all: 'The sharing of managerial knowledge is indispensable not only if power is to be shared but also for happiness.'[34] Lewis was undoubtedly ahead of his time, and with much to say to today's business generation. In fact, given the importance of knowledge to modern business, it could be argued that this link is even more critical today than ever before.

Perhaps most important of all though, John Spedan Lewis's business philosophy challenged the most fundamental question about business – what is it for? He thought it was wrong that the rewards of business should be shared amongst a few shareholders. Important as investment funding might be, he held the view that employees were much more responsible for business success, and as a result should reap more rewards from their labours. And perhaps even more enlightened for the early 1900s, he also insisted on transparency in the business, in the belief that fairness and transparency need to go together. Such issues are every bit as important today as they were at the turn of last century. As the global economy struggles to respond to a recession, it's not just business practices and ethics that are being scrutinized. Questions are being asked about the very purpose of business.

The legacy of leadership

Thinking about leaders as servants or stewards means thinking about their legacy. The legacy of John Spedan Lewis can be viewed in different ways. Fundamentally, the partnership principles are still very much the same today as they were in the early part of the last century. The organization still operates in a belief 'among top management that they are in effect the servants of the partners, who own the business and pay their salaries.'[35]

Perhaps another way to view Lewis's legacy is in some questions prompted by his success. How can an organization better share power, knowledge and profit? What would be the effect of more organizations making the happiness of their employees a higher priority? Why, if employee-owned businesses perform so well, are there so few of them? Whilst employee ownership may not be the answer for all businesses, or indeed for many, it may still be for some. And regardless, there may well be principles that any business can apply.

And there may be yet another way to view Lewis's legacy. Perhaps he has done more than leave the John Lewis Partnership as a great place to work. The business model he pioneered stands as a challenge for the future. Posing the question: 'How might business better serve society?' could be a far greater legacy still. Legacy is one key way in which we can see the principles of servant leadership put into practice. A second is the way in which leaders build loyalty, something we'll illustrate with shopping baskets and data-mining.

CASE STUDY   Dunnhumby and a basket full of loyalty

You may not have heard of Dunnhumby, but they may know much about you. Just how they do that, and why, is something we'll come to shortly. But first let's give you some background on this obscure but highly successful company. Dunnhumby began as a husband and wife data-mining business, working from their family home. From these very humble beginnings, the business now offers advice and insights to several major UK and US businesses. Data-mining is the practice of examining large, pre-existing databases in order to generate new information. Sifting through large volumes of data for client businesses probably doesn't sound the most exciting of occupations. So it's not surprising that Dunnhumby don't describe their work in these terms. Instead, co-founder and chairman, Clive Humby, prefers to position the business in this way: 'If companies put their customers first in every decision, they become the customer's first choice, which improves their brand value and their performance.'[36]

So how is it that Dunnhumby might know about you? Well, first ask yourself if you're a customer of Kroger (in the US), or Tesco (in the UK), or Casino (in France). If you answer yes, then the chances are Dunnhumby may know a good deal about you – or at least about people like you. The secret of Dunnhumby's success is that they're very good at looking in other people's shopping baskets. Well OK, perhaps they do a bit more than that, but arguably it's the same principle. In reality, they've made a successful business out of determining what kind of shopper you are, based on what you put in your shopping basket. To be more precise, Dunnhumby excels at building shopper profiles based on large-scale data analysis. We did say it didn't sound the most exciting of activities!

Dunnhumby may not be a widely known business, but there is no doubting their value to their clients. The success Tesco had with their Clubcard would not have been possible without Dunnhumby. When Tesco received their first report on the pilot for the scheme, they couldn't have been more surprised. Ian McClain, Tesco chairman at the time, remarked after the presentation of initial results: 'What scares me about that is that you know more about our customers in three months than I have from 30 years.'[37]

So why were those findings so startling? What Dunnhumby found was that a small number of Tesco's loyal customers accounted for most of their profitability. This was a good example of the 80/20 principle hidden in plain view, as this level of knowledge wasn't definitively known to Tesco prior to the pilot. It's one thing suspecting such a breakdown but it's quite another knowing it for sure. Even today 50–60 per cent of Tesco's business comes from 20 per cent of its customers.[38] But there was something else about the Dunnhumby approach that made all the difference – an uncommon view of loyalty.

The business community frequently uses the language of customer loyalty but not in the same way as Dunnhumby. What they do is turn thinking about customer loyalty upside down. Whereas most businesses try to build customer loyalty, Dunnhumby argue that it's far better to think about the reverse – businesses showing loyalty to customers. There is nothing subtle about this difference, it's a genuine example of upside-down thinking. And the results show that thinking this way can make all the difference. It's well known in business that it's far cheaper to keep an existing customer than to find a new one. But Dunnhumby also demonstrates the *value* of loyal customers to a business. They estimate that it takes between 12 and 20 new customers to match the value of one, committed customer. Given that so much effort goes into finding and keeping loyal customers, it's surely worthwhile developing customer loyalty schemes that really work. With Tesco, Dunnhumby proved the value of a scheme, which did just that. Clubcard proved that: 'Customer loyalty is not about customers demonstrating their loyalty to the company but rather the company showing loyalty to its customers.'[39]

Loyalty and the common touch

Tesco's Clubcard was designed to show the company's loyalty to its customers but it also had another clear benefit. Not only did the scheme turn thinking about loyalty upside down, it also addressed another fundamental issue for big business. One of the inherent risks faced by growing businesses is the loss of personal connection with customers. Effective customer loyalty schemes offer a way for businesses to be personal again. They help keep customers in touch with the company but just as importantly, they keep the company in touch with its customers. This doesn't just mean personalized addresses or greetings. For example, when Clubcard vouchers arrive in the mail, they are totally related to the customer's buying habits with Tesco. The scheme rewards loyal customers with discounted offers on products that are directly relevant and personalized. Here's how one of their marketing directors explained the offer: 'It's simple: the more you spend the more you are rewarded. It's fair, there are no gold or platinum versions. It is personal, giving offers that are based on what people buy.'[40]

Echoing some points made earlier, this marketing director neatly brings us back to common sense thinking: 'If this is common sense, it doesn't make it easy to do.' Going on to explain how the Tesco scheme had taken 10 years of improvement and development, he reminds us that simple and easy are not the same thing.

Dunnhumby have also applied their combination of common sense and upside-down thinking to a major US retailer. In 2002, Kroger was the second largest grocery retailer in the United States.[41] Kroger had been battling to challenge Walmart's dominance of the US market, a battle they were losing. When beginning to work with Dunnhumby, Kroger believed that their stores were performing well and what they needed was more customers. This seemed perfectly common sense. However, it wasn't the common sense that Dunnhumby sought. Closer scrutiny of the data revealed that even the best Kroger customers only spent up to a half of their shopping budget with the ambitious retailer. What Dunnhumby found was uncommon sense. Kroger didn't need more customers, it needed to persuade its existing customers to spend more. In fact, if they could persuade existing customers to spend their total shopping budget at Kroger, the company would triple its sales.

Loyalty and legacy help to build a picture of how servant leadership can be put into practice. We've seen how a focus on legacy has actually helped organizations to perform better and raised some challenging questions about the very purpose of a business. Then we saw how upside-down loyalty is a good example of leading with service. This uncommon insight turns loyalty on its head, challenging companies to be loyal to their customers. But leading with service also needs something else adding to the mix. This comes from some surprise findings from research into businesses that provide excellent service.

Simple leadership

In the previous chapter we mentioned Professor Robert Johnson's work with the Royal Automobile Club.[42] His research wasn't limited to just the one organization. In actual fact, Johnson worked with four other companies, all renowned for their service excellence: First Direct; Shangri-la Hotels; Singapore Airlines and Tesco. Johnson considered the relationship between how employees viewed their role, and their delivery of excellent customer service. What was the connection? These employees didn't view their work from technical or functional perspectives. They delivered excellent customer service because they believed their main role was to help people. These are rather startling insights, which prompt two very interesting questions. Firstly, what do they mean to organizations and to their leaders? And secondly, what were those organizations doing so differently, to lead to such a successful change of emphasis? That's what Johnson and his team set out to discover. Several of their findings were neither new nor surprising. One might expect such things as the importance of teamworking, customer-focused systems and procedures, and supportive management styles. But Johnson also discovered something that was more unusual – the importance of simplicity.

Johnson found that those businesses which best served their customers were, quite simply, the easiest to do business with. By way of contrast, the least happy customers were those who experienced the most difficult service processes. But it's important not to confuse simple with easy. It's not always easy to provide a simple service for your customers. Ease needs simplicity but simplicity can take a lot of thinking about. As the CEO of one computer company is alleged to have said: 'Simplicity takes a lot of code'.

We can think of simplicity in several ways. It can be thinking about a simple solution to the packaging design of a Tesco sandwich. It might be a more exclusive service feature, such as Virgin Atlantic's innovatory drive-thru check-in for their upper class customers. Or it could simply be the way RAC drivers think differently about the service they provide at the roadside. They don't just fix cars, they provide support with assurance for customers who are likely to be stressed, worried, or highly irritated. Perhaps one company, more than any other, has been associated with designs that are both simple and focused on the user experience – Apple.

CASE STUDY Simple success

In Chapter 1 we discussed how Steve Jobs rescued Apple, after returning to the company in 1997. What we didn't mention was the passion for simplicity, which was very much at the heart of his approach. But though famous for his simple, stylish product designs, Jobs's focus on simplicity wasn't just about aesthetics. For Jobs, simplicity was also about ease of use – as a means of overcoming complexity, not just avoiding it. 'It takes a lot of hard work to make something simple, to truly understand the underlying challenges and come up with elegant solutions.'[43]

Perhaps one of the best examples of this approach in action was Apple Stores. In the year 2000, Jobs hired Ron Johnson to oversee the creation of Apple's own network of retail stores. This was a counter-intuitive attempt to improve the sale of Apple products. Johnson recalls Jobs putting the entire Apple product line on a table – two desktop computers and two portables (there were no iPods, iPhones or iPads at that time). It's one thing having a very simple product range but it's quite another to build a successful retail network with so few items. But in essence, the answer to that problem was quite simple too. Apple had to make shopping in its stores an experience – an ownership experience. Johnson thought the most important aspect of the experience was that staff shouldn't focus on selling products. Instead they should be: '…focused on building relationships and trying to make people's lives better…Their job is to figure out what you need and help you get it, even if it's a product Apple doesn't carry.'[44]

Perhaps this concentration on the common touch explains why Apple seems to do more than just win loyal customers, it creates fans. But there were other counter-intuitive elements to Jobs's Apple Store plans. One journalist wrote: 'The most striking thing… is what you don't see… clutter… Jobs has focused Apple's resources on fewer than 20 products, and those have steadily been shrinking in size… the interiors, too, have been distilled to a minimum of elements'. He went on to quote Johnson himself, saying: 'We've gotten it down so there's only three materials we're using: glass, stainless steel, and wood.'[45]

But Jobs's idea wasn't counter-intuitive just because of minimalist store designs, minuscule product ranges or altruistic sales staff. The Apple Store idea had little support, either from inside the company or beyond. Many analysts and critics predicted that the Apple Store would be an expensive failure. The retail industry norm is to measure sales-per-square-foot of retail space. Apple, with its relatively small outlets, small product range and non-aggressive sales teams didn't seem to fit the bill at all. As the stores were about to launch, *Fortune* magazine published a quote from *Business Week* that seemed to sum up early criticism of the venture: 'I give them two years before they're turning out the lights on a very painful and expensive mistake.'[46]

But some years later, things were very different. When *Fortune* quoted the retail sales data for 2007, Best Buy was the leading electronics retailer with $930 per square-foot. Noting that world famous Tiffany and Co was taking $2,666, *Fortune* quipped: 'Audrey Hepburn liked Tiffany's for breakfast, but at $4,032 per square foot, Apple is eating everyone's lunch.' By 2011, according to the *New York Times*, Apple's figures for that year were 'higher than any other US retailer in $ per square foot... and almost double that of Tiffany... worldwide (Apple)... stores sold $16 billion in merchandise.'[47]

If the launch of Apple Stores attracted initial critics, it was also delayed due to Jobs's concerns about the store design. This element of the story also illustrates an important aspect of Apple Stores' success. In preparing for their launch, Apple built a prototype store in a warehouse. It was only when this was completed that Jobs realized a problem. Rather than a layout based on what *customers* wanted, the prototype had positioned products according to Apple's own internal product classifications. Logical as this might be on paper, it didn't reflect the reasons why customers might want to visit the shop. Apple Stores were meant to be all about the experience. Although a return to the drawing board delayed the launch, Jobs felt it made all the difference. In the re-design '...only a quarter of it was about product. The rest was arranged around interests: along the right wall, photos, videos, kids; on the left, problems. A third area – the Genius Bar in the back...'[48] allowed Apple users to get their equipment fixed.

In many ways the story of Apple Stores sums up the main themes we've so far explored in this chapter. Jobs's insistence that his stores be laid out to suit the customer rather than Apple's interests was a clear example of leading with service. Creating a sales force that was based on helping people rather than just selling to them shows how important the common touch can be. And the whole Apple Store concept was founded on minimalism, illustrating the power of small things and simple solutions. But perhaps we should also offer a note of caution at this point.

Simple but not sure-fire

You may remember that in Chapter 1, we suggested leaders should learn from the best, which was one way of seeing the sense before it becomes common sense. But we then went on to stress that, just because an idea works well somewhere else, there are no guarantees it will work in your situation. Even the best ideas need to be adapted and shaped to meet your particular context. It's dangerous to assume that a counter-intuitive approach such as Apple's will work everywhere else. That's what Ron Johnson seems to have done when he left Apple Stores for US retail giant J C Penney.

In an attempt to re-position Penney from its bargain-store roots to a more up-market operation, Johnson tried to be bold. He set out with the notion that 'Penney needed a little of Apple's magic'.[49] Trying to apply much of what he had learned with his former company, Johnson soon found that J C Penney was no Apple. Within a year of his arrival the business had lost $4.28 billion in sales and its shares were down about 55 per cent.[50] Seventeen months after his arrival, Johnson was fired. Bill Ackman, a principal shareholder in the company, later reflected: 'One of the big mistakes was perhaps too much change too quickly without adequate testing on what the impact would be…'.[51]

Big changes to the customer offer need careful implementation. When your customers are used to discounts and coupons, even if your intent is to find new ways to improve the customer experience, it pays to bring them with you, not leave them behind. As David Cush, the CEO of Virgin America remarked, whilst the ideas might have been good, you 'don't destroy your old revenue model before you have proved your new revenue model. That's the box that J C Penney has put themselves in.'

Success like Apple's might be possible when your products are iconic, and your customer base is more akin to a fanbase. But what if you're managing a less-glamorous business, like the 'dowdy department store' J C Penney?[52] Is it possible to lead with service and apply the common touch in a grocery business, selling everyday products? For an answer to that question we need to return to the fortunes of the UK retailer Tesco.

A simple thank-you

Earlier in this chapter we discussed the inverted leadership pyramid as a way of illustrating Sir Terry Leahy's 'reversing the flow'. There was one Tesco initiative that captures this notion, of serving the customer, better than any other. But as we trailed earlier, this wasn't an obvious idea and on face value it carried very high risks.

Who needs to shop there?

In 1993 Tesco was in a very difficult position. The *Times* newspaper captured the essence of the company's problem: 'if you want quality shop at Sainsbury, if you want price shop at the discounters. Tesco is stuck in the middle. Who needs to shop there?'[53] Tesco's position was summarized by Leahy as being 'stuck in the doldrums'. Tesco needed to build reasons for customers to shop with them, they needed to create loyalty. Not only did the company manage to do this, but within a decade they came to dominate UK retail sales and more. By the end of 1995, Tesco had overtaken Sainsbury to become the largest grocer in the UK. Two years later, Tesco had passed Marks & Spencer to become the number one retailer in the UK. In 2011, Tesco had around 30 per cent of the national grocery market and was the third largest retailer in the world, behind Walmart and Carrefour. By then, according to UK academics Nigel Piercy and David Cravens, it was 'nearly twice the size of its nearest competitors, Asda and Sainsbury.'[54]

How was this achieved? There were many reasons but according to Sir Terry Leahy, 'the launch of the Clubcard in February 1995 was, in my view, undoubtedly the most significant.'[55] And Leahy wasn't the only one to think so. Using an expression we'll return to in our concluding chapter, the BBC's Denise Winterman asserts that 'what really took Tesco to the top was watching customer behaviour. It was the first British supermarket to do so and it was a *game-changing* move.'[56] This is a view supported by Simon Knox, Emeritus Professor at Cranfield School of Management, citing the introduction of the Clubcard as 'the real change agent' underpinning Tesco's phenomenal growth.[57]

Yet it was not an easy idea to sell. The company had earlier closed its huge, stamp-collecting loyalty scheme[58] (Green Shield Stamps), which had in some ways defined an unsuccessful period in Tesco's history. And this previous failure led many to question the sense behind Leahy's new initiative. However, the card held the potential to reveal a vast amount of customer information for Tesco. And with positive indications from existing customers, Leahy went ahead with his game-changing initiative, with startling results. In the mature grocery market, a 1 or 2 per cent movement either side of the industry average was what could normally be expected. But as Leahy noted, without a hint of understatement: 'That morning, we were 11 per cent per cent ahead. I knew at that moment something had changed in the industry forever, and my life along with it.'[59] Even so conventional wisdom still decried the scheme. David Sainsbury believed the card didn't give enough value to customers. In his view the scheme would cost 'at least £10 million just to administer. That's wasted money, which brings no benefits at all to customers.'[60] Only six months following the launch of the Clubcard, the evidence was undeniable. Tesco reported 16 per cent increase in half-yearly pre-tax profits, and a 2.1 per cent increase in market share.[61]

Why was Clubcard such a spectacular success, where other loyalty schemes had failed? It was one of the world's first shopper loyalty cards but at its heart, the card epitomized a very simple idea. When customers joined the scheme, they were rewarded with a 1 per cent discount off all shopping in any Tesco store. In return, Clubcard gave Tesco vital data about their customers' purchases and purchase habits, which is the other startling statistic about Clubcard's success. At that time, in that industry, untargeted promotional efforts typically received a response rate of 1 per cent. Armed with Clubcard information, responses to Tesco's targeted promotions were between 10 and 30 times better. But Clubcard was more than just a successful loyalty card – it was a practical example of the value to be found in reversing the flow. Showing leadership that is focused on service to customers, and demonstrating the common touch, Leahy himself summarized why his loyalty scheme had succeeded where others had failed: 'It was a thank you, pure and simple.'[62]

Simple leadership is about making life easier for everyone. But leading with service is also about being at ease with those around you, whether you're talking with crowds or walking with kings.

Talking with crowds, walking with kings

If, one of Rudyard Kipling's most famous poems, includes these lines:

> *If you can talk with crowds and keep your virtue,*
> *Or walk with Kings – nor lose the common touch*

The common touch is all too easy to lose when people move into leadership roles. Sometimes this brings with it the notion that you have joined 'the other side'. Yesterday you were 'just' an employee, today you're management.

So it should not be forgotten that uncommon leadership is about keeping in touch. It's about being at ease with others and putting others at ease. To illustrate this point, we'll finish this chapter with three different perspectives, which will shed light on leadership with the common touch. First, we'll start with an example. Few business leaders have captured the public's perception of what it means to have the common touch, more than one UK entrepreneur. Then we'll consider how to guard against losing the common touch. Finally we'll explore the contrasting approaches used by two former British prime ministers, to shed light on what it means to lead with the common touch.

Sharing the common touch

The business leader often associated with the common touch is Sir Richard Branson. In 2009, Cancer Research UK conducted a poll[63] to find out which celebrity Britons would most like as their boss. Branson won the title, beating US President Barack Obama into second place. In 2013, the National Business awards conducted another poll, this time with over 1,000 employees and business leaders. Asked who they thought was the most inspirational leader, Branson won again, this time ahead of Bill Gates, Lord Alan Sugar and Steve Jobs. Several respondents cited Branson's tenacity and determination, borne of his oft-cast role as the underdog.

Perhaps the best example of this was when Branson's Virgin Atlantic locked horns with the UK's giant, national airline, British Airways (BA). Virgin took legal action over claims of BA's anti-competitive behaviour and a dirty-tricks campaign. The contest ended in 1993 when BA agreed to the largest, uncontested, out-of-court libel settlement in UK history. The case cost BA some £3 million in legal fees, plus around £600,000 paid to Branson and Virgin Atlantic. A gleeful UK press often portrayed Branson as a swashbuckling, man-of-the-people, entrepreneur. They characterized him as a modern-day David, battling Lord King's Goliath.

But there was one more twist to the story, which further reinforces Branson's image as a leader with the common touch. What did he do with the money he received from BA? As a thank-you present, he shared it with the employees of Virgin Atlantic. Of course, Sir Richard Branson isn't short of money and there is no doubting that he fought BA for principle rather than payment. So whilst the money may not have been a big thing to Branson, it certainly was for his employees. As we pointed out earlier in this chapter, it's the small things that count. But this story illustrates something else which we will discuss in the next chapter – Sharing – the final S in uncommon leadership.

Branson is a good example of someone who works at keeping the common touch, but how do you guard against losing it? Never forget that in leadership, as in life, it's about the small things.

A PhD in the common touch?

We often describe people who have moved into leadership roles as having lost touch – with customers, with people on the 'frontline', or with the reality of what is happening in the business. In one of his trademark, high-octane presentations, Tom Peters told a story of what it means for leaders to be in touch. He asked his audience to imagine having waited six months for that meeting with Mr/Ms Big. You finally get into the room for the five minutes you've been given, and guess what? He/she looks at you but doesn't see you. The boss is in the room but not in touch.

Peters uses this story to help him define excellent leadership. It also illustrates what we mean by leading with the common touch, a leader who is '… completely there for you.' Peters goes on to quote Dee Hock, the founder of Visa. According to Peters, Hock once proposed a 'short PhD in leadership', which echoes our earlier discussions on simplicity: 'Make a list of all the things done to you that you abhorred. Don't do them to others. Ever. Make another list of things done to you that you loved. Do them to others. Always.'[64]

Tom Peters suggests that for budding leaders, this is '99 per cent of what you need to know.' Well, that may be something of an *over*-simplification, but it's sound advice nonetheless. So sound that perhaps it could be re-labelled as a short PhD in the common touch.

Shining a light on leadership

When leaders have the common touch things are different, and people notice the difference. For example, Warren Bennis tells a story about William Gladstone and Benjamin Disraeli. These two 19th-century British prime ministers were brilliant politicians but bitter rivals. According to this story, each had a completely different impact on the people they met. It's said that when Gladstone invited you around for a meal, you left feeling he was the wittiest, most charming and most brilliant person in the world. When spending an evening with Disraeli, you left feeling that *you* were the wittiest, most charming and most brilliant person in the world. *When with Gladstone, he shone. When with Disraeli, you shone.*

The story makes two important points about leaders who have the common touch. Such leaders seem to have a knack for putting the people they lead at ease. This can often make people more receptive to what leaders have to say. It may even make them more likely to follow a leader. But leading with the common touch means more than that. It's more than encouraging people to be at ease, attentive and receptive. Leaders with the common touch do much more than just engage with their colleagues, they help bring out the best in them. They re-focus the leadership spotlight to help others shine.

From serving to sharing

This has been a chapter of upside-down thinking. To lead you need to serve. To lead you need to follow. To build loyalty you need to be loyal. To build a business with a legacy, turn around the purpose of the business, from shareholder profit to employee happiness. A David beats a Goliath, then shares his spoils. A priest shows respect, and a young boy sees a defining moment in his life.

Leading with service has explored both how leaders serve their colleagues, and how they serve their customers. Remember how Sir Terry Leahy ensured he was grounded in reality. He kept in touch by seeing what it was like to both work in the business, and to be a customer of the business. Leahy described his best leadership as sitting and listening, and letting customers take the lead. When Apple opened stores despite industry critics predicting failure, they found a way to win by discovering a distinctive way to serve their customers, leading with their customer experience. This leadership builds bridges and connects with employees and customers.

So next we turn to our final S in the 5-S leadership framework. There we'll try to answer the question: how can leaders share and spread leadership within their organizations?

Bibliography

1   Yunus, M (2007) *Banker to the Poor: Micro-lending and the battle against world poverty*, Philadelphia, Public Affairs

2   ibid

3   Yunus, M (2005) Eliminating poverty through market-based social entrepreneurship, *Global Urban Development Magazine*, **1** (1)

4   Yunus, M (2010) *Building Social Business: The new kind of capitalism that serves humanity's most pressing needs*, Philadelphia, Public Affairs

5   Grameen Bank (2011) [accessed 17 September 2011] Is Grameen Bank Different from Conventional Banks? Grameen Bank [Online] http://www.grameen-info.org/index.php?option=com_content&task=view&id=27&Itemid=176

6   Grameen Bank (2011) [accessed 17 September 2011] Grameen Bank at a Glance Grameen Bank [Online] http://www.grameen-info.org/index.php?option=com_content&task=view&id=26

7   ibid

8   Yunus, M (2010) *Building Social Business: The new kind of capitalism that serves humanity's most pressing needs*, Philadelphia, Public Affairs

9   Yunus, M (2009) [accessed 12 September 2013] Lifting people worldwide out of poverty, *Knowledge@Wharton* [Online] http://knowledge.wharton.upenn.edu/article.cfm?articleid=2243

10   BBC News (2003) [accessed 12 September 2013] Defining the moment [Online] http://news.bbc.co.uk/1/hi/in_depth/3051830.stm

11   Clarke, P J (2011) *Lives that Made a Difference*, Durham, Strategic Book Group

12   BBC News (2003) [accessed 12 September 2013] Defining the moment [Online] http://news.bbc.co.uk/1/hi/in_depth/3051830.stm

13   The British Sandwich Association (2013) [accessed on 17 September 2013] Facts about Sandwiches [Online] http://www.lovesarnies.com/yum/index.php/features-a-news/history-facts-and-figures/item/146-facts-about-sandwiches-did-you-know

14   Leahy, T (2010) *Management in Ten Words*, New York, Random House Business Books

15   ibid

16   Cooper, C (2000) Management blasted at nuclear plant, *People Management*, London, Chartered Institute of Personnel and Development

17 BBC News (2000) [accessed on 17th September 2013] BNFL Ends Japan Nuclear Row, *BBC News: UK Politics* [Online] http://news.bbc.co.uk/1/hi/uk/828046.stm

18 ibid

19 Forwood, M (2008) *The Legacy of Reprocessing in the United Kingdom*, International Panel on Fissile Materials

20 D'Arcy, C (2013) [accessed 17 September 2013] How Tesco is secretly taking over your high street, *MSN Money* [Online] http://money.uk.msn.com/features/how-tesco-is-secretly-taking-over-your-high-street

21 Leahy, T (2010) *Management in Ten Words*, New York, Random House Business Books

22 Humby, C, Hunt, T and Phillips, T (2004) *Scoring Points: How Tesco is winning customer loyalty*, London, Kogan Page

23 Leahy, T (2010) *Management in Ten Words*, New York, Random House Business Books

24 ibid

25 Greenleaf, R K (1982) [accessed 20 November 2013] What is Servant Leadership? *The Robert K Greenleaf Center for Servant Leadership* [Online] https://greenleaf.org/what-is-servant-leadership/

26 Handy, C (1999) *The Hungry Spirit – Beyond Capitalism: A quest for purpose in the modern world*, New York, Broadway Books

27 Isaacson, W (2012) [accessed 20 November 2013] The real leadership lessons of Steve Jobs, *Harvard Business Review*, [Online] http://hbr.org/2012/04/the-real-leadership-lessons-of-steve-jobs/ar/1

28 John Lewis Partnership [accessed 20 November 2013] About Us [Online] http://www.johnlewispartnership.co.uk/about.html

29 Confino, J (2012) [accessed 20 November 2013] John Lewis and the search for happiness *The Guardian/Professional/Guardian Sustainable Business* [Online] http://www.theguardian.com/sustainable-business/john-lewis-shared-ownership-business-model

30 John Lewis Partnership [accessed 20 November 2013] Our Strategy [Online] http://www.johnlewispartnership.co.uk/about/our-strategy.html

31 Lampel, J, Bhalla, A and Jha, P (2012) *The Employee Ownership Advantage: Benefits and consequences*, London, Department for Business, Innovation and Skills

32 Davies, W (2009) *Reinventing the Firm*, London, Demos

33 Kennedy, C (2003) *From Dynasties to Dotcoms: The rise fall and reinvention of British business in the last 100 years*, London, Kogan Page

34   Lewis, J S (1954) in: Witzel, M (2009) *Management History: Text and cases*, London, Routledge

35   Witzel, M (2009) *Management History: Text and cases*, London, Routledge

36   Humby, C and Popeck, V (2010) *Dunnhumby on Loyalty*, Dunnhumby

37   ibid

38   Hayward, M (2009) *Any Colour You Like As Long As It's Any Colour You Like*, Dunnhumby

39   Humby, C and Popeck, V (2010) *Dunnhumby on Loyalty*, Dunnhumby

40   Humby, C, Hunt, T and Phillips, T (2003) *Scoring Points: How Tesco is winning customer loyalty*, London, Kogan Page

41   Hayward, M (2009) *Any Colour You Like As Long As It's Any Colour You Like*, Dunnhumby

42   Johnston, R (2003) *Delivering Service Excellence: The view from the front line*, London, Institute of Customer Service

43   Isaacson, W (2012) [accessed 20 November 2013] The real leadership lessons of Steve Jobs, *Harvard Business Review*, [Online] http://hbr.org/2012/04/the-real-leadership-lessons-of-steve-jobs/ar/1

44   Johnson, R (2011) [accessed 20 November 2013] What I learned building the Apple Store, *Harvard Business Review* [Online] http://blogs.hbr.org/cs/2011/11/what_i_learned_building_the_ap.html

45   Useen, J (2011) [accessed 20 November 2013] How Apple became the best retailer in America, *CNN Money* [Online] http://tech.fortune.cnn.com/tag/gap/

46   Edwards, C (2001) [accessed 20 November 2013] Commentary: Sorry, Steve: here's why Apple stores won't work, *Bloomberg Business Week Magazine* [Online] http://www.businessweek.com/stories/2001-05-20/commentary-sorry-steve-heres-why-apple-stores-wont-work

47   Segal, D (2012) [accessed 23 June 2013] Apple's retail army, long on loyalty but short on pay, *The New York Times* [Online] http://www.nytimes.com/2012/06/24/business/apple-store-workers-loyal-but-short-on-pay.html?_r=1&

48   Useen, J (2007) [accessed 23 June 2013] Apple: America's best retailer, *CNN Money* [Online] http://money.cnn.com/magazines/fortune/fortune_archive/2007/03/19/8402321/

49   Clifford, S (2013) [accessed 23 June 2013] Chief talks of mistakes and big loss at J C Penney, *New York Times: Business Day* [Online] http://www.nytimes.com/2013/02/28/business/jc-penneys-chief-says-his-mistakes-led-to-big-loss.html

50   ibid

51   Denning, S (2013) [accessed 23 June 2013] J C Penney: was Ron Johnson's strategy wrong? *Forbes* [Online] http://www.forbes.com/sites/stevedenning/2013/04/09/j-c-penney-was-ron-johnsons-strategy-wrong/

52 Thau, B (2013) [accessed 23 June 2013] Ron Johnson speaks, calls reports on his J C Penney tenure 'Largely inaccurate and surprisingly uninformed', *Forbes* [Online] http://www.forbes.com/sites/barbarathau/2013/10/29/an-open-letter-to-ex-j-c-penney-ceo-ron-johnson-who-calls-reports-on-his-tenure-surprisingly-uninformed-when-youre-ready-can-we-talk/

53 Leahy, T (2010) *Management in Ten Words*, New York, Random House Business Books

54 Cravens, D W and Piercy, N F (2012) *Strategic Marketing*, New York, McGraw-Hill

55 Leahy, T (2010) *Management in Ten Words*, New York, Random House Business Books

56 Winterman, D (2013) [accessed 19 November 2013] Tesco: how one supermarket came to dominate, *BBC News Magazine* [Online] http://www.bbc.co.uk/news/magazine-23988795

57 Knox, S (2012) [accessed 10 November 2013] Tesco's growth success, *Cranfield University School of Management, Think* [Online] http://www.som.cranfield.ac.uk/som/p18725/Think-Cranfield/2012/November-2012/Tesco-s-Growth-Success

58 Humby, C, Hunt, T and Phillips, T (2004) *Scoring Points: How Tesco is winning customer loyalty*, London, Kogan Page

59 Leahy, T (2010) *Management in Ten Words*, New York, Random House Business Books

60 Peck, H C, Clark, M and Payne, A (2004) *Relationship Marketing for Competitive Advantage*, Oxford, Elsevier Butterworth-Heinemann

61 ibid

62 Leahy, T (2010) *Management in Ten Words*, New York, Random House Business Books

63 Cancer Research UK (2009) [Online] http://www.cancerresearchuk.org/about-us/cancer-news/press-release/branson-beats-obama-as-celebrity-dream-boss

64 Peters, T (2007) [accessed 20 November 2013] Gain respect by giving it [Online] http://www.youtube.com/watch?v=v-DYHdxcAw8

LEADING WITH PEOPLE

SHARING LEADERSHIP BY MAKING IT MORE COMMON

KEY TOPICS

- The case for shared leadership – when the ordinary becomes extraordinary.
- Sharing vision – compelling pictures and lazy leadership.
- Sharing enthusiasm – infectious leadership, bad apples and marital bliss.
- Sharing strengths – incompetence, mediocrity and excellence.
- Sharing influence – nudging leadership.
- Building human towers – a motto for shared leadership.

FIGURE 5.1 Sharing

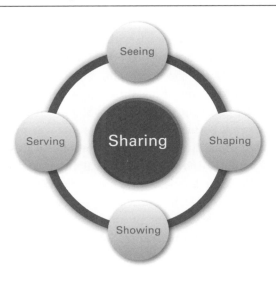

The case for shared leadership

So far we've explored how uncommon leaders:

- Find the sense before it becomes common.
- Make that sense common sense.
- Do the common things uncommonly well.
- Have the common touch to serve the needs of people, and the organization.

But if we are to make uncommon leadership a reality, then leadership needs to become far more common. For that to happen we need leadership to be shared more widely in our organizations. We need more leaders who can see the extraordinary in what might initially appear to be the ordinary.

When the ordinary becomes extraordinary

Why, in 2005, did a major-league US basketball team dare to discard all the conventional measures of success and buy an 'average' player? What did they know that others didn't? And what is the powerful, often-forgotten leadership lesson to be found in the answer to both questions? In 2005, the National Basketball Association's Houston Rockets found that most of its money was being spent in paying two superstar players. But despite their presence, the team was still performing poorly. The Rockets needed new talent but had no spare money to turn things around. Daryl Morey, the new general manager, had to think differently.

US pro-basketball had become awash with statistics. Conventional success measures, such as points scored, rebounds taken and shots blocked, made it easy to identify the top-performing players. But unable to afford conventional, Morey did something different – he opted for something unconventional. The player he recruited was Shane Battier. By most of the conventional measures, Battier was no superstar, he was simply average. In his 2008 *New York Times* article, Michael Lewis put it this way: 'Battier's game is a weird combination of obvious weaknesses and nearly invisible strengths.'[1] From the same article, Morey's own description of Battier went even further: 'He can't dribble, he's slow and hasn't got much body control.' Not the most inspiring assessment of any player, much less one who is supposed to turn around a losing team. So what had Morey seen in Battier that others hadn't? If, by all the normal measures, Battier really was only average, what made him so special for Morey? The answer to this question is at the heart of shared leadership. Michael Lewis summarized the real impact Battier had on his team: 'When he is on the court, his team-mates get better, often a lot better and his opponents get worse – often a lot worse.'

This is a counter-intuitive story in several ways. Necessity drove Daryl Morey to think differently and what he found provides a powerful lesson for leaders. Conventional performance measures were turned on their head by a player who was ordinary, but whose presence made his team extraordinary. Although his own game statistics were no better than average, when Battier played, his team-mates shone! Battier is what you might call a play-maker. He both brings out the best in his team-mates, and helps them exploit the synergy of effective teamwork.

When shared leadership makes sense

In our organizations, it's all too easy to focus on the 'super-stars'. These are the people who seem to perform really well when rated against individual performance measurements. Yet doing so can obscure the value of other performers, those who add value to the organization by bringing out the best in their colleagues. So the starting point in sharing leadership more widely is to help people perform better both as individuals, and as part of a team. Providing support for improved individual and collective performance can set the stage for greater benefits still. Encouraging people to take the lead in their areas of expertise, or to show initiative, creativity and teamwork, can help realize the benefits of real shared leadership.

When discussing leadership it's tempting to think in terms of the people at the 'top' of an organization. Even our earlier discussions on inverted pyramids and servant leadership might seem to imply that leadership comes from one person. But increasingly, effective leadership comes from encouraging wider responsibility *within* organizations. Flatter structures, cross-functional and project teams, and devolved responsibility all require the development of leadership skills all across the organization. This point is nicely illustrated in a UK Government report on leadership: 'Effective leadership runs through organizations like writing through a stick of rock [candy]'.[2]

Making leadership skills more common throughout the organization is a key feature of the uncommon approach to leadership. In any sector, the drive to foster collaboration and co-operation across professional and organizational boundaries clearly indicates the need for different approaches to leadership. More and more people will be expected to take the lead in their area of expertise. In many ways this is how it should be, people taking leadership and responsibility for what they know and do best. It makes sense to encourage leadership as a collective responsibility. Developing leadership skills at all levels is likely to enhance the performance of people, teams and the organization as a whole.

It has probably not escaped your attention that the 5-S uncommon leadership characteristics may seem demanding. In fact, you may be wondering if it's really possible to find them all in one leader. Which is another reason why the fifth 'S' is about shared leadership. Shared leadership isn't just a good idea because organizations need more people taking responsibility for leadership. It's also good because teams of leaders mean different strengths can be combined. Not many leaders will excel at every one of our 5-S characteristics. Some may be good at seeing the sense before it becomes common sense, others at doing the common things uncommonly well. With *teams* of leaders, different strengths can be combined to make overall leadership more effective:

It might be expecting too much to see all five uncommon leadership characteristics in one person, but in a team of leaders, that's a different story.

Teams of leaders

Whether referring to co-leadership, distributed leadership, collaborative leadership or shared leadership itself, the language of sharing features prominently in recent thinking on leadership. One reason for this emerging emphasis on shared leadership is because organizations are moving away from hierarchical structures towards more team-based environments. Alongside the introduction of flatter, team-based organizational structures, there is a growing emphasis on collaboration. This can be seen across functional areas *within* organizations, or increasingly it appears *between* organizations, as they share their expertise through partnerships and collaborative ventures. This shift is explained by three US researchers, who have been influential in setting the context for shared leadership: Craig Pearce; Charles Manz; and Henry Sims.[3] They argue that the growing interest in shared leadership is due to:

- Competition – driving firms to new forms and models of organizing, with teams being a central strand in these changes. Flatter structures often have fewer managers, and therefore need more leadership from within teams.

- The knowledge economy – in which different people will know best or better at different times. Knowledge workers often need to take a lead in their areas of expertise.

- Speed – in the current fast-paced, consumer-focused business world, organizations face increasing demands for rapid, responsive, delivery. Traditional, hierarchical structures are too slow. Leadership needs to be distributed and closer to the action.

- Complexity – the sheer complexity of business and the volume of information means that jobs are just too complex to be handled by a few senior leaders.

So fostering a sense of shared leadership through teams and individuals will be almost essential for businesses of the future. This adds up to a situation that begs several questions. Perhaps the first is the most obvious: Is the formal leader's role now impossibly complex? It also prompts us to wonder whether leadership by just a few formal leaders ever really was the best way to do things. Even if this were once true, it certainly raises doubts about such an approach to leadership given the pressures of current and future business environments.

A single, heroic leader or a team of rivals?

So given these fundamental questions, is the idea of a single, heroic leader really the right picture of leadership? Does the enduring emphasis on the individual leader help to obscure the value of a shared approach? After all, there can't be many leaders who have achieved success without the shared leadership of supporting people or teams. Yet the idea of individual leadership is hard to shift. Bolden[4] explains why this is the case with two, pointed quotes from US-academics James O'Toole, Edward Lawler and Jay Galbraith. Firstly, they recognized a common perception, that 'shared leadership for most people is simply counter-intuitive: leadership is obviously and manifestly an individual trait and activity'. But they go on to illustrate the paradox in this belief, referring to some of history's most famous, single, heroic leaders, such as Mahatma Gandhi and Martin Luther King, Jr: 'When the facts are fully assembled even the most fabled 'solitary' leaders relied on the support of a team of other effective leaders'.

Some famous leaders have even succeeded by sharing leadership with their rivals. Doris Kearns Goodwin's book, *Team of Rivals*, tells the story of Abraham Lincoln's pivotal 1861–65 political cabinet. Rather than shun his presidential rivals, Lincoln included them at the heart of US government. He wanted the best men working *with* him and *for* the nation, and not on the sidelines working against him. And rather than trying to lead alone, Lincoln and the country benefited from the shared leadership of some of the country's most capable politicians. *Team of Rivals* came to the attention of many when US President Barack Obama referred to the book after winning his first presidential election. When forming his own first cabinet, Obama sought to emulate Lincoln's counter-intuitive approach to shared leadership. Doris Kearns Goodwin captured a refreshing insight into shared leadership when she wrote about how Lincoln's political genius was:

> ... *revealed through his extraordinary array of personal qualities that enabled him to form friendships with men who had previously opposed him; to repair injured feelings that, left untended, might have escalated into permanent hostility; to assume responsibility for subordinates; to share credit with ease; and to learn from mistakes.*[5]

That's not a bad list of shared leadership qualities: the ability to build friendships, even amongst people you disagree with; to be emotionally intelligent, take responsibility, share credit with ease and to learn from mistakes. And not bad for a man who, when nominated for president at the 1860 Republican Convention, was described by the *New York Herald* as fourth-rate: 'The conduct of the Republican Party in this nomination is a remarkable indication of small intellect, growing smaller. They pass over... statesmen and able men, and they take up a fourth-rate lecturer, who cannot speak good grammar.'[6]

Adapting or embedding?

In stressing the value of emerging ideas on shared leadership, there is a risk that they can be over-emphasized. It can be all too easy to lose the value of what has gone before. So we're not suggesting you should disregard the importance of individual and formal leadership. These can and do go hand-in-hand with the concept of shared leadership. This is illustrated by the work of two MIT academics, Deborah Ancona and Elaine Backman,[7] working on an MIT project 'to identify DL [distributed leadership] practices, mapping their dynamics, and evaluating their effectiveness so that we know more about what it is and how to make it work at the firm level.'[8] Ancona and

Backman characterized four kinds of organization that experiment with shared leadership:

- Hierarchical organizations that introduce shared leadership practices as an 'overlay on a hierarchy'.

- Shared DNA organizations, like Google and W L Gore & Associates that minimize hierarchy and maximize collaboration.

- Nimble-networks composed of individuals and networks working semi-autonomously, such as Wikipedia and some of the growing share/open source initiatives.

- Cross-organizational collaborations, such as joint ventures or value chain collaborations.

But for some organizations, adaptation is not enough. The only way some businesses can live up to their vision is to ensure that shared leadership is embedded in all that they do. US academics Pierce, Manz and Sims capture this distinctive approach with reference to one well-known American airline. Renowned for its high levels of customer service, in a very competitive market, Southwest Airlines was the world's first low-cost airline. But unlike some of its direct competitors, the airline doesn't succeed by cutting corners and squeezing every possible overhead. It reaps the rewards of embedding shared leadership throughout the organization: 'Southwest Airlines is the only continuously profitable US airline over the past three decades.' What is their secret? According to Jim Parker, former CEO of Southwest,

> *Many people think that the source of our success is our cost structure – that we pay our people less than our competitors – but that simply is not true. The real source of our competitive advantage is our culture, which is based firmly on the principles of distributed and shared leadership.*[9]

So for organizations like Southwest Airlines, shared leadership is fundamental to their success and to the way they do business. But what does that mean in practice – how do they make it happen? Firstly, they pay particular attention to the way they recruit people. Herb Kelleher, founder of Southwest Airlines, put it this way: 'We believe that every person in the company is a leader in one way or another, no matter what their position in the company.'[10] This means the airline places a particular emphasis on recruiting people with the right attitude and with leadership potential. And there is something else that's different about their recruitment process. Interviews for new recruits involve a wide range of existing staff, ensuring decisions about job-offers are informed by those who know what's actually needed on the frontline. Then, echoing the 'bad apple' research we discuss later in this chapter, the company is very careful about ensuring they only keep the right people: 'We'll work with anybody that's trying. But if someone is exhibiting a poor attitude, or behavior that goes against our grain and our expectation, we get rid of bad apples as quickly as we can.'[11]

There is another counter-intuitive feature of the Southwest Airlines set-up. Although it's renowned as a successful, low-cost airline, the company has a higher supervisor–frontline employee ratio than any other airline. And according to Brandeis University's Dr Jody Gittell,[12] this is both critical to their success and clear evidence of their distributed leadership approach. At Southwest Airlines, decision-making is 'pushed down' the organization, closer to the customer interface and is therefore more responsive. And the company's extended network of leaders helps provide the coaching and counselling needed to make it work. Impressive as the Southwest Airlines example may be, there is another, even more radical example of shared leadership in action. This doesn't just challenge the notion of individual leadership. It makes us think about how leaders are appointed, and how they earn the right to lead.

Natural leaders or appointed leaders?

During a key scene in the 1995 movie *Braveheart*, Mel Gibson's William Wallace talks with Scotland's future king, Robert the Bruce. Wallace promises to follow Bruce if he would take the lead in fighting the English. But there is one, critical, unspoken question in the scene: who is the leader here? Robert the Bruce was a nobleman, and thus recognized as an 'official' leader, but at the time he was incapable of showing leadership. In contrast, Wallace lacked a noble rank, and had no power beyond the strength of his convictions and his undoubted ability to lead. Regardless of rank and position, these were more than enough for the many who *chose* to follow Wallace in his epic struggle. Robert the Bruce may have been later crowned king, but it was William Wallace who became one of the most famous leaders in Scottish history. Wallace's situation is a reminder of the challenging question we posed in Chapter 3: why should anyone be led by you? But the encounter between Wallace and Robert the Bruce prompts an even more challenging question, one very important to shared leadership: who decides who leads in your organization?

That's a question that W L Gore & Associates has addressed but with a very interesting twist. The world-renowned manufacturer of Goretex is no ordinary business. Like Southwest Airlines, it repeatedly ranks highly in US lists of best places to work. And Gore's different approach to work has underpinned its success all around the world. So how does W L Gore answer the question of how leaders are chosen? They ask their people who they *want* to lead them. Leadership at Gore is determined by 'followership'. Leaders emerge because they gain credibility with other associates. This is what Gore refers to as 'natural leadership,' an approach which is grounded in a very distinctive culture and structure.[13] Just like the UK's John Lewis (which refers to partners rather than employees), Gore is also owned by its workforce, who are called associates. At W L Gore & Associates:

> Everyone can quickly earn the credibility to define and drive projects. Sponsors [Gore terminology for managers] help associates chart a course in the organization that will offer personal fulfilment while maximizing their contribution to the enterprise. Leaders may be appointed, but are defined by 'followership.' More often, leaders emerge naturally by demonstrating special knowledge, skill, or experience that advances a business objective.'[14]

Leaders don't hold rank, title or privilege at W L Gore, so you might think not many associates would see themselves as a leader. Well you'd be wrong. In the annual employee survey, when they are asked the question: 'Do you consider yourself as a leader?' close to 50 per cent typically say they do.[15] This would seem to be a case of shared leadership on a grand scale.

You may recognize such 'leaders' in your own organization – people who are respected and listened to, but who don't necessarily hold a formal leadership position within the organization's structural hierarchy. Yet often these are the 'go-to' people, when things need to be done. Perhaps they are the people that others really recognize as leaders, even if employees don't get the opportunity to choose their leaders, like Gore's teams. The success of the Gore approach does make us wonder what leadership would be like if teams had more say in who leads them.

How Gore got to this position makes for interesting reading. When Bill and Vieve Gore founded the company in 1958, they wanted it to be a different kind of business. When previously working with Dupont, Bill Gore found that things seemed to work best when teams were created to work around projects and new ideas. Very often these teams worked outside of the formal structures and hierarchy of the company. Gore saw that there was a hidden 'real' way of working that had vitality and effectiveness, but one that rarely reflected Dupont's formal structure. As Bill Gore saw it: 'Every successful organization has an underground lattice. It's where the news spreads like lightning, where people can go around the organization to get things done.'[16]

In setting up his own business, Gore asked himself an interesting question: What would an organization be like if it was deliberately designed to capture these informal, 'real' ways of working? The W L Gore approach definitely provokes us to think differently about leaders and leadership. And Gore certainly offers a vision of leadership that is rooted in the concept of sharing. So how can your organization benefit from the advantages of a shared approach? Next we'll consider some ways to help build shared leadership.

Building shared leadership

Although shared leadership seems to make sense, it is no easy matter to make it work. It means meeting this mighty challenge of 'getting people to think of themselves as leaders or as having a leadership role.'[17] This begins with enabling people to perform well and to feel a part of the organization. As US leadership thinker Warren Bennis stresses: 'Good leaders make people feel that they're at the very heart of things, not at the periphery. Everyone feels that he or she makes a difference to the success of the organization. When that happens people feel centered and that gives their work meaning.'

To build shared leadership, we think it's helpful for leaders to 'share' some key themes with their colleagues. So in the rest of this chapter, we'll consider four different ways to think about sharing leadership:

1 sharing vision;
2 sharing enthusiasm;
3 sharing strengths;
4 sharing influence.

We'll begin with the most important of these, and in doing so return to some of the ideas we introduced in Chapter 1. If leaders are to build shared leadership, the best place to start is by developing a shared vision. To illustrate this point we take one, final look at the stonecutter story with a twist. Then we consider some surprising further research about people who see their work as a calling, and the impact this has on those they work with.

But sharing a vision is only the start, shared leadership means also sharing enthusiasm. So the next theme examines the importance of developing and encouraging enthusiasm. It looks at how organizations can benefit from enthusiasm through positive or 'infectious' leadership, and at the dangers of negativity exemplified by poor or 'infected' leadership, and the tolerance of 'bad apples'. There are some surprising answers to this issue, partly from research into marital harmony.

The third theme considers how we can build more leadership capability in others by encouraging them to use their strengths. This theme also addresses the importance of synergy, by building teams of people with individual but aligned complementary strengths. Shared leadership can't really be separated from shared learning. Leadership is an inherently social process and building more leadership capacity means learning and sharing together. The final theme builds on shared knowledge by considering the importance of shared influence in and between organizations. We examine some insights from behavioural science on how to lead by 'nudging' good behaviour. And we also consider the influence that middle managers can have, located as they are at the heart of organizations. Then we finish the chapter with an interesting story, which leaves us with a motto for shared leadership.

Sharing vision

First and foremost, if you want to encourage shared leadership you'll need people to *want* to be part of what's happening. That means developing a common sense of where you are going, and of what you want to achieve together. To see how leaders might do this, we'll turn to a third and final version of the stonecutter story. This version contains a subtle change of focus, which makes all the difference when thinking about shared leadership.

In the first version of the story, we highlighted the difference it can make when someone sees their work as contributing to something bigger. Our discussion there led to thinking about how people perceive their work and the impact this has on how well they do it. In the second version, we noted the tension that can result from a focus on just doing a good job, although in itself a good thing, without being concerned about the bigger picture. Peter Drucker identified this as a potential problem, where people focus too much on their own area without real concern for the wider impact on the organization. For example, individual team members may do their own k well, but without really engaging with the team as a whole. Or worse still, where silo working can encourage barriers to communication and obscure a focus on organization-wide objectives.

But this final version of the stonecutter story contains an added twist. It ends with an indication of the value of shared leadership.

'I am helping Sir Christopher Wren...'

This time our stonecutters are building London's magnificent St Paul's Cathedral, designed by the great British architect, Sir Christopher Wren. In this version of the story, the third stonecutter's response illustrates what can happen when employees feel they have a share in what the leader is trying to do. As in the earlier versions, the replies from the first two stonecutters were broadly the same – one felt he was cutting stone while the other felt he was earning a day's wage. But this time the third stonecutter answered: 'I am helping Sir Christopher Wren build a magnificent cathedral to the glory of God.'[18]

At face value, there may seem little difference in the three versions of the story. But the final twist is really quite significant. In this version, the third stonecutter is doing more than building a cathedral, he sees himself as *helping Sir Christopher Wren*. This stonecutter identifies with the leader, and sees his own role as one of offering direct support. It also shows two other things. The man has both connected with Wren's vision, and has taken a share in its success. The lesson is a valuable one: in order to build shared leadership, it's essential to share the vision. When leaders work with others to find the sense before it becomes common, then to make that sense common for the organization, they begin to create the conditions for shared leadership.

But did the third stonecutter's reply demonstrate shared leadership, or just someone happy in his work? Simply having the vision is not enough. Shared leadership requires leaders to have the ability to show that vision, to share it, and to inspire others to understand and work towards it. The third stonecutter only becomes a leader when he helps his workmates to share his view of his work – when more of them say they're not simply doing their job, but they're also helping Sir Christopher Wren to build a magnificent Cathedral. As Peter Senge has put it in *The Fifth Discipline*, the responsibility of a leader is not just to share a vision but to build a shared vision.[19] Once this is done, then shared leadership becomes a possibility.

Compelling pictures

As you may remember, our previous stonecutter story led us to think about how people view their work. Amy Wrzesniewski and her colleagues suggested there were three kinds of work orientations:

1 People who see work as just a job.

2 People who see work as a career.

3 People for whom work is a calling.

It's one thing to recognize that your view of work impacts how *you* feel and what you do, but Wrzesniewski went on to ask an even more interesting question: does having a different view of work impact on the way you work with others? Or putting the question another way: which work orientation do you think is more likely to make for good teamwork – doing a job, developing a career or seeing work as a calling? Wrzesniewski and her colleagues found some interesting insights, which they described as a 'compelling picture.'[20]

People who see their work as a calling (like our third stonecutter) tend to work far more effectively in teams than those who see their work as a career. And having more of these people in your team is likely to make it far more productive. Work-groups with a higher proportion of people for whom work is a calling reported some interesting findings. These showed a stronger, overall sense of team identity, less conflict, more faith and trust in management, more commitment to the team itself, and healthier group process such as more communication. But another, perhaps even more surprising point emerged from this research. Finding that people with a sense of calling contribute well in teams might be interesting but not necessarily surprising. But what about those people who see their work more as a career? You might expect that someone committed to developing a career would be productive and effective. This might be true but such an orientation does not necessarily make a team more productive and effective.

It begs the question: to what extent does a focus on career progression affect commitment to teamwork and team vision? Surprisingly, Wrzesniewski and her team found that work-groups with more career-oriented members had the reverse effect. They showed less commitment to the team, less faith and trust in management, and a weaker identification with the team.

It turns out that the third stonecutter's 'calling' orientation would work far better in a team setting, and would probably produce far better outcomes. According to Wrzesniewski and colleagues, it's people with a stronger sense of purpose and vision in what they do, those with a calling that perform better together. But building teams like this does more than increase productivity and help reap the rewards of synergy. It also helps lay the foundations for shared responsibility, and from there, shared leadership. Of course, it's much easier to develop a shared vision when people feel empowered. So long as empowered people are 'aligned'.

Shared empowerment

We've probably all worked with someone who is full of energy and bright ideas. And when that enthusiasm is coupled with a natural propensity for action, to start lots of things off, surely that's a good thing? It can be, but not when these live-wires continually go charging-off in different directions, taking colleagues, time and resources with them. It's one thing to have such people in our organizations, and to empower them to act. But such energy and enthusiasm are only of real value when they are properly aligned.

In his seminal book mentioned above, *The Fifth Discipline*, Peter Senge captured the essence of this energetic but directionless activity very well. Senge symbolized the organization as a large arrow, clearly pointing in just the one direction. But Senge cleverly depicted numerous smaller arrows within the organization, each representing individuals or groups of people. Some were pointing the same way as the bigger arrow, aligned with the organization's goals. But others clearly weren't, something Senge called empowerment without alignment.

The problem with unaligned empowerment is the potential damage it can do to the organization. Allowing people to go with ideas that are *too* far adrift from the general direction of the organizational arrow can be damaging at best, disastrous at worst. Taking Senge's idea a step further, perhaps we should think of our organizations as arrow-shaped balloons, each containing numerous smaller, sharper arrows. Allowing these to travel too far off course can cause the sides of the balloon to bulge, making it lose shape or aerodynamic efficiency. Or worse still, these errant arrows may puncture the bigger balloon, causing a slow descent or perhaps even a catastrophic crash. This is a powerful image, which underlines an important point. Empowerment works best when people are clear about the direction in which they are going. Healthy, growing organizations thrive best when visions are shared, actions aligned, and people are empowered to help achieve them both.

Lazy leadership

So if enthusiasm without direction can be a dangerous thing in any organization, it can be fatal on the battlefield. Just ask Napoleon. He blamed his final defeat at the battle of Waterloo partly on one subordinate who led repeated, futile cavalry attacks against the unbroken, British infantry 'squares'. Marshall Ney may have shown enthusiastic and active leadership, but the outcome was disastrous for the French army. It is said that Napoleon had his own leadership model,[21] characterizing leaders in terms of their intelligence and their industry. This suggests leaders can be either:

- intelligent and energetic;
- intelligent and lazy;
- stupid and energetic;
- stupid and lazy.

But which, according to Napoleon, was the best type of leader? You might expect it's someone who is intelligent and energetic – but that wouldn't be Napoleon's opinion. Such leaders might be likely to do too much. They may well concentrate on sensible ideas and implement them with unfaltering energy, but too much energy, however intelligent, might also lead to over-stretching or endless turmoil. And what about Napoleon's view of the worst kind of leader? The most obvious choice might seem to be the combination of stupidity and laziness. But for Napoleon, the worst leaders were stupid and energetic, because they waste resources on pointless actions.

This leaves the stupid and lazy leader, who is too lethargic to do any damage (and therefore not too bad an option). It also leaves one final leadership type, that which Napoleon considered to be the best. For him, the best leaders are intelligent and lazy. Why? Because they will have good ideas, but won't put them into practice themselves. Instead, such leaders will delegate to those most capable of implementing their ideas sensibly. But whilst Napoleon's point is thought-provoking, we're not really advocating lazy leadership. What we are proposing is leadership that combines enthusiasm with direction. Because one of the best things about enthusiasm is that it can be infectious, which is what we'll look at next.

Sharing enthusiasm

Enthusiasm without direction can lead to chaos, but what about direction without enthusiasm? This can result in an equally frustrating outcome. After all, who will buy into a vision when even the leader doesn't show enthusiasm? So the next theme on shared leadership is shared enthusiasm. In this section we'll examine the importance of enthusiasm at work, and how the impact of negativity can be a real threat to shared leadership – one that can't be ignored. But first let's take a look at contagious leadership because, as Ralph Waldo Emerson once said: 'Nothing great was ever accomplished without enthusiasm.'

Infectious or infected leadership?

Do your moods and emotions matter much to the colleagues around you? Well, they may matter a good deal more than you realize. It's quite possible that many leaders are unaware of the importance of their mood. And of the powerful messages they can convey through the expression of their emotions – deliberate or accidental. Moods and emotions can be contagious, just as laughter is often called infectious. Given that leaders are critically placed to influence what happens in organizations, it must then follow that their moods and emotions are arguably more important than most. And if that's true, then you might say their moods are more infectious than most. In fact you might say that leaders are highly contagious! So it's not surprising that Daniel Goleman (the writer and thinker behind emotional intelligence) thinks it pays for leaders to be optimists. As Winston Churchill once famously said: 'I'm an optimist, it doesn't seem to be much use being anything else.'

Of course we're not advocating indiscriminate or blind optimism. A leader's mood needs to match or relate to any given situation or climate. But there should be a healthy optimism about how these situations are approached. Why? Because, as Goleman said: 'good moods galvanize good performance.' In 'Primal Leadership', a *Harvard Business Review* article, Goleman and his colleagues made another interesting point. According to them, numerous studies 'show that when a leader is in a happy mood, the people around him view everything in a more positive light. That, in turn, makes them optimistic about achieving their goals.'[22]

Most people would probably agree with these sentiments, at least anecdotally. What's interesting about Goleman's claim is that it suggests a leader's mood can do more than affect the mood of others. It may also affect their performance. So there is evidence that a leader's optimism can be infectious – others can catch your energy, passion and affirmative attitude ✓ to work and life. And if this is true, then just imagine the impact of a *group* of leaders working together, all sharing a positive, optimistic purpose. This is another key, synergistic benefit of shared leadership. You might remember our earlier discussion of tipping point leadership, in which we used Chan Kim's and Professor Renée Mauborgne's definition of a tipping point. They argued that tipping points occur when: 'the energy and belief in an organization reaches a level that brings about change quickly.'[23]

Reaching this point will be far more likely when leaders encourage that belief with positive attitudes and approaches. And sharing these can lead to infectious leadership. Of course, we're well aware that infection can be a two-way street! There is always the possibility that leaders may be susceptible to the mood and emotions of others. This can be especially important in relation to key people in our lives. This prompts us to ask: to what extent do we catch the mood of others, perhaps without realizing it?

Before answering that question it's important to note that we are not advocating a negative-free zone. As we shall see, some forms of negativity have their place. In the next section we'll see just how powerful such negativity can be, by looking at some challenging insights. For example, we'll discuss the link between a team's exposure to negativity and its lower productivity and impaired performance. We'll also consider whether leaders and teams can learn anything from some ground-breaking research into negativity within marriages. The answers may surprise you and offer some insights into how leaders might challenge the power of negativity by fighting back.

From bad apples to slackers, downers and jerks

Have you ever noticed how one member of a team who is constantly negative, complaining or clearly unhappy can affect the mood of the whole team? The effect of such people can often seem pervasive, having a much greater impact than you might have expected. Eliza Byington had such an experience, working in a job that didn't seem a very happy place at all. But it wasn't until a colleague suddenly had some time off through illness that she realized where the problem lay. The mood in her team changed completely and everybody was happier, right up until her absent colleague returned to work. This person wasn't a leader, or a particularly prominent member of the team, but still had an adverse impact on the team, which was both profound and simple to explain – chronic negativity.

Byington was married to Will Felps, a doctoral student at the University of Washington Business School. On hearing about this 'bad apple' effect from his wife, Felps was prompted to begin a research study. He teamed up with Professor Terence Mitchell to investigate several published studies on how teams and groups interact. They wanted to see if there was any evidence on the impact of bad apples on teams, and any insights they could glean and share. Their research revealed three characteristics in these bad apples, which they referred to as 'the three most salient and important behaviors of a negative [team] member.' Time and again, bad apples upset their colleagues by: withholding effort; continually being negative, and by violating important personal norms, such as making fun of someone, saying something hurtful, acting rudely or making inappropriate comments. Stanford University's Professor Bob Sutton put these in layman's terms, referring to the three negative types as slackers, downers and jerks.[24]

Felps went on to test his ideas in a further study. He set up groups of students and gave them a problem to solve which required a group decision, within a 45-minute period.[25] Unknown to the students, Felps planted an actor into each group, tasked with exhibiting one of the three negative behaviours Felps had identified in his previous research. What Felps discovered was the second disturbing insight he'd gleaned from his research into bad apples. Negativity doesn't just affect how others feel at work. It can also have a significant adverse effect on team performance. Just how significant will give any leader pause for thought. Felps estimated that a team that includes just one negative or disruptive person can see a decline in performance of up to 30 per cent to 40 per cent, when compared with teams with no bad apples.

One group did buck the trend because a student in the team didn't get frustrated or decide to switch off. Instead he listened, questioned, checked for clarity then brought the team back to focus on its goals. In doing so he kept the team engaged and managed to overcome the actor's negative influence. But this example was an isolated exception. By far the most common result of the deliberately disruptive behaviour was a disrupted team, which struggled to function or achieve its goals. But Felps observed something even more significant in this experiment. Not only did the teams become less effective. Many team members began to adopt the disruptive behaviours they were seeing in the actor, becoming negative themselves towards others in the group. Even in teams, bad apples can contaminate the rest of the barrel. Discussing his study with Ira Glass on the radio programme *This American Life*,[26] Felps explained what had surprised him the most. Predictably, the teams started out being positive and energized but what struck Felps was that 'by the end they are like him (the actor), all with heads on the desk.'

Of course Felps's experiment was with students rather than real workplace teams. But it did support his earlier work with his wife and Terence Mitchell, studying numerous published reports on bad apple behaviour. And although it's true that not every team will lose 30 per cent to 40 per cent of its effectiveness as a result of bad apples, there is still enough evidence to suggest we need to take it seriously. However we try to quantify their impact, it doesn't take much to recognize the negative impacts that can occur when people withhold effort, are continually negative, or violate important personal norms. Felps and his colleagues did add a caveat, which it's worth mentioning here. Not everyone who challenges or argues should be labelled as a bad apple. Teams need people in them who are prepared to question and offer a contrasting viewpoint. Such people, called 'positive deviants' by Felps, might be mistakenly labelled as troublemakers. But in reality they can provide the challenge that teams need, in order to become more creative or to think differently.

The kind of bad apple behaviour which Felps and his colleagues identified can be far more disruptive than we realize. Not only does negative behaviour tend to weigh us down and absorb a great deal of effort, but its effects can be long-lasting. This is an aspect underlined by Jonathan Haidt in his book, *The Happiness Hypothesis*. Haidt argues that a relationship conflict, such as we might experience with an annoying office colleague, 'is one of the surest ways to reduce your happiness. You never adapt to interpersonal conflict, it damages every day, even days when you don't see the other person but ruminate about the conflict nevertheless.'[27]

So it's clear that the bad apple effect isn't the only piece of research to highlight the disruptive power of negativity. And interestingly, we can find some clues on how to manage it by looking at findings from other research studies.

Bad apples and marital bliss

In a challenging argument, which draws together several research, strands, Roy Baumeister[28] and his colleagues made a thought-provoking assertion. Bad emotions are stronger than good. Having examined a wide range of evidence, Baumeister and his team painted a pervasive picture:

> Bad emotions, bad parents, and bad feedback have more impact than good ones, and bad information is processed more thoroughly than good. The self is more motivated to avoid bad self-definition than to pursue good ones. Bad impressions and bad stereotypes are quicker to form and more resistant to disconfirmation than good ones.[29]

And they found similar results relating to a disturbingly wide range of circumstances. One source they referred to illustrates the strength of negativity from an unexpected perspective – John Gottman's well-known study of romantic relationships and marriage. Gottman and his team made video recordings of married couples both in a laboratory setting and at home. By analysing the ratio between positive and negative interactions during the subjects' conversations, the researchers found they could make a pretty accurate prediction about whether or not a couple would stay together. Where positive interactions outweighed the negatives by a ratio was 5 to 1, there was a much higher likelihood that the relationship would last. As Gottman explained:

> the balance between negativity and positivity appears to be the key dynamic in what amounts to the emotional ecology of every marriage... That magic ratio is 5 to 1. As long as there is five times as much positive feeling and interaction between husband and wife as there is negative, the marriage was likely to be stable over time.[30]

Perhaps our working relationships could benefit from some of this magic too!

There is no doubt from all of the research we have discussed that leaders need to address negativity in the workplace. This is especially important if the aim is to encourage shared leadership. Felps's slackers, downers and jerks need to be recognized and dealt with. Whilst we have talked much about being positive, leaders cannot leave the negative unchecked. Because, according to Felps, Mitchell and Byington, when bad apple behaviours 'unfold at work, it consumes inordinate amounts of time, psychological resources, and emotional energy.'[31]

But how do leaders fight back? As we asked earlier, how do you guard against negative moods infecting your workplace? The first suggestion probably sounds very obvious – try to spot negativity early, and deal with it, before it takes root. Though if it's too late for that, take heart. Positivity can overcome negativity, but for it to do so leaders need to work at switching the balance heavily in favour of the positive. And the most important lesson we can learn may seem rather counter-intuitive. Because bad is stronger than good, reducing or eliminating negativity will have a bigger impact than trying to increase positivity.

So, as we have now seen, just as infectious moods can improve performance, infected moods can impair it. But this takes us to another interesting point and a salient question. If you are leading a team that seems to be down or negative, have they caught the mood from you? A negative team is bad enough but it's potentially far more damaging when the cause of that negativity is infected leadership.

In medicine, an inoculation broadly gives your body a tiny sample of a disease, to help stop you getting the real thing. Your body reacts to the sample and builds antibodies, priming them for future action. Perhaps we can also use inoculations as a leadership analogy. When a leader's mood, words or actions seem unconvincing or even negative, are we inoculating our teams, priming them for future action – or inaction? Is just a taste of unconvincing leadership likely to make it far harder to convince them later, perhaps when it is more critical? It's rare to see a team motivated and enthused by the organization's vision, when their leader isn't. You don't often see people stretching themselves when their leaders have low expectations of them. Remember the Golem effect – when leaders have low expectations of their staff, people tend to perform poorly.

Whilst negativity can be extremely damaging in the workplace, it would be remiss to ignore the fact that negative isn't always bad. So we'll return to the idea of feedback to redress that balance.

When negative can be positive

In Chapter 3 we have promoted positive feedback, and to some extent questioned the role of negative feedback. It would seem that negative feedback has received an increasingly bad press. Is this merited? What's wrong with negative feedback? Nothing and everything! Used appropriately it can be very effective. Used inappropriately, it can be devastating. It may well be that in your workplace negative feedback predominates and a healthy dose of positive feedback might actually start to change the motivational focus.

But can negative feedback be used positively? Recent research[32] has found that people's response to feedback may actually change over time, in relation to a particular goal they are pursuing. So for example, when people are uncommitted to a goal, positive feedback is more motivational. That is, it increases their commitment. However, as people become committed to a goal, they appreciate feedback that tells them how they are progressing. This kind of feedback will often be negative; pointing out what is not working or what needs to be changed. Negative feedback therefore can have a positive effect, but to do so it requires leaders to think about the purpose of the feedback and the position of the person who will be receiving the feedback.[33]

These findings are similar to what Kirschenbaum found in the bowling story we recounted in Chapter 3. When people are proficient and experienced, they are more likely to appreciate negative feedback, which tells them where they are going wrong in order to get better.

How positive beats negative can be expressed in another way. Do you build on strengths more than correcting weaknesses? Nobody is good at everything, but do they need to be? Next we'll take a look at the importance of sharing strengths. After all, no organization builds competitive advantage based on its weaknesses.

Sharing strengths – incompetence, mediocrity and excellence

The late Peter Drucker is perhaps the most famous of modern, management thinkers. Drucker believed that the main responsibility of managers is to achieve the best results from the resources available to their organizations.

FIGURE 5.2 The three levels of strengths-based management

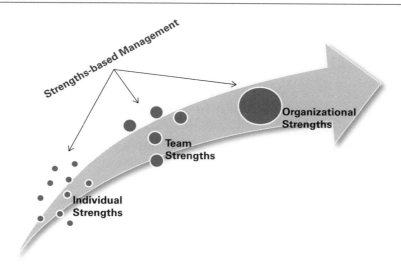

But he also believed that one of the best ways to do this is by building on strengths. For Drucker, this made obvious common sense: 'It takes far less energy to move from first-rate performance to excellence than it does to move from incompetence to mediocrity.'[34]

But in many organizations, far too much time is spent trying to address weaknesses. By contrast, nowhere near enough time is spent on helping people to get better at what they are good at, and then making a contribution. We'll look at strengths at three different levels: individuals; teams; and organizations as a whole.

What are strengths?

According to Peter Drucker, a strength is something you are already good at, where there is clear evidence from feedback that this is the case. Strengths can manifest themselves in several different ways. Individuals may be particularly strong in the way they *do* things, such as applying practical skills or expertise. Or we could interpret expertise in a more general way, to include the abilities, experience and attitudes people need to do their jobs.

Strengths may also relate to the way people think or reason, perhaps in an ability to think creatively or laterally. Others may have an abundance of personal or professional contacts, through well-developed networks. It may be that someone has a particular strength in creating opportunities, or perhaps they are good at bringing out the best in others. Earlier we talked about Shane Battier as an example of someone whose crucial individual strength was just this, rather than the technical expertise of playing basketball.

This brings us to the core issue in managing strengths. Whilst it is important to identify and develop individual strengths, the most value comes from combining these through teamwork. What makes the difference is when individuals with complementary skills come together, bringing out the best in each other to achieve the organization's objectives.

Team strengths

All too often performance management tends to concentrate on the individual, even when what really matters is how they work together as a team. The language of performance management is often about the individual and his or her line manager. Goals are set individually and performance is reviewed individually. There are real risks associated with agreeing individual goals without thought to their effect on the whole team. Without alignment of team and individual goals, one person may develop or achieve on a personal level, but this may be at odds with another colleague's goals, or be of little value to the team as a whole.

Wrzesniewski's research shows that people who focus on their own professional careers often don't really help their teams perform. These people may be good individually, but the team performance is not what it should be. As Charles Handy once said: 'No-one in their right mind would put 11 bowlers in a cricket team, or try to make a football team out of 11 goalkeepers.'[35]

Yet how often do we think about the complementary skills that people bring, or recognize the Shane Battiers amongst us, whose real strength is helping others to shine?

Sharing through collaboration – leading with other organizations

Alongside the well-established notion of competitive advantage, often cited as the private sector's raison d'être, the concept of collaborative advantage has firmly taken root. The central idea behind collaborative advantage is that significant value can be achieved by thinking of the network of relationships surrounding the organization. To put it another way, this means seeing organizations as a 'family.'[36] The language used to describe business relationships is beginning to reflect this changed way of thinking. Words such as partnerships, alliances, networks, and collaboration are in common use, pointing to the new focus on finding ways to combine the benefits of related networks of organizations and suppliers.

It's instructive to note how some of the early thinking about collaborative advantage was fundamentally linked to the importance of 'value' and 'relationships'. This is nowhere better illustrated than in the work of Rosabeth Moss Kanter, the leading US management thinker and Harvard academic. She suggested three principles on which to build collaboration:

1 Yield benefits and open possibilities beyond the original reason for collaborating.

2 Create value together (collaboration), rather than simply exchanging, getting something back in return for what you put in.

3 Build relationships across organizations – these are a key business asset and 'knowing how to nurture them is an essential managerial skill.'[37]

The distinctive nature of collaboration is further emphasized by Strathclyde Business School academic Chris Huxham.[38] She stressed the importance of synergy as a primary benefit of collaboration. For Huxham, collaboration should result in something being achieved that could not have been attained by any one organization acting alone.

Like Kanter, Huxham saw the role of nurturing as being critical to sustaining the collaboration. The key to gaining collaborative advantage does not lie in effective systems, processes and mechanisms. It comes through building and maintaining good relationships. This means the focus is on nurturing trust and creating value together, rather than merely aiming to get something back in return.

In the last chapter we introduced another good example of the value of shared leadership at organizational level – the Grameen Bank. Not only a radical bank for the poor, Grameen is also innovatory in the way it is building partnerships. Not satisfied with providing finance to the underprivileged of

Bangladesh, Yunus Muhammed is sharing his leadership approach through several new business partnerships, amongst them: Grameen Danone; Grameen Veolia; and Grameen Intel.

One of the first partnerships was with French company Danone, developing a nutritional yoghurt drink for poor children. The key challenge was to produce a health drink which was affordable for some of the world's poorest people yet which would still return value for the manufacturer. Grameen Danone succeeded in making a viable drink that contains all the nutrients that are missing from a poor child's diet.[39] Just two cups of the yoghurt per week, for eight or nine months, turned malnourished children into healthy, playful youngsters. How was this possible? The answer echoed the counter-intuitive approach so typical of Grameen.

Danone has created a purpose-built manufacturing facility, with a long-term plan to develop more plants that will service local communities. Although the existing facility is still not profitable, there are signs of future commercial viability, 'having generated the first positive gross margin in the fourth quarter of 2010'.[40] And this is within Danone's normal commercial business payback period of three years (although not within some over-optimistic initial predictions for the joint venture project, considering the novelty and difficulty of the task). Of course returning value to the manufacturer is not just about profit. Danone is also reaping other rewards from the partnership, including some valuable new insights into working with developing countries. So despite some early start-up difficulties, the joint venture is realizing some real mutual benefits, including 'manifold positive livelihood outcomes' in the area surrounding the first plant. Shared leadership at its humanitarian best.

It's clear that Danone and Grameen have *learned* much through their collaboration. So next we'll discuss a useful tool to help leaders ensure knowledge is shared more widely, both within and between organizations. It's time for a 'T' break.

Sharing knowledge with a 'T' break

Knowledge and learning can get stuck. Too often they stick in parts of the organization and don't get shared more widely. At times we may not be aware that there is knowledge in the organization to solve a particular issue. Think back to the Sternins' approach. They looked for things that were

FIGURE 5.3 Sharing knowledge with a 'T break'

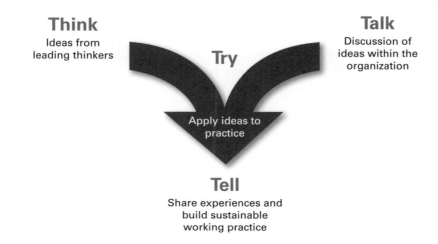

Think
Ideas from
leading thinkers

Try

Talk
Discussion of
ideas within the
organization

Apply ideas to
practice

Tell
Share experiences and
build sustainable
working practice

working and asked why, so they could spread that knowledge more widely. So next we'll look at how leaders can encourage the sharing of knowledge and experience throughout their organizations.

We should never overlook the resources that surround us every day. Shared leadership is about creating a fertile environment in which we can all learn and draw inspiration, both from our own experience and from the vast pool of knowledge and experience that surrounds us. It's true that a good deal of knowledge is gained from external sources, but there is also a surprising amount to be gleaned from knowledge within the organization and from shared experience. One way to lead the way in sharing knowledge is to encourage use of a 'T' break:

- *Think* about it.
- *Talk* about it.
- *Try* it.
- *Tell* others about it.

Compelling insights – think about it!

Thinking time is often in short supply, especially in busy organizations operating in today's fast-changing business environment. Yet most of us would intuitively recognize the power of stepping back and reflecting, on ideas, knowledge, experience and practices. But how many of us routinely do this? How much easier would it be to share knowledge and experience if we gave ourselves more time and space? The 'T' break technique can help reap the benefits of regular time allowed for thinking about issues and opportunities within the business. When time is so precious, it's important to use a process that helps filter and focus ideas and insights, to provide challenge and to encourage action. When thinking is informed by fresh insight and new ideas that promote debate, you have the potential for compelling insights.

That is one of the ideas behind this book. We have brought together a number of ideas and insights to both challenge thinking and to offer fresh perspectives. So consider how any of these might impact on your own practice, and how you can share them within your organization. Thinking is about finding the sense before it becomes common, so make time to think. Here are some suggestions to get you started:

- Use *Uncommon Leadership* to give you a structure for thinking about your own leadership, and elsewhere in your organization. Take each of the 5 S's in turn and think through what strikes you and what resonates. Where might some of the ideas have impact in your organization?

- Are there any counter-intuitive ideas that might hold a key? Where are things going right in the organization? What is surprising about this? What about potential tipping points?

- To make the most of exploring these ideas you are best finding out what others think. What do your customers think? For example, Tesco focused relentlessly on identifying their customers' aspirations and what they actually needed.

- What about front-line staff? Few people know better where there might be opportunities, but are they encouraged or empowered to contribute?

- Use the ideas from Chapter 2 about learning from the best.

Effective learning requires time to think, but to share insights and knowledge, you also need to talk. So, why not think about some of the ideas that have resonated with you as you have read this book, and discuss those ideas with some of your colleagues. Talking about ideas and insights is the next stage of the 'T' break technique.

Significant conversations – talk about it!   ✓

If organizations are to prevent ideas being stuck or hidden then leaders need to talk with each other more often. It's surprising how much can be learned simply by talking with, and listening to, others. But we don't mean ordinary conversations or small talk here. We mean talking in order to take advantage of the vast pool of resources and experience within your organization. The kind of talking that brings leaders and managers together to discuss insights and fresh thinking. That's when you begin to foster *significant conversations*. These are the substantial and meaningful discussions that can often reveal helpful and sometimes surprising ideas, and some practical suggestions to make the most of them. Think about how you might build more significant conversations into your regular routine. One obvious way is to use the 'T' break technique. It's a straightforward yet powerful way to help get leaders talking together. Here are five helpful suggestions to get you started with some significant conversations:

1 Ask someone for their views on ideas or issues. For example, if they could change something, what would it be and why?

2 Where is the pain in your processes? Where do things go wrong, or what is costing you in time and money?

3 What do staff and customers find so frustrating? What do they wish they could do?

4 Who else could be your customers? Who else do you customers buy from?

5 What ideas might work? How can we try this to see if it does what we hoped?

That final point leads us to the next of our four T's. Thinking and talking are of little use if you don't try things out.

Putting learning to work – try it!

Putting the learning gained from insights and conversations to work is the next step in sharing knowledge via the 'T' break technique. This means applying the practical suggestions arising from your significant conversations. Above all this phase is about putting learning to work. For example, find ways to test any promising ideas emerging from the think and talk phases of the technique. Perhaps experiment through pilot, assessment and refinement before rolling out anything major. Involve your colleagues in the process and outcomes then learn from the experience and share this in any subsequent discussions.

Building sustainable practice – tell others about it!

The 'T' break technique both encourages shared knowledge and shared leadership. It can also result in a virtuous circle. People bring their education and experience to work. Sharing and building on these can benefit leaders, their colleagues and their organizations.

Shared learning and experience will spread successful ideas and help build better practice. This phase of the 'T' break is about asking leaders to share ideas on what works and what doesn't, and why. Considering what they might do next, and discussing how new ideas might be applied more widely in the organization, also takes us back to the very first step in the technique. Because the 'T' break technique works best as a cyclical tool. Once ideas have been applied and learning shared, it's time to return to the thinking step and to start the whole process over again.

There are always more possibilities springing from new practices that have been applied. Think about the new capabilities that you now have and how you can capitalize on them. Are other things now possible, because of the changes you have made? Often when you introduce new ideas, other potential improvements emerge. Achieving the benefits of shared leadership will be much easier with a process that brings:

- compelling insights, together with...;

- significant conversations that encourage...;

- learning to be applied to the workplace and...;

- lessons shared to spread good practice throughout the organization.

So far we have discussed three key themes in relation to shared leadership. But it could be argued that the one remaining theme informs them all. One of the fundamental aspects of a leader's role is to be able to influence people. So next we'll turn to some thoughts on sharing influence.

Sharing influence

At the beginning of this chapter we outlined some reasons for the growing focus on shared leadership. These include increasing use of project teams and cross-functional roles within organizations, as well as greater demands for collaboration between organizations. Arguably, these changes to the way we work are making a leader's ability to influence more critical than ever. This is because they are often leading people who report to other managers, in other departments, or even in other organizations. Such circumstances mean leaders can no longer rely on the power of their position within the organization, they need to apply the power of influence. So let's return to the world of behavioural science for some guidance on how to share influence effectively.

Nudge leadership

Behavioural sciences are providing new insights into how we behave. As we mentioned in Chapter 2, the defining idea behind 'nudge' is that we have two ways of thinking: the rational and the intuitive. The rational, deliberative approach says that we come to decisions and think in a logical, linear way. However, there is much evidence to suggest that often, we really make choices using a more subtle, instinctive approach. We are actually far more affected by the *context* of the choice than we might admit or often recognize. How does this relate to leaders? Persuasion and influence are two critical leadership skills. The message of nudge leadership is that influencing your colleagues is often easier if you go 'with the grain' of human behaviour. So let's look at a straightforward example of this kind of influencing in action.

In Chapter 3 we referred to the work of Stanford academic Albert Bandura. In addition to being an expert on the relationship between self-confidence and success, Bandura has also written about the way we frame feedback. Identical or equivalent facts can be fed back to individuals in very different ways. For example, in any given situation, we can choose whether to give positive or negative feedback. Bandura used as an example his colleague Jourden's work, in 1992. Jourden used a simulated organization in which feedback to different individuals was factually correct, but one set of feedback emphasized the positive, the other emphasized the negative. So if individuals performed at 75 per cent of a standard, the positive feedback highlighted 75 per cent progress already achieved. The negative feedback highlighted the 25 per cent shortfall. What did he find? Emphasizing gains rather than shortfall enhanced 'perceived self-efficacy, aspirations, efficient analytical skills, self-satisfaction and performance accomplishments.'[41] Clearly, a very different outcome can be achieved by what may seem to be relatively small differences in the way we frame things.

Framing is just one of several techniques to help us influence others. Here are some more nudge strategies that you and your colleagues might find useful. They are based on work done for the UK government, which has resulted in a model called MINDSPACE.[42] In essence, people are more likely to be supportive of your ideas when you put them forward in ways that accord with the way they tend to think. Below we've identified seven influencing strategies to help you develop this critical leadership skill:

1 *Reciprocity* (give and take). People are far more likely to be willing to give something themselves if *you* give *them* something first. So leaders should show the way, by being generous with their time, advice, support, or interest in others. As a former Yahoo! executive once said:

> *Business people who are the busiest, the happiest, and the most prosperous are the ones who are the most generous with their knowledge and their expertise. People who love what they're doing, who love to learn new things, to meet new people, and to share what and whom they know with others: these are the people who wind up creating the new economic value and, as a result, moving their companies forward.*[43]

2 *Who gives the message matters* (the weight we give to information greatly depends on the messenger). Think about how you are perceived by others. The degree to which you have built up trust and respect will significantly affect the way people respond to what you say and ask of them.

3 *Salience* (our attention is drawn to the novel and to what is relevant to us). Think about the few significant things you need to focus on. Connect them to your colleagues by making your priorities relevant to them. Think of ways to share your ideas that will have impact on those receiving them.

4 *Stressing social norms* (we are strongly influenced by what others do). Emphasize that many people already support the approach you

are putting forward, or want to do so (when that is the case). How can you build a shared sense of agreement?

5 *Framing* (presenting an issue in order to encourage a certain response). How can you make the issue or decision easier for people to make? Nudging is partly about encouraging automatic decisions, or constructing 'choice architecture' so that positive decisions are easy to make – often by default.

6 *Commitment* (we tend to seek to be consistent with our public promises). Make commitments and try to keep them. Seek ways for people to commit together.

7 *Emotions* (our emotional associations can powerfully shape our actions). Connect ideas to what people feel strongly about. Most of us have a strong sense of pride in the job that we do and who we do it for. Think about how you connect with these emotions.

If you want to engage more people in sharing leadership you'll need to be persuasive in influencing them to *want* to take a lead. Think about how you might use these nudging approaches to show the way in your organization. But it's important to remember that using behavioural science to your advantage should be done in conjunction with some of the lessons from earlier chapters. They are not tricks for manipulating behaviour and conjuring the responses we want. They should be harnessed and used as a means to build genuine trust, co-operation, engagement and confidence in the way forward.

Influence by what you say or by what you do?

There is a well-known saying that you can tell a person by the company he or she keeps. It could also be said that you can tell a company by the people it keeps, or perhaps even more pointedly, by the people it promotes!

The tension between getting results and getting on in organizations was the basis of some interesting research carried out over a four-year period. Led by US management professor Fred Luthans, the researchers set out to determine what made managers successful and what made them effective. Some might say the results confirmed what we intuitively think. Successful managers were significantly better at networking and building relationships. They tended to see the management of people as the least important aspect of their job. In contrast, effective managers were very good at communication and people management, but fared poorly at networking.

Of the managers studied by Luthans and his researchers, only 10 per cent were found to be both successful and effective. Unsurprisingly these were effective networkers, communicators and people managers.[44] This study is not alone in making such a point. In their Harvard article, 'The smart talk trap', Jeffrey Pfeffer and Bob Sutton referred to studies which highlight that people who talk more than others in groups tend to come out on top. They cited a classic book by Bernard Bass, which made an interesting point. Namely, that people who talk more often and for longer, are more likely to surface as group leaders – 'regardless of the quality of their comments.'[45] Contrast this with the way W L Gore selects leaders, as we discussed earlier in this chapter.

What does this tell us? Firstly, that organizations need to consider the basis on which people are really being promoted. Is promotion based on what's best for the organization or because those promoted are best at promoting themselves? Secondly, that individuals would be wise to remember the value organizations seem to place on networking and talking. Without becoming a successful manager, the value of your ability to be effective will be limited. So make sure you don't just focus on results, remember to network and speak up! Effective shared leadership requires a combination of both.

A bad influence or unrecognized heroes?

In considering the benefits of shared leadership, it's well worth thinking about one group who are arguably best placed to have the most impact – middle managers. Unfortunately, leaders and managers in the middle of our organizations often get a bad press. They have typically been described as being a problem as much as an asset. Often, middle managers are negatively associated with such things as:

- Building empires.
- Acting as a 'permafrost' preventing vision from becoming reality.
- Defensive behaviour, holding on to the status quo.
- Resisting change.

Yet there is evidence to suggest that this might be unfair. A six-year research study, 'In praise of middle managers', examined factors relating to successful change in organizations. It provided an interesting and contradictory view to the perceived wisdom about this group of managers. Starkly contrasting with views that middle managers are part of the problem, this study suggests quite the opposite. Not only are they part of the solution, they are the essential ingredient. Why? Because everything has to go through the middle of the organization. And if the middle doesn't work then you've got a problem. 'Middle managers, it turns out, make valuable contributions to the realization of radical change at a company – contributions that go largely unrecognized.'[46]

Of course, this isn't necessarily the story for every leader and manager in the middle. But the study found good evidence that, where change was successful, it was because of effective middle leaders and managers. So what were effective middle-managers doing to make change so successful? What stood out was their ability to manage tensions and balance competing demands. Leaders and managers in the middle are particularly adept at 'not just – but also' leadership. This means they are able to:

- Not just… translate vision – they also know how to take action and ✔ implement it.
- Not just… network – they also effectively influence others.

Not just… translate vision

Translating vision might also be called 'middle vision' and it's a crucial skill. It's about being:

- far enough away from the frontline to see the bigger picture;
- near enough to translate into a tangible reality;
- uniquely placed to interpret broad organizational visions into something that makes sense to your colleagues.

Middle managers are not just well-placed to be able to interpret and communicate vision. They are adept at managing any disconnect between that vision and the reality of an existing situation. And they are also well placed to make things happen – knowing what to do. Middle managers generally know how to get things done, what will work and what won't. Because:

- They know better than others where the problems are.
- Everything goes through the middle.

Not just... networking

The second major tension that middle managers address very well is the balance between networking and influencing. Leaders in the middle of our organizations tend to have very effective networks. They know who knows, who can and who cares. You might remember these are Reg Revans' 'Three Who's', which we referred to in Chapter 1.[47] Revans talked about engaging these three essential groups of people, whenever we want to make sense of a situation. Leaders and managers in the middle of an organization tend to have extensive and effective webs of relationships, both internally and externally. But they also bring other benefits, which are critical to developing a sense of shared leadership. Being uniquely placed in the middle, they:

- often have the trust and respect of their colleagues;
- are aware of their own emotions and of those around them;
- know the right strings to pull;
- know who the key opinion-formers are in their areas and how to influence them;
- have an in-depth knowledge of how things work;
- are very well-connected – networking is particularly important for shared leadership.

So is it time to change the message regarding leaders and managers in the middle of our organizations? Are they really a bad influence or are they the unsung heroes, pivotal to developing shared leadership? It does beg the question, which we addressed in Chapter 3: do we get the leaders we expect in our organizations?

Building human towers – a motto for shared leadership

One of Barcelona's most famous landmarks is Antoni Gaudi's stunning but incomplete cathedral, *La Sagrada Família*. But outside the slowly growing spires of this edifice, you'll often see other towers being built. A Catalan tradition dating back to the 18th century is to build human towers. Each tower is made up of circles of people, each interlocking arms to form a platform for the next (smaller) circle to climb on their shoulders. Gradually this human tower will grow to five or six people high until one single person tops the tower in triumph. The teams who build these human towers are known as *castellers*, and they have an interesting motto made up of just four terms:

- strength;
- balance;
- courage;
- common sense.

This motto may be both accurate and motivational for the *castellers*, but it can also be very useful for organizational leaders.

Strength

Think about putting the right people in the right place, and using their strengths. The base of a human tower has the strongest members of the group, the smaller and lighter group members climb to the higher stages of the tower. We've already seen the advantages of getting people to work to their strengths, it's easier and far more effective to build on strengths.

Balance

For the *castellers* this is clearly essential but balance is also essential in organizations. In any team you need complementary skills, to achieve optimum results and to balance the workload. As we've seen earlier, middle managers are very well placed to balance the tensions between different tiers of the organization.

Courage

Castellers need courage to climb to the heights they reach. Courage is based on the trust and support they have from their team members. Courage is needed in organizations too. It's needed for teams to help them stay true to their convictions. Just as innovation and making bold decisions can also require courage, and trust in the support of your colleagues. And of course, leaders will often need courage to apply some of the uncommon ideas we've discussed throughout this book.

Common sense

For *castellers*, the most obvious common sense is to practise, practise, practise. And when building their towers, common sense dictates that they stop at any sign of weakness or imbalance. Just like organizations, success needs to be built on a sure and firm basis. And just like organizations, common sense is a vital ingredient in ensuring this happens.

As Spain's *castellers* regularly demonstrate, rarely do we achieve much without the support of those around us. But what else have we learned from the likes of Lincoln building a team of rivals, or from W L Gore's associates selecting their own leaders? It's that encouraging shared leadership is perhaps one of the best ways to get the most from our organizations. And in many ways, that's really only common sense. In our final chapter, we turn to some practical advice on how to become an uncommon leader. By identifying the five key leadership roles that will help you to see, shape, show, serve and share.

Bibliography

1   Lewis, M (2009) [accessed 2 September 2013] The no-stats all-star, *The New York Times Magazine*. [Online] http://www.nytimes.com/2009/02/15/magazine/15Battier-t.html?pagewanted=all&_r=0

2   Department for Business, Innovation and Skills; Leadership and Management Network Group (LMNG) (2012) *Leadership and management in the UK – the key to sustainable growth*. Department for Business, Innovation and Skills

3   Pearce, C Manz and C Sims Jr, P (2009) Where do we go from here? Is shared leadership the key to team success? *Organizational Dynamics*, **38** (3) July–September 2009, pp 234–38

4   Bolden, R (2011) Distributed Leadership in Organizations: A review of theory and research, *International Journal of Management Reviews*, **13** (3) pp 251–69

5   Goodwin, D K (2009) *Team of Rivals: The political genius of Abraham Lincoln*, London, Penguin Books

6   ibid

7   Ancona, D and Backman, E (2012) Distributed leadership: going from pyramids to networks, *Leadership Excellence*, **27** (1)

8   ibid

9 Pearce, C Manz and C Sims Jr, P (2009) Where do we go from here? Is shared leadership the key to team success? *Organizational Dynamics*, **38** (3) July–September 2009, pp 234–238

10 Cohen, A, Watkinson, J and Boone, J (2005) Southwest Airlines CEO grounded in real world, *Babson Insight*, Babson Executive Education Center

11 Cohen, A and Rao, J (2006) *Creating a Great Spirit of Service at Southwest Airlines: An Interview with Colleen Barrett, President.* Babson Executive Education

12 Gittell, J (2005) *The Southwest Airlines Way: Using the power of relationships to achieve high performance.* New York, McGraw-Hill

13 Shipper, F, Manz, C and Stewart, G (2010) Case study: W L Gore & Associates: developing global teams to meet 21st-century challenges, in M S, Hitt, R D Ireland and R E Hoskisson, (2013) *Strategic Management: Concepts and cases: competitiveness and globalization*, 10th edition, Southwestern, Cengage Learning

14 W L Gore & Associates [accessed on 2 November 2013] About Gore: Our Culture [Online] http://www.gore.com/en_gb/aboutus/culture/index.html

15 Bell, A (2009) W L Gore & Associates, Inc: Natural Leadership'. Cited in Avery, G *Understanding Leadership: Paradigms and Cases*, London, Sage Publications Ltd

16 Manz, C, Shipper, F and Stewart, G L (2009) Everyone a team leader: shared influence at W L. Gore & Associates, *Organizational Dynamics,* July–September **38** (3) pp 239–44

17 Turnbull James, K (2011) *Leadership in context Lessons from new leadership theory and current leadership development practice*, London, The Kings Fund

18 Ziglar, Z (2006) *Better Than Good,* Nashville, Thomas Nelson Inc, p 171

19 Senge, P (1990) *The Fifth Discipline: The art and practice of the learning organization*, London, Doubleday

20 Cameron, K, Dutton, J and Quinn, R E (eds) (2003) *Positive Organizational Scholarship: Foundations of a new discipline*, Berrett Koehler

21 Sheard, A G and Kakabadse, A P (2004) A process perspective on leadership and team development, *Journal of Management Development*, **23** (1) pp 7–106

22 Goleman, D, Boyatzis, R and McKee, A (2001), Primal leadership: the hidden driver of great performance, *Harvard Business Review* (December)

23 Kim, C and Mauborgne, R (2003) Tipping point leadership, *Harvard Business Review* (April)

24 Sutton, R (2011) [accessed on 2 November 2013] How a few bad apples ruin everything, *The Wall Street Journal* [Online] http://online.wsj.com/news/articles/SB10001424052970203499704576622550325233260

25 Churchman, P (2009) [accessed on 2 November 2013] When you work with a jerk: the bad apples study, *The Glasshammer: smart women in numbers*. [Online] http://www.theglasshammer.com/news/2009/04/28/when-you-work-with-a-jerk-the-bad-apples-study/

26 *This American Life* [accessed 2 November 2013] [Online] http://www.thisamericanlife.org/radio-archives/episode/370/Ruining-It-for-the-Rest-of-Us?act=0

27 Haidt, J (2006) *The Happiness Hypothesis: Finding modern truth in ancient wisdom,* London, Arrow Books

28 Baumeister, R F, Bratslavsky, E, Finkenauer, C and Vohs, K D (2001) Bad is stronger than good, *Review of General Psychology*, 5 (4) pp 323–70

29 ibid

30 Gottman, J and Silver, N (1994) [accessed 2 November 2013] What makes marriages work? *Psychology today* [Online] http://www.psychologytoday.com/articles/200910/what-makes-marriage-work

31 Felps, W, Mitchell, T R and Byington, E (2006) How, when, and why bad apples spoil the barrel: negative group members and dysfunctional groups, *Research in Organizational Behavior*, 27 pp 175–222

32 Fishbach, A, Eyal, T and Finkelstein, S (2010) How positive and negative feedback motivate goal pursuit, *Social and Personality Psychology Compass* 4 (8) pp 517–30

33 Halvorson, H G (2013) [accessed 2 November 2013] Sometimes negative feedback is best, *Harvard Business Review: Blog* [Online] http://blogs.hbr.org/cs/2013/01/sometimes_negative_feedback_is.html

34 Drucker, P (2005) *The Daily Drucker: 366 Days of insight and motivation for getting the right things done,* Oxford, Elsevier Butterworth-Heinemann

35 Handy, C (1999) *Inside Organizations: 21 ideas for managers.* London, Penguin Books

36 Prahalad, C K and Ramaswamy, V (2000) [accessed 2 November 2013] Co-opting customer competence, *Harvard Business School* [Online] http://hbswk.hbs.edu/archive/1299.html

37 Kanter, R M (1994) [accessed 2 November 2013] Collaborative advantage: the art of alliances, *Harvard Business Review* [Online] http://hbr.org/1994/07/collaborative-advantage-the-art-of-alliances/ar/1

38 Huxham, C (2003) Theorizing collaboration practice, *Public Management Review*, 5 (3) pp 401–23

39 Yunus, M (2009) [accessed 2 November 2013] Lifting people worldwide out of poverty, *Knowledge@Wharton* [Online] http://knowledge.wharton.upenn.edu/article.cfm?articleid=2243

40 Humberg, K M (2011) *Poverty Reduction through Social Business? Lessons learnt from Grameen joint ventures in Bangladesh*, Oekom Verlag Gmbh

41 Bandura, A (1993) Perceived self-efficacy in cognitive development and functioning, *Educational Psychologist*, **28** (2), pp 117–48

42 Dolan, P, Hallsworth, M, Halpern, D, King, D and Vlaev, I (2010) *MINDSPACE: Influencing behaviour through public policy*, Institute for Government

43 Sanders, T (2003) *Love Is the Killer App: How to win business and influence friends,* New York, Crown Business

44 Luthans, F (1988) Successful vs effective real managers, *Academy of Management Executive*, **2** (2) pp 127–32

45 Pfeffer, J and Sutton, R (1999) [accessed 2 November 2013] The smart-talk trap, *Harvard Business Review* [Online] http://hbr.org/1999/05/the-smart-talk-trap/ar/1

46 Huy, Q N (2001) [accessed 2 November 2013] In praise of middle managers, *Harvard Business Review* [Online] http://hbr.org/2001/09/in-praise-of-middle-managers/ar/1

47 Revans, R (1998) *ABC of Action Learning*, London, Lemon and Crane

CONCLUSION
BUILDING COMPETITIVE ADVANTAGE THROUGH UNCOMMON LEADERSHIP ROLES

KEY TOPICS
- Pathfinders.
- Game-changers.
- Rain-makers.
- Bridge-builders.
- Play-makers.
- Saliency, sagacity and serendipity.

FIGURE 6.1 The 5-S leadership framework

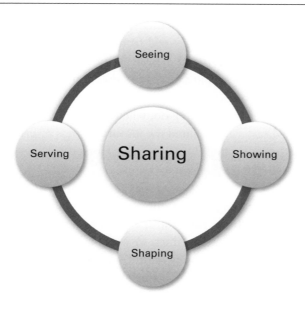

Building uncommon competitive advantage

When does a strength become an advantage? Just because an organization is good at something doesn't necessarily mean it has a clear advantage. Many organizations have similar strengths, which can therefore mean none has any real advantage over another. To answer our question, a strength becomes a real advantage when it is applied to a promising opportunity. And crucially, some advantages are more powerful than others. In many ways, that's what this book has been written to do: to help you find and develop an advantage. But not just any advantage. At the heart of uncommon leadership is the idea of realizing a very powerful advantage. That of finding the sense before it becomes common sense: an uncommon advantage.

Uncommon Leadership is about how you can build competitive advantage by thinking differently. This is what Richard Rumelt referred to as 'an insightful framing of a competitive situation [which] can create whole new patterns of advantage and weakness. The most powerful strategies arise from such game-changing insights.'[1] With each 'S' in the leadership framework, there is an uncommon advantage. The first and most significant is the advantage gained through what Rumelt calls insights and game-changers.

In our chapter on seeing the sense before it becomes common, we saw how the Sternins and Bill Bratton demonstrated this, finding uncommon sense in difficult situations and turning it to their advantage. In Chapter 2 we talked about the real advantage to be gained from putting that uncommon sense into action, that of transforming a business or a situation. One powerful example was shown in Richard Branson's creation of a successful airline, simply because he thought he could provide a better service. Another was in the uncommon sense of making do, when resources are constrained. The Apollo 13 near-disaster highlighted the resourcefulness of bricolage leaders, thinking differently to find ways through, sometimes by realizing that answers can be hidden in plain view.

Then we saw the advantage of not only doing the things that matter, but of doing them *really well*. Or better still, adding value by doing them better than anyone else. In fact, doing them so well that others might pay to see you deliver memorable performances. In Chapter 3 we also saw how small things can have a big impact, for better and for worse. As Gerald Ratner discovered to his cost, how crucial it is to ensure that what you say resonates with what you do. Sometimes an advantage can be lost surprisingly quickly!

In Chapter 4 we discussed an often-overlooked advantage, one that might even be called a missing advantage. This is the advantage of leadership with service, which we addressed from two key perspectives. Such a focus provides an employee advantage of engaged staff contributing to new ideas which in turn, provide customers with memorable experiences. What emerges from this is a powerful customer advantage. This is the advantage gained when customers become advocates or when they themselves begin to participate in your business. When they move from being a spectator, watching your employees perform on the business 'stage', to becoming part of the performance themselves. Increasingly this kind of customer advantage is being seen as particularly important.

Our fifth 'S' highlights the value of shared leadership. It is the advantage gained when leaders help to develop and co-ordinate strengths, for individuals, for teams, and for organizations as a whole. There is real collaborative advantage to be gained from the synergies of shared leadership, either internal to the organization, or through partnership with others.

The 5-S leadership framework and uncommon leadership roles

This book has been structured around our model to help you think differently about leadership. For each element in the 5-S leadership framework: seeing; showing; shaping; serving; and sharing, there is an associated 'uncommon' aspect which helps to explain the theme. So throughout each section we have explored what it means to become an uncommon leader, by:

- finding the sense before it becomes common;
- making that sense common sense;
- doing the common things uncommonly well;
- having the common touch to serve the needs of people and the organization;
- leading with others by making leadership more common.

As we have just seen, each of these uncommon themes points to an advantage from thinking differently, as the book's sub-title suggests. But it's not enough to just think differently. Gaining competitive advantage means taking action. So we'll finish the book by identifying five key leadership roles to help you turn our ideas into uncommon competitive advantages. Five leadership roles, delivering five uncommon advantages:

1 pathfinders;

2 game-changers;

3 rain-makers;

4 bridge-builders;

5 play-makers.

FIGURE 6.2   The roles of uncommon leadership

Pathfinders ...

see

- Leading with vision
- Finding the sense before it becomes common
- Delivering the advantage of innovation

Game-changers ...

shape

- Leading with action
- Making that sense common sense
- Delivering the advantage of transformation

Rain-makers ...

show

- Leading with purpose
- Doing the common things uncommonly well
- Delivering the advantage of value and excellence

Bridge-builders ...

serve

- Leading with service
- Applying the common touch
- Delivering the advantage of service

Play-makers ...

share

- Leading with others
- Making leadership more common
- Delivering the collaborative advantage

Seeing – leading with vision requires *pathfinders*

Competitive advantage through thinking differently means finding the sense before it becomes common sense. It's about an *uncommon advantage* or the advantage of innovation, of not just finding the sense but of doing so before others do. To do this organizations need pathfinder leaders – people who lead with vision and find the sense before it becomes common. According to one dictionary definition, a pathfinder is: 'A person who makes or finds a way, especially through unexplored areas or fields of knowledge.'[2]

Jerry and Monique Sternin are examples of pathfinder leaders. They certainly made sense of a difficult situation, finding ways through a seemingly intractable problem: addressing child malnourishment in a hostile context despite being short on time and money. They had no choice but to find a way to make change happen quickly. They did this by applying a counter-intuitive idea. Instead of fixing their thoughts on what was wrong, they noticed what seemed right – that some children were healthy. Bill Bratton also applied counter-intuitive ideas to the issues facing the New York City Transit Police. He found ways to bring energy and belief together, to create a tipping point where seemingly impossible change became possible.

Pathfinder leaders lead with vision, showing us the way through difficulties or the way to overcome obstacles. When vision is unformed, or becomes blurred or obscured, pathfinder leaders find ways to clarify what needs to be done. That way may be based on pragmatism, because sometimes that's all that can be done. Alternatively, when carrying on as usual is not an option, when more radical ways forward are required, pathfinder leaders may take a leap of faith. On other occasions, such as that faced by the Sternins and Bill Bratton, pathfinder leaders combine the two.

Pathfinders in action

We think leaders who demonstrate the uncommon characteristics discussed in Chapter 1 are pathfinder leaders. They are the people who lead with vision and find the sense before it becomes common. In organizations, pathfinder leaders:

- make sense of confusing messages or context;
- seek out new ways to do business;

- hold competing tensions;
- create the conditions where small changes can have a big impact;
- maintain optimism;
- lead with vision;
- find the sense before it becomes common;
- show the way through difficult times.

Both Bratton and the Sternins found the sense before it became common sense. Each led with vision, based on a guiding principle and uncommon insight. This enabled them to shed light onto the path they were taking, so that others could see what they were seeing. But, although finding uncommon sense is vital, this alone is not enough. Successful organizations must translate uncommon sense into common practice. To do the first you need pathfinder leaders, but for the second you need a different focus.

Shaping – leading with action requires game-changers

Competitive advantage through being different means turning uncommon sense into common sense. This is the advantage of transformation, of doing the right things that will change the nature of the business. To do this you need game-changer leaders who can take the insight of uncommon sense and make it into the 'new' common sense for their organization.

In Chapter 2 we drew on the thought-provoking examples of leaders who have become game-changers. For example, Tony Hsieh at Zappos and Tesco's Sir Terry Leahy. Both focused on shaping their organizational culture so that they could deliver their strategy. But it's worth noting that these aren't ordinary business stories. Zappos has become one of the most successful online retailers in the US. Tesco has seen similar dramatic success, passing its rivals to become the UK's number one retailer.

You may remember that at the start of this chapter we used the story of Konosuko Matsushita to illustrate the power of common sense. Matsushita built a giant, multi-national corporation, most famous for its electrical appliance brands: National, Panasonic and Technics. We told his story to point out that, even in the face of severe constraints, Matsushita held onto his principles and found a way to keep his workforce employed. When other companies were making staff redundant, he managed to retain them. In doing so, he asked many of his production staff to change roles in the short term, switching to sales in order to help them sell more products. This was a flexible resource strategy straight from the bricolage leadership manual.

These were examples of game-changers altering the face and fortunes of individual companies. But what about someone who wanted to change a whole industry? Then take the example of Richard Branson, the UK entrepreneur. When he decided to enter the airline business, it was out of frustration with the service he experienced as a customer. Branson knew he could do better. But what's telling about Branson's approach, and what makes him a game-changer, is that he not only saw the opportunity to create his own airline business. He was sure he could be successful and in the process, 'change the whole industry'.[3]

Game-changers in action

So what does this all tell us? It tells us that game-changers are resourceful leaders. They craft creative solutions by thinking differently about the resources they've got, rather than wishing for the things they don't have. They see the potential when resources are re-purposed, to achieve outcomes beyond what was thought possible. As the phrase suggests, game-changers change the rules.

Game-changers find the sense before it becomes common. Then, crucially, they make that new sense common sense in their organizations. By doing so they change some of the rules about how things are done. Game-changers are particularly important in difficult times because they look to turn conventional wisdom on its head. When resources are stretched, game-changers transform situations by seeking creative combinations to achieve more with less. They are bricoleurs, crafting different uses and solutions from existing stretched resources. Game-changer leaders are adept at:

- Sense giving – they are able to influence with logos, ethos and pathos.

- Seeing flexibility – when others see only restrictions, game-changers find ways around restrictions.

- Challenging underlying assumptions.

- Adapting strategy to reflect emerging priorities.

- Applying bricolage leadership – releasing or re-purposing resources.

- Showing resilience – an ability to bounce back and remain positive even in tough situations.

When it comes to leadership, game-changers make uncommon sense into sense for their organization. To use Sir Terry Leahy's words, you could say that game-changers 'drive home the simple things that really matter'.[4] Charles Handy captures the heart of this idea – that of constantly reinforcing the common cause:

> *Presidents, leaders, to be effective have to represent the whole to the parts and to the world outside. They may live in the centre but they must not be the centre. To reinforce the common sense they must be a constant teacher, ever travelling, ever talking, ever listening, the chief missionary of the common cause.[5]*

That's not a bad way to sum up a game-changer's role: the chief missionary of the common cause. But turning new common sense into practical reality, in order to realize opportunities and potential, requires a different set of skills. Making the right things happen also requires the talents of rain-makers.

Showing – leading with purpose requires rain-makers

The third competitive advantage builds on the second. It's not enough to do the right things to differentiate your business from others. You need to excel at doing them, to do the common things uncommonly well. Competitive advantage through doing the right things well is the advantage of value through excellence. Leaders who are rain-makers put the first two advantages to work. They can be seen as connecting the transformed business to opportunities. They combine innovation and direction to add value, making excellent customer experience and satisfaction core to the organization.

You could say that rain-makers have always been thought of as people who are well-connected. The name originated in tribal traditions where someone with a perceived connection to the gods or to nature could call for rain to fall. The term seems to have been first used in the business world in reference to the legal profession, during the 20th century. Like their tribal equivalents, business rain-makers also seemed to exert influence, through their connections and experience, which enabled them to secure business deals with apparent ease. In our view, rain-makers do more than just bring business into an organization, though this is an important part of the idea. We also think that rain-makers bring things to fruition. They capitalize on the pathfinder's ideas and the game-changer's resourcefulness, creating value for their customers and for their organizations.

Of course, doing things with comparative ease it not always easy to do. It requires doing what you do really well, where experience and competence make everything *look* easy. Apparent ease comes when competence and excellence combine. Excellence that is focused on the customer-experience sells itself. Remember our discussion of Zappos, an organization that spent comparatively more of its money and effort on existing customers than on trying to gain new customers? So in many ways, rain-makers do what Peter Drucker once advocated as an aim of marketing: 'To know and understand the customer so well that the product or service fits [him or] her and sells itself.'[6]

Rain-maker leaders add value by bringing insights and ideas to fruition. They connect good ideas and great practices to customers and opportunities. Henry Stewart at Happy Ltd and Tony Hseih of Zappos made their businesses open for all to see. In doing so, they have people queuing and paying to see how they do business. Rain-makers are also in touch. Like Sir Terry Leahy, they are attuned to their customers, their industries and their business. These leaders are also adept at adding value, finding new opportunities to connect their business with customers.

You may remember in Chapter 2 we mentioned J D Rockefeller's definition of success: doing the common things uncommonly well. But how does Mohammad Yunus, the founder of Grameen Bank define success? That's exactly what he was asked in an interview at Wharton, the world's first collegiate business school. He defined success as doing what you set out to do: 'We wanted to bring credit to poor people and savings services to poor people.' But what he then went on to explain echoes some of the lessons from the next-mile story, which we told later in that chapter. In the face of critics who said his idea wouldn't work, Yunus said: 'We hoped that it would and it did.' Then, the critics countered: 'Well, it may work in one village, but it won't work for two villages.' But Yunus proved them wrong again, only to find the critics were now saying: 'Maybe in 10 villages it won't work. If you grow big, it will collapse. You are stretching your luck too much.' But again Yunus was able to say to the critics: 'We did it.' 'So,' he concluded, 'that is a success, even beyond what we imagined.' Like next-mile leadership, success can be taking one step at a time. Or creating a bank for the poor, one village at a time. Then, as small steps become big leaps, so the rain spreads.[7]

Rain-makers in action

In 1968, 3M scientist Dr Spencer Silver[8] discovered a formula for a glue that didn't seem to work properly. It was sticky, but didn't stick. Another failed experiment? Possibly, if not for the predicament of a colleague. Silver's colleague Art Fry was experiencing a very frustrating problem. Whilst singing in the church choir his bookmarks kept falling out of the hymnal, causing him to lose his page. Fry needed a repositionable note, one that would stick, but would not remain stuck. Six years after Silver's 'failed' experiment, Fry remembered his colleague's low-tack glue. And so, 3M's ubiquitous Post-it® Notes were born. You may think the story ends here and that the rest is history, but connecting a problem to a possible solution was only the beginning.

Rain-makers find ways to make things work, to grow and to develop. They:

- connect customer need to services and products;
- convert problems into opportunities;
- convey confidence tempered with realism;
- create a customer need.

On his return to Apple, Steve Jobs was interviewed by *Business Week*.[9] What he said in response to a question about market research was revealing. 'A lot of times, people don't know what they want until you show it to them.' Jobs clearly did not have a conventional view of marketing research, rather like the late Anita Roddick, whom we referred to in Chapter 1. For her, 'running a company on market research is like driving while looking in the rear view mirror.' Steve Jobs was a rain-maker at work, creating something which people will know they want once they see it. But to say that rain-makers don't pay much attention to market research would be an over-simplification. In the same interview, Jobs explained his approach, revealing a subtle but vital characteristic which rain-makers possess: 'We also watch industry trends pretty carefully. But in the end, for something this complicated (the iMac), it's really hard to design products by focus groups.' That's the twist which rain-makers bring. Like Jobs, rain-makers are in touch, watching trends, sensing where things are changing, and where opportunity is hiding. It could be said that rain-makers have the half-full view of life but it's more than that. When the glass is empty, they recognize that it can still be filled again. Rain-makers not only seek to water the seeds planted by game-changers so that they are fruitful for the business, they also encourage others to be rain-makers too.

Our first three uncommon leadership roles were about challenging conventional wisdom, asking different questions and connecting the new common sense to opportunities. These can give organizations competitive advantage through innovation, direction and excellence. But you also need to build a strong sense of togetherness within an organization and then help people to fulfil their potential. So our final two roles are crucial to helping the uncommon sense flourish throughout an organization.

Serving – leading with service requires bridge-builders

The fourth advantage of uncommon leadership is the *customer advantage*. But in reality, fostering a sense of leadership with service can help to realize two advantages: employee advantage and customer advantage. And the key to achieving these is through bridge-builder leaders who display the common touch.

We call them bridge-builder leaders because these are the people who excel at building trust and support within an organization. They are adept at keeping everything and everyone together. Bridge-builder leaders are also great at making connections both inside and outside of the organization. The power of external bridge-building can be seen both in the way organizations relate to each other, and in the way they relate to their customers. Underpinning each of these strengths is the most critical: their ability to emphasize the importance of service.

Bridge-builders are often the 'go-to' people in an organization. Trusted and relied upon, they are in touch with the feelings of their colleagues. And this often leads them to be moved to respond, by demonstrating the common touch. Remember how Muhammad Yunus was inspired by the plight of the hard-working poor of Bangladesh? And of his determination to create a sustainable way forward that connected with people's needs? Yunus demonstrated how to build a bridge between the unacceptable present and the desirable future, through his common touch.

It can be all too easy for leaders to be consumed by the problems at hand. And in doing so, it can be just as easy to lose the power of noticing the small things. Bridge-builders are skilled at finding the small things that can have big impact and making the most of them. And this can also help them to demonstrate the power of the common touch. Noticing the small things, and caring enough to do something about them, can make a lasting impression on the people we work with.

In the face of a complex business environment, with constantly competing demands, energy can be sapped from even the best of teams. So it's important to realize another advantage of bridge-builders, as sources of energy. It's worth thinking about how these last two attributes might be combined. What if noticing one, comparatively small thing could make all the difference to energy in your workforce? For example, if there were only one thing you could do to improve health and well-being, and performance at work, what would you choose? You might quite reasonably answer with:

- improve the working environment;
- introduce more flexible working hours;
- implement a structured health and well-being programme at work.

All of these may have merit, but here's an interesting insight from Dame Carol Black who chaired an independent review of the health of the UK workforce. Having studied the evidence, Black made one simple suggestion:

If I could wave a magic wand, the one thing I would do is to improve the relationship between line managers and employees... health and

wellbeing is not just a medical issue. Good line management can promote better health and well-being and improved performance.[10]

Remember that Black's comments weren't simply anecdotal. Having analysed a comprehensive array of evidence, she argued that the relationship between a manager and employee has a significant effect, not just on health and well-being, but crucially on performance. Many organizations invest a good deal of effort and resource in developing their people but how many invest time in systematically developing better relationships? When the relationship between manager and employee is good, then people tend to feel better and function well. How many health and well-being programmes in our organizations have better manager and employee relationships at the core of the initiative? Managers can have a significant impact on those around us, an impact that is better for people's health and well-being and improves performance. Bridge-builders help to ensure that these vital relationships in the organization work, fostering well-being and performance.

Bridge-builders in action

In the introduction to *Uncommon Leadership*, you may remember we discussed the work of Ronald Heifetz, on adaptive leadership. His idea, that leaders need to be capable of switching between the balcony and the dance floor, relates equally well to bridge-builders. They see the bigger picture – the view from the balcony, but they are still grounded in reality – when down on the dance floor. We explored this in Chapter 4, with Sir Terry Leahy advocating the importance of keeping in touch with his workforce, experiencing the reality of how the business worked, and of listening to his customers. So bridge-builder leaders demonstrate the following uncommon characteristics of a good leader. They:

- *Build* – a sense of togetherness.
- *Encourage* – cooperation.
- *Serve* – colleagues and customers.

Bridge-builders create that essential sense of togetherness and bonding. And it's when this begins to work that our final leadership role really makes an impact.

Sharing – leading with others requires play-makers

Our final advantage is based on the idea of shared leadership, bringing about *collaborative advantage*. To achieve this you need play-makers – people who can connect strengths, nurture performance and create synergy.

Play-makers take the sense of togetherness and cohesion created by bridge-builders and use this to help bring out the best in people. Remember how Shane Battier transformed his team's performances, even though some only perceived him as an average player? This is an important lesson for any leader – their own performance is dependent on the people they lead and manage.

To succeed in modern business, organizations need to ensure they harness all the attributes of the talent they employ. Play-maker leaders are the key to achieving this. They are particularly adept at helping others to use their strengths to the best effect. They galvanize the strengths and commitment of those around them, particularly in team situations. Play-makers motivate, facilitate and develop teams.

Play-maker leaders also have a key role in spreading leadership more widely throughout the organization. They encourage others to take the lead, and excel at devolving responsibility, empowering action and encouraging others to take a lead. They also have a central role in sharing leadership beyond the organization, through co-operative activities that help realize collaborative advantage.

Like any other strategic options open to organizations, there are no guarantees that collaborations will succeed. In our discussion of collaboration in Chapter 5, we highlighted the work of Moss Kanter and Huxham. Both stressed that, for collaborations to succeed, organizations need to:

1 *Seek collaborative advantage.* By thinking about how you can gain benefits and open possibilities, beyond the original reason for collaborating. Think about how, with your collaborative partner, you can create value (for others) rather than simply exchange it (for yourselves). Specifically, what value do you create for the customer?

2 *Nurture relationships and a culture of sharing.* By making relationship building a priority so identify the right people to nurture relationships, and build trust between the partners (bridge-builders). Spend time understanding the different perspectives represented in the collaboration. Put those with strengths in these areas into the right roles to build a 'coalition of the willing'.

Play-makers in action

All too often we don't realize the knowledge and potential within the teams or groups of people we have assembled. In many cases, we already have the insight and knowledge needed to solve problems, or identify innovative ways forward, within our organizations. But often that knowledge and expertise remains dormant or under-used without the skills of play-makers. As we have seen, the most critical of these skills is the ability to share leadership, both within and between organizations. In Chapter 5 we discussed examples of both kinds of shared leadership in action: W L Gore & Associates; and the Grameen Bank.

At Gore, teams form quickly around problems that need to be solved, or to capitalize on opportunities that arise. The responsiveness of Gore's teams is due to two main factors: they have a fluid structure; and leadership is shared widely throughout the organization. In fact, the teams themselves decide which team-member is the best person to lead in any given situation. This is an example of embedded, internal shared leadership at its best.

Collaboration happens for many reasons but one features very highly: the ability to achieve something important that couldn't be done by individual organizations alone. When Grameen Bank wanted to meet the nutritional needs of children in the communities it served, it turned to the expertise and skills of big business. Its collaboration with Danone demonstrated the obvious advantages to be gained from leadership shared between organizations. Grameen collaborated with Danone to produce a drink that was low-priced, high in nutrition and tasty. The result was a clear benefit to Grameen's customers, as their health improved in a cost-efficient way. And there was also clear benefit for Danone, as it learned how to use low-tech production and distribution methods, not to mention some vital lessons about working in emerging markets. This was an example of external, shared leadership, or collaboration, at its best.

It's true that working well together takes time and effort. It also takes persistence to foster effective collaboration. But there is no doubt that teams and organizations can go much further when they reap the synergistic benefits of shared leadership. There is an old African proverb which makes this point far better than we could: 'If you want to go fast, walk alone. If you want to go far, walk together.'

An uncommon advantage – saliency, sagacity and serendipity

When we set out to write this book, we wanted to encourage thinking about leadership from a range of different perspectives. One aim was to surface the things that good leaders had in common, and to suggest ways to make these more common in organizations. We wanted to stimulate thinking and practice that would act as a springboard for better leadership in better organizations. And the key to this was encouraging leaders to think differently.

But just thinking differently is not enough. Business leaders need to develop competitive advantage, by challenging conventional wisdom, by asking different questions, and by connecting the 'new' common sense to opportunities. There is much in this book to help you do that but perhaps the best way for you to get started is to look at *Uncommon Leadership* through these three lenses. Think about:

- *Saliency* – emphasizing the striking or the significant. What particularly struck you, perhaps having special meaning for you or your current situation?

- *Sagacity* – sharing knowledge and developing wisdom. What connected with your own experience and knowledge, and the wisdom of those around you?

- *Serendipity* – capitalizing on unexpected or fortuitous discoveries. What unexpected, surprising insights resonated with you, and how might these realize new opportunities?

Is it time to make uncommon leadership more common? We think it is.

Bibliography

1   Rumelt, R (2011) *Good Strategy Bad Strategy: The difference and why it matters*, New York, Random House

2   Collins (1998) *The New Collins Concise Dictionary of the English Language*, London, Collins

3   Handy, C (1999) *The New Alchemists: How visionary people make something out of nothing*, London, Random House Group

4   Leahy, T (2012) *Management in Ten Words*, London, Random House Business Books

5   Handy, C (2002) *The Empty Raincoat: Making sense of the future*, London, Arrow Books

6   Drucker, P (1973) *Management: Tasks, responsibilities, practices*, London, HarperCollins Publishers

7   Yunus, M (2009) [accessed 12 September 2013, online] *Lifting People Worldwide out of Poverty*, Knowledge@Wharton, http://knowledge.wharton. upenn.edu/article.cfm?articleid=2243

8   *Post-it® Notes ...Little sticky notes that revolutionized messages* (No date) [accessed 21 February 2014, online] http://www.3m.com/cms/ca/en/1-30/ rFzeEA/view.html

9   Bloomberg (1998) [accessed 20 November 2013] Steve Jobs on Apple's Resurgence: 'Not a one-man show' *Business Week* [Online] http://www .businessweek.com/bwdaily/dnflash/may1998/nf80512d.htm

10 Macleod, D and Clarke, N (2009) *Engaging for Success: Enhancing performance through employee engagement*, Department for Business, Innovation and Skills

Bibliography

INDEX

● ● ● ● ●

NB: for entries beginning 'leading with' on contents pages *see* action; purpose; service *and* vision

page numbers in *italics* indicate Figures

Also available from Kogan Page

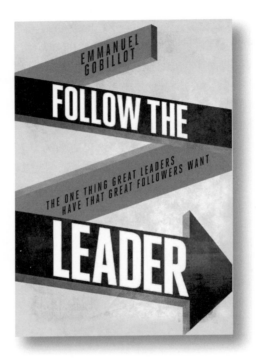

Find out more; visit www.koganpage.com and
sign up for offers and regular e-newsletters.

Also available from Kogan Page

Find out more; visit www.koganpage.com and
sign up for offers and regular e-newsletters.

Also available from Kogan Page

Also available from Kogan Page

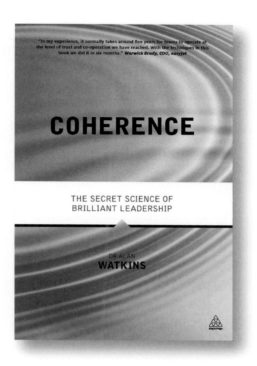

"In my experience, it normally takes around five years for teams to operate at the level of trust and co-operation we have reached. With the techniques in this book we did it in six months." *Warwick Brady, COO, easyJet*

COHERENCE

THE SECRET SCIENCE OF
BRILLIANT LEADERSHIP

DR ALAN
WATKINS

Find out more; visit www.koganpage.com and
sign up for offers and regular e-newsletters.

KoganPage

Also available from Kogan Page

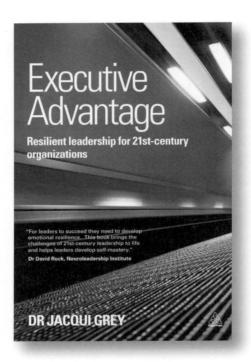